Don't Worry, Be Happy

Thomas Krause

Translation: Stephan Waba

Contents

PART 1

PART 2

PART 3

Preface

*"Stories help children sleep but also
awaken adults."*

[Dr. Jorge Bucay]

"Where would I be today had I not spent my semester abroad in Bali in 2009 and met Sami, a traditional Balinese healer?" This question can only be answered in a hypothetical way. What I certainly can say, however, is that up to that moment, I had been on a misguided path. Then I met Sami, my friend and mentor. He taught me that we could create our world the way we dream it. We just have to understand that everything comes into existence from within ourselves and everything happens through us. His key message is "Change the world — start with yourself," which has stuck with me like a mantra and which he not only taught me through his words, but also showed me constantly. Sometimes it seems to me that very little has changed in all the years since my semester abroad — but beneath the surface nothing is the same anymore.

In this book, I would like to share with you my personal metamorphosis and the insights I have gained since my first encounter with Sami. I intentionally provide very profound insights into my emotional and mental world, and I am aware that I've been very open and have revealed myself completely. Even if openness serves as a breeding ground for vulnerability, I believe that our lives should not remain a well-kept secret.

Only by sharing our story can we be an inspiration to others and help them discover the untapped resources within themselves.

While writing this book, I was asked by a friend how I actually came to know how to write a book. I didn't have any response for her, except a clueless look and a monologue that was full of more silence than answers. After all, I had not given it any thought beforehand, much less acquired any special knowledge. Rather, I simply felt I had to write the book. It was important that I relieved myself of the pressure of having to be perfect from the beginning or to launch an impeccable product on the market. It may be said that diamonds only emerge under pressure. That may be the case, but for me, pressure is always something that goes hand in hand with stress. Moreover, stress, in turn, is nothing but a brake on my wheels of self-fulfillment.

There was also a voice inside me that had very high demands on content and the quality of writing. I had to consciously detach myself from this internal tension and practice embracing my own imperfections. If I had not done that, you would not be holding this book in your hands right now.

Everything in it is my very own story and does not hold any claim to be true for anyone else. Only a few small details of the book originate from my imagination and are fabricated. Both for the sake of adding cool elements, and to clarify my individual findings even more thoroughly. Other details have to be kept secret for the simple reason of not inflicting shame on my parents.

To visually accompany what I have written, I have included pictures for some of the chapters. You can find them on Instagram under the hashtag *#Balichyhealing_book.*

On that note, I wish you an exciting and inspiring journey — wherever it may take you.
Don't Worry, Be HAPPY

Thomas

PART 1

a.) On the wrong path without any sense of direction

1. Who I am or who I think I am

> *"Whether you think you can, or you think you cannot — you are right."*
>
> *[Henry Ford]*

The foundation for a happy life is most certainly laid in childhood. Following this assumption, the conditions for me in the here and now could not be better. After all, my memories of this time are filled with boundless ease, joy and enthusiasm. I am incredibly grateful that I was allowed to grow up in such a well-protected way. My parents simply facilitated everything for me and always permitted all kinds of freedom. I never betrayed their trust. Or rather, I never let them catch me. Of course, I was also subjected to the customary difficulties of any adolescent. Still, there was this positive attitude that allowed me to approach life with a certain carefree attitude.

Today, at the age of 22, much of that has faded, and I ask myself how I could have lost all that so easily over the last few years: "Why did I lose this boundless ease? Why is it suddenly so important to me what others think of me? Where do all the doubts and fears come from that never existed before? Why do I experience real feelings of happiness so rarely?"

I could not give a genuine answer to the question of what I would like to become one day, neither as a child nor in my teens, let alone today. For this planlessness, the field of economics provides me with a welcoming home. Studying this subject at Stuttgart Hohenheim University is definitely no walk in the park. Incredibly smart people, among whom there is already a lot of competition, surround me. Moreover, one exam is chasing the next and I hardly have time to catch my breath. Just thinking about the upcoming exam period makes me sweat and creates stress pimples all over my body. It is not just the number of exams, but rather the complexity of the subject and the amount of learning, that makes the exams seem like unconquerable monsters. Every semester, six to nine of these beasts have to be defeated, only to find myself facing the same challenges in the following semester.

If my studies were at least fun, or even just a little bit interesting, then none of this probably would be such a burden for me at the moment. I do not really feel like I belong. Rather, I feel like a complete outcast in my degree program. Like someone who simply neither belongs there nor wants to belong. I cannot and do not want to talk to my fellow students about the supposedly exciting world of business administration and economics and share a common interest, nor do I visually fit the image of a typical business student. I tend to prefer unironed t-shirts, flip-flops and jeans instead of loafers, a polo shirt with khaki pants and a pair of horn-rimmed glasses.

While many of my fellow students already have their first experiences in the professional world during their studies interning in consulting firms and thus have a clear idea of the path they want to take after graduation, I solely focus on passing my exams. Much like a soccer player is planning from game to game, I am planning from semester to semester.

I am already dreading my mandatory three-month internship. I try to delay it as long as possible, hoping to find a friend who is willing to confirm that I have completed one without having to do anything. It is not only that I simply have no desire for the practical part of my studies. To be honest, I also have to admit to myself that I am extremely afraid of failing and not being able to meet the requirements. I can neither easily transfer the knowledge I learned during my studies, nor do I have any true practical skills. In the same way, I simply lack faith in myself.

Unfortunately, student life in Hohenheim is not very befitting for students either. At least not in the sense that I have always imagined it. (Hollywood, with its films such as *Old School*, is not completely guiltless in setting up these high expectations.) In addition to the people there, who tend to dance to a different beat, this is also due to the geographic location. The hottest pubs near the university are "Red Onion Saloon" or "The Old Town Pub." Since the university is located in the countryside between Stuttgart airport and the city center, you have to travel by car to get to the parties, or you have to start drinking early so you're sufficiently drunk by 9 p.m. which allows you just enough time to catch the last bus back to the city. Otherwise, in the villages around campus, the streets are deserted pretty much exactly at 8 p.m. The area for student recruitment for the University of Hohenheim is huge in any direction. Many of my fellow students commute to the university, and for this reason, it is difficult to establish a sizable network of friends who meet after lectures for true student life.

Despite my unsatisfactory situation, I still pursue my studies and invest a lot of time and energy. In doing so, I continue to follow my parents' advice to obtain a university degree, the completion of which will give me promising opportunities on the job market. Meanwhile, I know that I will probably not be happy in the process.

I have chosen this path because so far, I have lacked a sense of purpose. I consider it my punishment for the fact that I have never really thought about my future career beyond high school, but only considered the future from school year to school year. In retrospect, there are many things I could have done differently at the end of my school years to allow myself some time to make the right decision for my vocational future. One of the first things that comes to mind is traveling.

However, it is too late for that now. I will soon have completed the four-semester basic course, and I am already trapped too deeply in the abyss of economics to throw it all away now. My efforts must not have been in vain. Furthermore, I lack alternatives. Moreover, I have no idea what else I could do. I am left with the hope that by the time I complete my studies, enough time will have passed so that I know where to find happiness in my career.

In contrast to me, my sister, who is two years older than me, had known since elementary school that she wanted to become a police officer. After graduating from school with a perfect score of 1.3 on her exams, she turned her dream into reality and embarked on a career as a police officer. By her early twenties, she already owned a condo. Furthermore, she has always had stable, solid partnerships, most of which have lasted for several years.

I probably have the same expectations of a respectable life in terms of "building a house, planting a tree and having children" for myself. Even if no one has ever expressed this to me so clearly, I think it also corresponds to the desires of those around me.

Both my father and my mother work as civil servants. It is difficult for me to judge whether they are happy in their professions. I was raised to believe that happiness is outweighed by a secure job and decent income. I have often felt the disappointment of my parents when I blew their expectations and left school with mediocre to sub-par grades. Unfortunately, I could not offer the same purposefulness and determination of my sister. This may be the fate of the second-born. Therefore, I put extreme pressure on myself to finish my studies with a good average grade. Even if I have to face the situation right now and do without many of the pleasures of life.

I usually compensate for challenges in my studies with sports. Handball, to be precise. I spend time in the gym four times a week. I gladly embrace this commitment, both physically and in terms of time, because of my passion for this sport. In fact, I am so ambitious that I am currently earning money with it. I have been a handball player with all my heart and soul since I was six years old. The sport provides me with an identity. Handball is something I am extremely good at. Better than many others. This is where I get my self-confidence. In sports, I feel free. When my body is fully engaged in action, there is no room for the big trains of thought to which I otherwise feel exposed as a head-driven person. Losing is extremely difficult for me, and I wish I could show this determination and self-confidence outside the gym as well.

Financially, I try to stand on my own two feet as much as possible. Therefore, in addition to my perceived existence as a handball pro, I have had a part-time job at German Post for quite some time. There are no fixed working hours. Depending on demand, I am contacted, or I can volunteer to work myself. The job gives me the maximum flexibility I was looking for as a student. In the mail center, I usually have to sort several bundled catalogs by postal code and transfer them from one pallet to another. With each lift, several kilos of weight are placed on my shoulders and back. One bundle after the other. Pallet after pallet. Depending on my workout and lecture times, sometimes I work during the day, sometimes at night. I do not have to think too hard there. This job is simply a physically exhausting task. It is by no means the answer to quick and easy money. Accordingly, I usually come home from work completely exhausted. With a few Euros more in my bank account, but without any energy to do anything other than lazily hanging around in front of the TV or just sleeping.

2. Drunk as a skunk

"Alcohol may be man's worst enemy,
but the bible says love your enemy."

[Frank Sinatra]

They say one should enjoy celebrations as they come. I have been living up to this motto for quite some time now and never miss an opportunity. In fact, how much I enjoy celebrations is almost exclusively determined by the amount of alcohol I consume. Or rather, by the consumption of alcohol in quantities that far exceed indulgence. Not to mention all the cigarettes, which I crave constantly after the fourth beer and turn me into a chain smoker.

Alcohol is something that I can't do without, and I have trained my body to become a veritable alcohol destruction machine. Over the years, this has increasingly spiraled out of control. Starting out with secretly buying bottles of sangria or *alcopops* at the corner drugstore and occasionally crossing the line of what is forbidden, alcohol has become an integral part of my weekends.

I cannot really work out why I always slip back into the habit. While intoxicated, there is always something to laugh about. It is never tedious. Some of the funniest things tend to happen. Moreover, for me, as a single male, the most important aspect is that I can hit on girls without any problems. While I can only think of some extremely awkward pick-up lines when I am sober, approaching girls when I am drunk is a piece of cake. Dancing up to a girl is also a safe bet when I'm drinking. The only explanation I can give is that I must have Latin blood in my veins. Because when I am drunk, I become like a beast on the dance floor, swaying my hips like a real Latino. At least, that is how I feel in those moments.

I attribute my nonchalance in dealing with women under the influence of alcohol to the fact that I simply do not care at all about being rejected (which has unfortunately happened a few too many times in the past). Without fear of being exposed or painfully turned down again, I just go for it without a care in the world. And with each success, this belief is reinforced further. When sober, there is something that somehow constantly holds me back, that makes me stiffen up and feel less cool than I really am.

After all, it is not that I am totally tight-assed when it comes to interacting with women in general. Quite the opposite. If I am familiar with a girl even very casually, I feel extremely confident and can be myself. Nevertheless, among my acquaintances, I have already failed with all the women who would qualify as potential girlfriends for me. Therefore, it is absolutely imperative for me to get to know new women. And exactly therein rests my problem.

Generally, it is quite difficult to meet an attractive girl at all. The Stuttgart women are not particularly known for their open nature, and they often stick their noses very high up in the air. Maybe it is just that I feel that way because I regularly get turned down by them. Getting to know a woman like that does not just happen. It requires courage and initiative to approach someone. Nevertheless, I lack the guts to do so. I have no idea what to say without appearing cheeky or even blunt.

I have also entertained the idea of attending an adult education course to be hit by Cupid's arrow. Of course, I would always have the option to register with one of the numerous singles' sites on the Internet. But I do not consider that a good option at the moment. Somehow, I prefer to date a real person, whom I can directly compare to my visual expectations, and not to deal with someone who might pretend to be someone she is not at all. Furthermore, by using a singles' portal, I would be admitting to myself that I am no longer able to get to know someone in the traditional way. In the past, it has always turned out somehow. I'm not ready to go quite that far yet. In that case, I may as well place a single ad in the regional newspaper under the pseudonym "Lonesome Cowboy 85." Thus, the only way for me to get to know people is by partying.

Therefore, to remain competitive in the contest for the most attractive ladies, I need the much-loved high proof magic potion. My recent experiences when I have been able to score with women almost exclusively under the influence of alcohol have revealed to me the secret of life: "If you drink alcohol, you will be successful with women. Your buddies will be amazed; your self-esteem will appreciate the boost. If you do not drink, do not bother trying at all. That will never work anyway."

This assumption is corroborated by a multitude of testimonials that prove all of this almost scientifically, thus establishing it as my very own truth, which cannot be contested. A study remains a study, whether it is reliable or not: getting to know women without boozing is hopeless.

Playing the bore in a group of drinking enthusiasts and staying sober also requires a sturdy character, which I currently do not possess. I cannot find a satisfactory answer to the question of why I am not joining in the drinking. Unfortunately, one is constantly exposed to this kind of conflict. To be honest, I am usually one of the first to criticize a nondrinker in a group. To me, this represents a social problem. The longing to belong is part of our nature.

I wonder how many brain cells have died through my alcohol excesses alone in the last few years. It is hard to imagine what a smart brain I would be otherwise! I would surely be just a small step away from winning the Nobel Prize. I would certainly have invented miracle cures for cancer and AIDS!

3. Fighting the symptoms of physical disease

"It is far more important to know what person the disease has than what disease the person has."

[*Hippocrates*]

Apart from the negative side effects of my studies and my limited love life, I would generally describe myself as a cheerful person. I enjoy laughing a lot as often as possible. I am a real joker who is full of nonsense. My sense of humor always appears whenever the constant search for ultimate happiness and love, as well as the worries of everyday life related to my professional career, do not haunt me. This joker in me is, metaphorically speaking, permanently locked in a cage which is covered with a cloth in a small storage cabinet. Currently, there is no room for him because my life is defined by permanent weakness. Often, I lack the drive for even the simplest things of everyday life. As a result, I am overwhelmed by many things.

At the moment I almost exclusively find myself in this state. I suspect this is related to the fact that I have been struggling with severe pain in my hip and lower back area for quite some time. It is difficult to pinpoint exactly what this pain is. Sometimes it is located in the hip area, sometimes it moves to the lumbar area, and sometimes it even radiates to the upper back region. For the sake of simplicity, I have told my handball coach and teammates that I have a back injury and will have to take a break for an undefined period of time. The pain is almost omnipresent. Not only during stressful periods, but now I am also having increasing problems in everyday life. I even have to cut back on certain routine things right now. I can no longer do my exhausting work at the post office.

Unfortunately, there is no improvement in sight at this time. Meanwhile, I have visited just about every orthopedist in the area. The diagnosis is *hip dysplasia*. Or a crooked back. Or something in between. Or rather, there is no such thing as a definitive diagnosis. Even after months of treatment with various therapies, there is no improvement. My perception of doctors as demigods in white robes who can solve any problem with the right advice and the right therapy has been shattered. The little boy inside me, who has believed this all his life, is now bitterly disappointed. I feel left alone with my problems.

Currently, all hopes rest on my new physiotherapist. He is extremely competent and very motivated, but he can only help me to a certain extent with my backache. After his treatments, I usually feel much better. Unfortunately, this improvement is not yet truly lasting.

It takes an enormous amount of time and effort for me to get to his practice. Since I do not own a car, I have to resort to the services of my rattling student bike. It takes almost thirty minutes to get there on this diva of semi-flat tires and squeaky hinges. Therefore, the two treatments per week cost me a total of about three hours of time, which is counterbalanced by a benefit of sixty minutes of treatment with only modest improvement. Not to mention the time required for regular doctor visits.

To make matters worse, I have had inflamed eyes in addition to my back problems for almost five months now. Both eyes are affected by a kind of conjunctivitis. Only, conjunctivitis should ease relatively soon after the use of appropriate eye drops. My eye inflammation, on the other hand, has persisted stubbornly for such a long time now.

In addition to the medical visits for my back problems, I have already consulted two ophthalmologists. They have both diagnosed me with conjunctivitis. But, they still owe me an explanation as to why the inflammation did not improve even after several types of eye drops.

I had every possible medical test done. Allergy test at the dermatologist: negative. Examination of my organs by an internist: no results. Furthermore, I took an autohaemotherapy with an alternative practitioner, which was expensive, but had no effect. I do not want to know how much time I have spent in doctors' waiting rooms in the last half year, only to be just as sick as before. Or much worse, just as unaware and in the dark as before.

It is a really depressing feeling when, as in my case, you have two serious illnesses whose causes are unclear. As a result, nothing substantial can be done for recovery. Instead, there is a lot of trial and error about what might help. The doctors' motivation to earn money with the treatments often seems to me to be a higher priority than the success of the treatment itself.

I just came from another treatment with my physiotherapist. I had to ride my bike home for half an hour through the pouring rain. Now I am soaking wet. No part of my body is dry any longer. Additionally, I am completely frozen to the bone. And to make matters worse, I again feel only minimal relief from my pain. At this moment, my exterior exactly mirrors the emotional state within me. I am completely powerless. Not just physically, but more so mentally. I can no longer handle my frustration and bitterly burst into tears. I feel as miserable as sin and whine to myself. Like a baby crying for its mother. A waterfall of salty tears is pouring down my cheeks. My eyes are burning and bright red. Even more than usual. When my flatmate Markus registers the sounds of despair, he joins me in the kitchen to comfort me. He wraps his arm around my shoulders and asks in a gentle tone, "Hey little tiger, what's wrong with you?"

"Everything's fine, I just have something in my eye," I reply to him. Real men just do not show emotion. We both start laughing, as he could hear my wailing even with the door to his room closed and the music turned up. My red, swollen eyes leave no room for any other interpretations anyway. My flippant remark is no more than a brief emotional ray of hope. A short rebound. I quickly find my way back to the track of profound frustration. Again, I howl away like a mad dog on ecstasy. Now, finally, my frustration forces its way out. I have to share my feelings and I can no longer hold them back: "You know, I am just investing so much time and energy to finally get healthy again. It costs me so much physical and mental strength to constantly race to the doctor or physio, only to find myself in almost the same condition as before. I want to be fit again and feel the joy of life inside me. There is not much of that right now. It just does not get better. On the contrary, I have the feeling that it is getting worse. I am treading water and notice how my energy is fading. And there is simply no one who can help me. I am just disappointed right now. I no longer know what else I could do. Nothing seems to help. Everything feels so extremely exhausting. Every day is a burden, and I am glad when I am lying down at night and have managed to finish the day. This cannot go on like this forever. Why is this happening to me, of all people?"

"Cheer up, it'll be all right," Markus the Wise replies to me. Of course, I am not really inspired by his advice. What else is he supposed to say? But at least he stands by me and lends me his ear. It feels good to complain to him about my suffering. There is a good reason for the saying: A problem shared is a problem halved. No one who has not experienced something like this firsthand will have better advice for my current situation.

Although I had been so confident that I would be strong enough to overcome this physical low, I wanted to defy the recommendation of my family doctor with all my might. During my first visit, he had already advised me to stop playing handball because of my back and hip problems and the risk of permanent damage to my entire body. I was supposed to switch to swimming or cycling! "That ignorant bastard," I had said to myself at the time. "I will show him. Swimming or cycling. Why not halma or golf? I am not 100 years old yet, so maybe I can do that in the last days of my life. As if you could just quit after seventeen years in this sport. Just like that, simply switch to a different sport. What is he thinking?"

My family doctor was not at all aware of the importance I attach to this sport. Particularly not its social and emotional aspects. Handball provided regular structure to my everyday life and even the weekends, and filled them with life. This team sport has always been the source from which I derived my strength. "And I am supposed to leave all that behind now? What am I expected to do with my spare time without handball?"

At that time, I decided to muster all the strength I could to stick it to my GP and get back on my feet. Given my current level of frustration, I feel like I am helpless against my situation. I give up. A cold beer and a cigarette accompanied by Markus the Wise on our balcony allows me to endure the situation for a brief moment.

A few days later, I cancel my handball contract. I just cannot stand the fact that I am condemned to watch the games and still get paid for it. That is not at all in line with my ethical sportsman's code. The pressure I put on myself to get back on the field as quickly as possible has gotten out of hand.

Considering my decision to quit, the disappointment is enormous and depression is not far off. In fact, it might have been breathing down my neck for quite some time. In those days, many tears are shed.

4. Define yourself by your environment

*"To be yourself in a world that is
constantly trying to change you is the
greatest accomplishment."*

[Ralph Waldo Emerson]

In the weeks that follow, I feel consistently empty. It is not just the situation itself, that I've lost handball, a critical purpose in my life. Rather, I am simply completely dissatisfied with how my life has been going recently, and especially with myself. I glance into the mirror of our shared bathroom and regard my red, inflamed eyes. Eyes in general bear an exceptional meaning for me. Not only do we perceive the outside world through them. We also have the opportunity to express ourselves through them without using words. Through eye contact, we can get extremely close emotionally, reveal our emotions and perceive what others around us are thinking and feeling. It is said that our eyes are the "windows of the soul." But my soul must be possessed by the devil. For what I see is more than frightening. Since my eyes are not only red, but also dry as hell and burning, I try to avoid any eye contact with others. I do not even know if I am doing that consciously. I feel ashamed of my red eyes about as much as a woman who has been given a black eye by her husband. Moreover, dark circles have appeared under my eyes, which make me look like a drug addict, or someone who has given up on life. Considering my appearance, I do not really appear self-confident to the people around me. Being asked by others if I have been drinking is a breeding ground for my insecurity. Unfortunately, I often get asked this question, which humiliates me anew every time. With my eye inflammation, regrettably, I can no longer wear contact lenses. So instead of looking like *Superman*, I appear to my fellow human beings like the stripped-down version of *Clark Kent*.

The dissatisfaction that stems from my health problems is increasingly being spread to the rest of my life. I keep standing in front of the mirror and realize once again that I am not particularly satisfied with my appearance in general. I run my hand through my hair and pull it back into a ponytail and am faced with the truth. What I see is my high forehead and seemingly endless stretches of receding hairline. It just looks like crap, and I positively accept that I do not fit the ideal for attractiveness even in the darkest corners of this world. Since it is embarrassing for me to have a bald spot at the age of 23, I have been trying to cover up this optical flaw for a few years now. All it takes is properly aligning the hair and a sufficient dose of hairspray to keep it in place. My nemesis in my efforts are usually strong wind or rain, which bring down this laboriously erected wall and reveal the bald spot to the world around me. Once the high forehead and the receding hairline are exposed, I feel vulnerable and open to attack. I can see myself in five to ten years when it gets really embarrassing, and I am forced to comb the almost shoulder-length hair of my monk's wreath from one side over the other just to hide my baldness. The worst is if someone tries to tousle my hair. There are some people in my inner circle of friends who simply do not possess any sensitivity and are blind to the inner damage they are doing to me. I absolutely cannot handle that. I become even more insecure than I already am and start to find this part of my body more repulsive, if not to hate it. Furthermore, I am accompanied by the constant fear of being exposed by others. And there is simply nothing I can do to change that. After all, I was born with this appearance and simply cannot do anything about it. Of course, I will continue to try to style my hair with hairspray to keep my receding hairline as hidden as possible. Furthermore, wearing caps is a sensible and casual alternative.

Besides my looks, I am not particularly satisfied with myself as a person, that is, with the part of me that cannot be seen directly in the mirror. On the one hand, there is my lack of memory. I simply cannot remember anything. Strangely enough, this does not include bullshit. I call it the "shit filter." Be it a good joke, a stupid saying or an embarrassing mishap —I inevitably remember every detail. Possibly, even for the rest of my life. If, on the other hand, it concerns important matters such as mathematical formulas, legal texts, names, dates or similar things of importance that I urgently need to keep in mind, they are forgotten quickly. I am not obtuse or dumb, but compared to my highly gifted fellow students, I often regard myself as substandard. While they read the most complex texts once and internalize them right away, I often have problems even understanding the headline. While I study for weeks for an exam and cannot concentrate on anything else, many of my fellow students only have to invest a few days for preparation —with the same or even better results. Of course, this is poison for my already tarnished self-confidence. Except for sports, there is nothing I am really good at. Nothing in which I have real talents.

What would really do me good now would be a steady girlfriend. Someone who adores me and through whom I could finally improve my self-esteem again. Someone who tells me that she loves me the way I am and with whom I can be completely myself. Looking in a mirror, I have no valid arguments why I should be rated better than my competitors on the male market. Therefore, I do not give up hope that eventually something more will come out of a drunken romance.

It is crucial to me what others think of me, and not just when it comes to women. This ever-present thought prevents me from developing fully. It is some kind of invisible protection that constantly subjects me to check whether I satisfy the opinion of those around me or not which influences my emotional state enormously. If I am liked and met with acceptance, I feel good and my self-worth experiences a high. If exactly the opposite is the case, I feel low and worthless.

Now, after standing in front of the mirror for about five minutes, my back pain is already kicking back in. The pain starts to intensify, and my body sends me the unmistakable signal that I should lie down again. The only reason I do not lie down in front of the TV in resignation is that at the same moment I am called into the living room by Markus the Wise:

"You have mail from the University of Applied Sciences Dortmund."

His words abruptly thrust me into a state of positive excitement. I rush to him and snatch the letter from his hands. Giving in to my back's desire, I sit down on the sofa and open the envelope with a devastating tear. I can hardly believe it. What I see there brightens my outlook at the speed of light.

"Yeaaaaaah! Wohhhoooo," I release an indefinable sound that is supposed to be an expression of my joy.

"How aaaaaaawesome!" I inform Markus.

"I got an acceptance letter for the semester abroad in Bali in just under four months."

An overflow of joy washes over me. "This is happening just at the right time," I state confidently, enjoying the euphoria that gives me great hope at this moment.

b.) A new perspective

1. Vacation semester in Bali

> *"I have chosen to be happy, it is good for*
> *my health."*
>
> [*Voltaire*]

By choosing the vacation island of Bali for my semester abroad, I deliberately chose a place that offers me optimal conditions to consciously take a break from my stressful everyday life. I want to completely let go of all the suffering that has now accompanied me for so long. And above all, to taste the sweet nectar of life again. Almost one and a half years of back pain and almost an entire year of inflamed red eyes are behind me. This difficult time should now finally come to an end.

Except for applying for my visa, getting my rabies shots, packing my travel backpack and exercising to build muscles that are ready to show off at the beach, there has been virtually no preparation. I rely entirely on the recommendation of a fellow student who was there last year. He encouraged me to spend the semester abroad, not least with the words "It was the best time of my life."

I did not have the slightest idea about the country and its people. To my shame, I have to confess that until recently, I was not even aware that the destination for my trip was part of Indonesia. I also had to take this opportunity to find out where Indonesia is located in the first place.

It is a strange feeling to be away from home for such a long time, for the first time in my life. Moreover, it is so damn far away from home. In addition, in Asia, a completely unknown world awaits me.

My parents are supporting me as usual, wherever they can. Since I have been unable to work for the past year and a half due to my back pain, it would not be possible for me to complete the semester abroad without their financial support. For now, the last time they are assisting me is driving me to Frankfurt airport by car. We bid farewell with a loving embrace and look deep into each other's eyes once more. The look on my mother's face suggests something like "Take care of yourself and come home safe and sound." My father's look, on the other hand, expresses something more in the category of "Do not fuck around, kid." I cut off the cord and my independence increases with every step I take away from my parents. Alone, I walk to the check-in desk to meet two fellow students from my university in Stuttgart Hohenheim. I do not look back, but only ahead. With a spirited high-five, I briefly greet my fellow students. It does not take many words to notice the anticipation in the air. We proceed through passport control and the security check. Until boarding, we are fantasizing about what, we hope, will be the wildest time of our lives in the coming six months. Fully charged with endorphins, we board the plane, heading for the sun.

Despite all the excitement and feelings of happiness, my eyes are shut before takeoff and don't open again until ten hours into the flight. Apparently, the reason for these hours of sleep is the comatose level of intoxication I indulged in at my farewell party the night before. Therefore, I am reasonably well rested when our plane finally touches down in Bali after a total of eighteen hours of flight time. The moment shortly before landing, when the song "Life in Technicolor" by Coldplay pierces my ears at full volume and the orange horizon of the sunset in all its beauty through the window enchants my eyes, is absolute magic and gives me goose bumps down to my toes.

The heat that awaits us in Bali even forty-five minutes after sunset is suffocating. Sweat is running down my entire body. My deodorant has already failed miserably as we emerge from the air-conditioned plane. Following a brief stopover at the *Imigrasi* counter, which we are able to clear seamlessly thanks to our previously applied for visa, we continue on to the baggage carousel. Here it becomes apparent for the first time that everything in Asia is a bit more disorganized than in our European homeland. Even after thirty minutes, there is no sign of a single suitcase. Overall, it takes us almost one hour to collect our entire group's luggage. Right next to the baggage carousel, helpful locals are standing by, ready to take our backpacks and haul them to the cab stands at the exit. Our momentary astonishment at how accommodating the people here are is somewhat dampened when our Balinese sherpas hold out their hands for us to pay for their services. Since we are only carrying Euros, we are forced to stop at the nearby ATM, which is fortunately only a few feet away, to get our hands on some local cash. One transaction later, I am suddenly a millionaire. Thanks to the Indonesian Rupee. It feels good, even if I am only a Rupee Baron and not a millionaire in Euros.

"I am a fucking millionaire," I inform my two fellow students immediately of my newfound wealth, waving the bills in my hands like crazy. Completely overwhelmed with the new currency, I settle the debt with my personal sherpa. Since the machine has only issued me ten 100,000 IDR bills, I have no other option when choosing my tip than to generously part with one of these bills. I am aware at this moment that I am not getting a good deal, although I have no real idea of what value this bill corresponds to in Euros. I just hope my sherpa appreciates my generosity.

A colorful hustle and bustle awaits us at the cab stand. Everybody —cab driver or private citizen —tries to offer us their driving services. A small crowd forms around the three clueless fools from Germany, and we finally try to find the two most trustworthy drivers. Since three of us with all our luggage do not fit into one vehicle, I have to take a cab alone, which follows the other cab carrying my fellow students.

It feels sticky and there is a foreign scent in the air. The background noise and hectic pace of the crowded traffic immediately add to the stress. At the very first turn after leaving the airport, we lose touch with my classmates in the cab in front of us in the darkness that has already set in. Suddenly, I find myself alone in a gloomy cab with a persistently smoking driver named Ketut, whom I unceremoniously name Helmut (in reference to the probably best-known German chain smoker: former German Chancellor Helmut Schmidt) due to his considerable nicotine consumption. I have no idea where we are going and whether I am about to be robbed and chopped into pieces with all my luggage. Considering Helmut's open and warm-hearted nature, this is rather unlikely, but since I am not familiar with the surroundings and the people here at the other end of the world, I let caution prevail for now. I therefore find nothing wrong with mentally playing out the worst-case scenario.

With the firm goal in mind of not being hacked to pieces or ripped off on the fare due to my lack of local knowledge, I come up with a congenial plan that I immediately put into action. I pull out my cell phone and fake a call to my fellow passengers in the other cab: "Yeah, hi, we are close to that bar we went to last time. Where are you? Ah...mmmhhh...OK. We must be very close to you guys! Ah...OK, see you in a couple of minutes! We meet there."

With this fake call, I think I masterfully made the driver believe that I was familiar with the surroundings and that I knew exactly what was going on. Immediately after the imaginary end of the phone call, I realize how idiotic and incredibly embarrassing this actually has been.

Helmut is not impressed by any of this and is entirely focused on driving and smoking. "And why do I even experience such paranoia? Maybe because of the tiredness that prevails by now despite all the exciting first impressions?"

28

Fortunately, Helmut knows the address of our backpacker hostel, which allows us to arrive independently of the cab somewhere in front of us. When we finally arrive at our temporary lodging in Kuta after about twenty-five minutes of driving, the other two are already waiting for me in the lobby with a cold beer in their hands. It feels good to finally be here after all the travel hassles, and I hope that this feeling will be reinforced in the next half year.

After several days of painstaking investigation, I and my two fellow students from Hohenheim have rented a villa in the southwest part of Bali in Seminyak, which has its own swimming pool and separate rooms with air conditioning. We also have a living room lounge including a hammock, an open kitchen, a huge TV area and a wonderful garden. Everyone has to pay only $290 dollars per month. The housecleaner and pool boy are already included in the price, of course. Yes, we even have our own staff. After all, you never know if and when one will be in a position to afford such comforts again. We therefore take full advantage of all our resources. So, my parents' money is well spent! My expectations were far exceeded, and it still seems surreal that one could easily shoot an episode of *MTV Cribs* in our very own villa.

In general, one can do extremely well in Bali even on a limited student budget thanks to the low cost of living. It is therefore completely normal and very affordable to have breakfast, lunch and dinner in one of the numerous restaurants or *warungs*, as the local food stalls are called in Indonesia.

Therefore, we were able to bypass all the annoying shopping, cooking and dishwashing tasks this way too. A ninety-minute full-body massage in a wellness salon costs the equivalent of $11 dollars. Cigarettes are about ninety cents a pack. A beer is about as cheap. Likewise, a liter of gasoline costs the equivalent of only about twenty-six cents. The monthly rent for my scooter is less than $50 dollars.

The luxury in which I live does not solely manifest itself in the money I spend. I am totally fascinated by the diversity of the island. In the north, there are volcanoes, mountains, lakes, forests and the jungle. In the south, you find a rather sparse landscape. Beautiful rice fields extend in the middle part of the island. I did not expect too much from the beaches. Being surrounded by the beauty of nature turns the island into a real paradise. All the scenic images on my camera could easily be used for a travel brochure.

Despite the beautiful surroundings, I am most impressed by the culture. The Hindu religion is quite influential. It is omnipresent in everyday life. While in Germany, the Christian religion is limited to an occasional visit to church or a few sporadic rituals and is otherwise mostly forgotten, religion in this country is a full-time job where people are in constant interaction with the Gods. Ceremonies with wreaths of flowers, offerings and incense take place around every corner. At any given time, one encounters people dressed appropriately for a ceremony with robes and headdresses. The sound of chimes from the backyards is regularly heard, which has a very calming effect. Everywhere you can find small as well as large temples.

The Hindu religion is also evident in the behavior of the people. The belief in karma is only one of the reasons why people are so incredibly open, helpful and friendly. If you do good things, good things will happen to you. Basically, it takes some getting used to for a German to get a warm smile from almost everyone on the street or to be addressed in a friendly manner. In this country, this is completely normal.

Meanwhile, I have settled in comfortably on the Island of the Gods. In the two and a half months I have been here, I have established a huge network of friends. It consists exclusively of German students from my study abroad program, in which a total of 190 students from various universities in Germany are participating. The days usually end rather late because there is always something to celebrate. Wednesday is the new Friday and Thursday is the new Saturday, which means that the party goes on not only on weekends, but also during the week. A pool party here, a pool party there. Dancing shirtless in swimming trunks until late at night with like-minded people under a starry sky by the pool and celebrating life to the fullest does have something to do with making my student dreams coming true. It feels as if life itself is giving me a conciliatory French kiss.

On a normal day, we spend a lot of time together on the beach. Our favorite activities include surfing, playing soccer and volleyball, listening to music, reading, playing cards, drinking iced coffee, or just hanging out. We often take trips together and get to know the island in all its beauty. From time to time, we also end up at the university. I admit to being a chronic procrastinator. If my fellow students did not regularly forge my signature on the attendance list, I would probably have an attendance rate of less than twenty percent. Or rather, an attendance rate on the beach of eighty percent. Moreover, the university classes only take place from Monday to Wednesday anyway. Nevertheless, I have promised myself that I will deliberately allow myself this time off. For this reason, I will continue to stick to this decision and I do not have a guilty conscience about not showing up there more often than is absolutely necessary. I am surprised myself that I am so faithful to this intention without fear of imminent consequences, and in a way it also makes me proud.

I could say that over the weeks, a feeling of letting go and freedom has set in. It's not difficult if you have no obligations worth mentioning and the beach is right in front of your door. I enjoy this sense of living to the fullest, as I completely lacked it in the weeks, months, if not years leading up to my trip to Bali. Nevertheless, I do continue to complain of physical discomfort. My back pain is definitely improving and I'm making progress in healing. Meanwhile, I can even go jogging or surfing on the beach without pain. Now the pain often becomes noticeable only after the exercise. Furthermore, there is still some eye inflammation, which is noticeable through the dryness and slight redness of my eyes, but really only affects me when wearing contact lenses.

Fortunately, I hardly have to struggle with lack of energy and drive anymore. Except, of course, on those days when I am completely devastated by the consequences of a hangover, and I am forced to lie down again and again. But those days do not count, as they are willfully induced and not at all regretted. Due to the diversions at the beach, I am so busy with other things that I hardly pay any attention to the physical problems that continue to arise, and therefore they no longer dominate my daily life.

In order to further intensify this positive change and to ensure its lasting effects, I have decided to consult a local healer. I heard that there is someone who works miracles. Mark and Ruby, two acquaintances of mine who have settled down in Bali to run their own fashion line, raved about him with high praises and could warmly recommend a visit to him based on their own experiences. Mark, for example, complained of respiratory problems for several months, and instead of help, met only perplexed expressions from his doctors. It took the healer only two sessions to completely resolve his ailments. This is precisely the kind of help I was looking for. Except for his cell phone number and the stories of my acquaintances, I have no other idea about what to expect from him. There is no homepage. When I dial his number to schedule an appointment with him, a man answers in a deep and cheerful voice: "Hello, Sami speaking. What can I do for you?"

2. An encounter of change

"If you do what you've always done,
you'll get what you've always gotten."

[*Tony Robbins*]

Two days after our phone call, I already have my first
appointment for treatment. I am a little excited. After all, so far,
I am only familiar with the conventional therapies of German
medicine. I expect a lot from the session and hope for a
complete cure of my physical complaints. Or at least for a
proper diagnosis. I do not have a clear picture of Sami in my
mind. After all the stories of Mark and Ruby, I imagine him as
a kind of medicine man in traditional garb, with gray hair and
a long beard. A visual mix of *Mr. Myiagi*, *Obi Wan Kenobi* and
Gandalf the White.

I take my scooter to Kuta, the tourist center and party
capital of the island. In the midst of the foreigners, already
drunk in the afternoon, I turn left from the tourist strip into a
small side street. After about four hundred and fifty feet, a sign
on the right side of the alley with the words *Bali Chy Healing*
indicates that I have reached my destination. Since I am a few
minutes early, I have some time to examine the exterior of the
clinic. The facade is slightly run down. Several posters are
displayed on it, faded by the rain and barely legible. Two small
stone statues stand to the left and right of the entrance. Both of
them look quite battered. One of the statues even has a large

part broken off. Without the recommendation of my acquaintances, I would never have found my way here. The area doesn't look very appealing. Before I enter the clinic right on time, I knock on the door and timidly announce my arrival: "Hello, anybody there?"

No one answers, and so I remain standing in the doorway like a shy deer for now. When I get no response even after my second attempt, I take off my flip-flops, following the country's customs, and cautiously venture through the door. I notice a slightly musty, moldy smell, paired with the scent of incense sticks. I survey the entire premises from the entryway. The clinic is divided into two rooms. In the larger room there are two massage tables with stools. To maintain privacy, these are largely hidden behind two large partition curtains. In the room in front, there is a small office, where I now stand around waiting cluelessly. On the walls, there are mysterious images, which I am unable to decipher. In addition, the entire room is plastered with diagrams on which you can see reflex zones, body postures or energy lines. Behind the desk, there is a large shelf with herbs stored in jars. Off to the side are small vials of indefinable liquids. Next to the desk, leeches are kept in an aquarium. Stacked on a bookshelf are countless tomes on healing.

"There's definitely healing in the air here," I observe. Even though everything looks rather run-down to me. Therefore, I am a bit skeptical.

A Balinese-looking man, who must be in his mid-forties, appears from the back room. Contrary to my expectations, his strong build, his long silk trousers and polo shirt, his short hair and his reading glasses on his nose are very different from the man I had imagined. He flashes a nice smile at me and greets me with the words: "Hi, I am Sami, please have a seat. What can I do for you? You come to see me for what?"

At first, I think to myself that I am dealing with *Yoda* from Star Wars, who never quite grasped how to construct grammatically correct sentences. I comply with his request and take a seat on the chair in front of the desk, introduce myself briefly and tell him that I am currently "studying" in Bali. Then I begin to describe to him how my back and hip pain started, what I tried so far for my healing, and how the pains still appear after such a long time. Furthermore, I describe to him my eye problems, which he has already noticed due to the slight redness that still persists.

"OK, ok, enough information I get. No problem, I can help you. Please follow me. With massage we start."

"Alright, you are the boss, *Yoda*!" I joke to myself and follow him into his treatment room. I strip down to my boxers and lie down on my belly on one of the two beds. He rubs me with some oil smelling of herbs and starts to massage me, beginning at the feet. At first, we talk a little and I have slight problems understanding his Balinese English style of speaking. He works his way along every part of my body, from bottom to top. When he has reached my back and completely mangles it with his elbow, I have to surrender and end our conversation effective immediately due to the tremendous pain. I grab the crossbars under the massage table so tightly with my hands that I have serious doubts whether they can resist my force. He proceeds to tear apart my butt cheeks, triceps and neck before standing behind me and asking me to turn to the other side with the instruction "face up." I follow his instructions and roll over onto my back, only to be subjected to the entire procedure again on the front of my body with my face contorted in pain. When he is finally done with the torture and has completely massaged my whole body from top to bottom once, he reaches for a towel that is placed next to the massage bed, wraps it around my neck and wraps my head with it in a tight noose.

"Relax," he whispers to me. With a firm grip, he holds the other end of the towel loop with both hands. He rocks it gently from left to right so that my head swings ever so slightly in this motion. With an abrupt jerk, he pulls the towel back towards him, completely unexpectedly and with all his might. My spine is stretched out and there seems to be a cracking sound in every vertebra. That came as a surprise. I had not expected it. For a brief moment, my breath caught in my throat and I gasped for air. I cannot help myself and let out a: "Whoa, FUCK." Considering my shortness of breath, however, I cannot muster more than a pitiful yip from my lips.

"This is part of chiropractic" he lets me know and then frees me from the bonds of the towel. I lie on the bed as if I'd just lost a fight in a boxing match and keep my eyes closed. He grants me a few moments in this position. Then he takes a seat directly behind me on a chair and holds my head in his hands. I fear further acts of torture. Again, I hear Sami say "Relax," which now, as experience has shown, does not bode well.

Contrary to my fears, though, I am rewarded with a gentle touch of his hands. I perceive a kind of current, but have no idea what exactly he is doing to me. In any case, it feels pleasant, which is why I fully surrender to this state of relaxation. I am completely calm inside. After about ten more minutes, the almost ninety-minute treatment is over for the moment. I eagerly await the upcoming consultation to find out about the cause of my problems and what I can do to fix them. After all, Mark and Ruby had let me know in advance that a consultation is an important part of his holistic treatment. Therefore, my expectations were shattered when Sami promptly bids me farewell and tells me on the way out: "Please come back in three days. Another massage I give you. Then I can see where your body is reacting. Please have a rest today. Fever you can get tonight. Please drink a lot."

On the doorstep, we agree on another appointment and I pay him 350,000 Rupees, which is the equivalent of about $32 dollars. Curious as I am, I would have hoped for a diagnosis and suggestions from him today. Regardless, the fact that my session was obviously different from that of my acquaintance alone clarifies it for me that he responds in a highly individualized way to the problems of his patients and does not just follow a standard program. I follow his advice and let the day quietly fade away. I do not get a fever, but I still feel the effects of the massage hours later.

Three days later, Sami welcomes me to the clinic and then follows the same procedure as during our first session: a short greeting, followed by an approximately seventy-minute disintegration of my entire body in the form of his massage, followed by placing his hands on me. Unlike at our first meeting, this time he reserves time for me at the end for an in-depth consultation in his healer headquarters —his small office. He reaches for his notepad and reveals to me his holistic healing concept: "This is effecting this. This is effecting this. This is connected to this. Kidney here...lower back there...This is connected to this. This is caused by this. And this is caused by this. Everything is connected. Your body is connected to your mind and your emotions," and so on and so forth. He explains to me that my eye problems are not isolated from my hip and lumbar problems, and that they are interrelated.

"Liver and stomach problems you have," is his final diagnosis. I am quite puzzled by this, as I was previously unaware of these alleged problems. I have never had any pain or other abnormalities in any of my organs. Even the examinations at an internist in Germany did not show anything in this regard. I am amazed because this is the first time that I've heard all my physical problems are associated with each other. "You always live under pressure. You live under stress," Sami adds as an explanation. "These organ problems are the result of your lifestyle. Your way of thinking, acting and the emotions you have. And the eye and back problems are the result of your organ problems. Your body is a mirror that reflects your inner problems. It warns you. Looking within for solutions you should!"

He gives me the advice to start meditating to create some space of awareness in my constantly flowing stream of thoughts. A simple breathing exercise, which he immediately shows me, will have to do for starters: "Deep inhale, watch your breath and count till three, hold breath for six seconds and exhale count nine seconds!" He also suggests that I start yoga and change my diet specifically: "Physically, it is very good to eat green vegetables and drink green tea. And generally very important for you, do not make yourself too much stress. Do not live too much under pressure. Life is very simple. Enjoy life. Don't worry, be HAPPY."

I note everything down to the smallest detail on a separate sheet of paper and continue to listen carefully to his words.

"And most important for your liver: stop drinking alcohol!"

My jaw drops in sync with his words. I refuse to believe what he is telling me right now.

"Yeah, sure *Yoda*!" I grumble inwardly sarcastically, registering the admonishing tone behind his words. I suspect that he has deliberately saved the unpleasant part for the end because immediately after that, the second session is over. Instead of ninety minutes, he took a whole two hours for me. Although I want to give him a little more money than for my first treatment, he flatly refuses to accept it.

"Well, then I will just buy a beer with the money," my inner voice rumbles with a grim sense of humor. With a handshake, I thank him for his help and then ride home on my scooter. He has given me plenty of recommendations but I do not quite know how to deal with them all right now.

> *"Every time you are tempted to react in*
> *the same old way, ask if you want to be*
> *a prisoner of the past or a pioneer of the*
> *future."*
>
> *[Deepak Chopra]*

I keep my encounter with this extraordinary person to myself for the moment and do not even tell my closest confidants here on the Island of the Gods about it. I have the firm belief that what he set in motion for me during the treatment and the input he gave me afterward have great potential to bring about a lasting positive change in my life. After a long period of searching, in this man, I have at last found someone who makes me truly and completely feel understood. Sami is someone who has deep compassion for my emotional and physical suffering. Not to mention, I consider him by far the most competent therapist I have confided in over the years. With him, my faith in a permanent recovery has returned. I am furthermore fascinated by his personality, as his extremely cheerful, authentic and charismatic, but also somehow mysterious nature, exerts a certain attraction on me. However, at the moment I do not know how to apply all his advice.

Particularly with regard to abstaining from alcohol, I find myself in a veritable dilemma: the little angel on my left says that I should follow his instructions to the letter, and for my own well-being, abstain from alcohol for now. The little devil on my right, on the other hand, makes it clear to me that the semester abroad with its exuberant pool and beach parties is neither the right time nor Bali the right place for this celibacy. So, it certainly makes the more powerful case. In addition, there is no guarantee that this sacrifice will give me one hundred percent certainty that I will be fully recovered. I simply lack the last bit of conviction. I therefore decide not to change my lifestyle for now and to give myself some time to think about it.

Furthermore, I continue to enjoy the remaining time of my semester abroad to the fullest and revel in the simplicity of the life offered to me here. Since Sami's treatments, there has been some further improvement in my symptoms, but to say he has worked miracles would be a bit of an exaggeration. Regardless, the positive feeling prevails that I have been given both the right tools and the appropriate knowledge to bring about change myself at any time. Sami's advice has etched itself into my subconscious, and so I actually do not drink a sip of alcohol without his admonishing words ringing in my ears and thus giving me a guilty conscience.

With each additional day on the beach, the semester abroad draws inexorably to a close. After five and a half months in the bright sunshine, the wet season has arrived, which is now accompanied by daily monsoon-like downpours. The final exams at the university were a joke and I passed with top grades. Furthermore, my certificate shows an attendance rate of just over ninety percent. Exactly how this all came about is a secret I will take to my grave. Or rather: which must never find its way to the ears of a professor, lecturer or future employer. In any case, we have already been given our farewells, which means that from now on, we no longer have to officially appear at the university.

Every day, another fellow student starts his journey back home, and my network of friends continues to dissolve more and more. So, this is undoubtedly the right time for me to soon pack up and leave myself. Looking back, this was definitely the most amazing time in my life. I made so many new friends. The island enchanted and captivated me. I will carry all the great memories with a warm feeling in my heart for a lifetime. I have made a start on a change in my life, not least because I have also decided not to drink anything during the last two weeks of my stay and to devote myself entirely to pursuing a healthy lifestyle according to Sami's advice.

The imminent return to Germany is not particularly difficult for me because the last days on Bali are marked by days of continuous rain. Unfortunately, this makes it almost impossible to spend time on the beach. Our student life can no longer be maintained as usual under these conditions. It is simply time to go. I am also looking forward to having my family and friends close to me again soon. I would never have imagined it, but there are already countless things that I have started to miss now towards the end.

4. Bye bye comfort zone

> *"Change only takes place through action, not through meditation and prayer."*
>
> *[Dalai Lama]*

I spend the first weeks back in Germany as if in a frenzy. Family, friends and schnitzel with fries are my drugs. With my renewed zest for life, I can now experience my old life in an entirely different way. I realize that Germany is a great home and that I lead a really privileged life.

It is hard to describe, but I have the feeling that a lot has changed since my time in Bali. Not so much on the outside, but on the inside of me. I am invigorated and liberated. All of a sudden, I am enjoying so many things again. "Was it the sun that infused me with new life energy? Or was it since I had no serious commitments in Bali? Was it because I only did what filled me with joy? Did the poverty and the living conditions of the locals in Bali make me a more humble person? Was it the infinite freedom, free from society and regulations, that I felt there?" Probably the answer lies right in the middle and is a blend of all of the above. Equally, I am convinced that meeting Sami has revealed to me an entirely new perspective on life. I am no longer the same as I was before my journey.

I continue to adhere to my new lifestyle even after returning home. This revolves mainly around abstaining from alcohol. I present a whole new side of myself to my environment. Among my friends, though, I am met with only limited acceptance. It does not take long before I am given the nickname "Teetotal-Tom," which from now on makes me the most boring member of our group. A clear indication of what my friends think of my new way of life.

It is only now that it becomes clear to me what an integral part alcohol really plays in our society. People drink on every occasion. And actually, there is nothing wrong with that. It is sociable and usually encourages an exuberant mood. Nonetheless, since I tend to drink non-carbonated water right now, I do not feel quite socially acceptable myself. When asked why I do not drink, I came up with the excuse that several doctors have advised me to be a little more considerate of my liver and cut back for now, due to poor blood test results. When I reflect on the honest answer: "[...] that is what a Balinese healer advised me to do so that I can get my back pain and red eyes under control and finally regain my full strength," I can already hear their criticizing voices and their laughter. I probably would have reacted the same way before my semester abroad. To spare myself this ridicule, I keep this secret to myself for the moment.

But it is not only because of the resistance I experience from my environment that I find it difficult to abstain from alcohol. I do not miss anything in a physical sense, nor do I feel some kind of addiction. Rather, my belief that I can only have fun and hit it off with girls under the influence of alcohol continues to prevail. I am unable to overcome this right now.

46

Consumption has always —even if it was only for a short period of time —bestowed on me qualities that I do not have access to when I am sober: Self-confidence, openness, or courage. And, of course, for a long time alcohol served as a cure to numb my fear of rejection. The consequence of my abstinence is that I completely lack these qualities when dealing with women. My chances of dating someone are thus dwindling, if not hopeless.

In addition to my radical treatment in dealing with alcohol, my lifestyle also includes taking conscious care of my diet. This includes, as prescribed by Sami, the preferred consumption of vegetables. Not to forget fruit. Furthermore, I hardly eat any sugar. I have also decided to avoid any kind of meat from now on. I quickly realized that as a vegetarian, you could not eat sausages either. And no salami, no ham and —oh no —no schnitzel. I practically avoid anything that tastes really good. This sacrifice does not last long, either, until I am nicknamed "Tofu-Tom" within my circle of friends. Every time we barbecue and I place my meat substitute in the form of cheese, tofu sausages or zucchini slices next to juicy steaks and real sausages on the grill, I regret this decision anew. But when it comes to my health, I am prepared to do without a lot. Even if the envy of meat continuously drives me to despair.

I continue to do Sami's breathing meditation almost daily. I would love to delve deeper into this whole subject. Furthermore, I notice that it helps me to calm down and that it does me a lot of good.

Finally, I am determined to try my hand at yoga soon. As of now, I have no clue what yoga actually is. Something about stretching, I would have said spontaneously. And toning exercises. Something that usually only girls do. Since my financial scope as a student is very limited, I have no idea where I could practice it at all at an affordable price. Therefore, I feel compelled to let the subject rest for now. I am still open to maybe trying it in the future, if I find a convenient and affordable opportunity to do so. Too much change at once is not good, either.

Apart from that, I am pursuing my life in the usual way as far as possible: I am studying hard, and experiencing a lot of stress, but I am not having much fun. I have also returned to work at the post office. To my great joy, I was able to start playing handball again due to my improved physical well-being. Admittedly, I can only do so in the third team in the district league without any real sporting ambition, but still. After all, it has a lot to do with socializing and the beer (or in my case, the apple juice spritzer) in the dressing room.

Thank goodness my health has improved to a pretty satisfactory level. Meanwhile, I have almost no problems in everyday life. It is only after greater exertion, such as after a workout, that I continue to struggle with pain in the lumbar region. Just the fact that I can do sports again feels like a miracle to me. My eyes are occasionally red, but it is no longer a permanent condition. I am very proud of myself, as I attribute this success to my discipline, to which I have already devoted much of my time in the more than three months since

I returned from my semester abroad. And all this improvement has happened without the help of any doctors, alternative practitioners or physiotherapists. I have a powerful feeling that I can heal my body with my own energy and that I can control my life myself. Nevertheless, deep inside I feel that, in addition to my regained health, I am still missing something elementary to my happiness: love!

5. Love, who is that?

"All you need is Love"

[John Lennon]

I cannot complain at all about a lack of experiences with women. Only, unfortunately, many of them were negative. Until my first really painful experience with my then girlfriend at the age of 18, I could claim to have been a real ladies' man.

My preference has been clearly defined over the years. Looks play a particularly important role for me. I like blond women, tanned, with an athletic physique, beautiful lips and a casual style. In the best case, she should be someone who is a great sport. Someone up for any kind of shit. I have set the bar very high with my demands, and I am aware of that.

In my life, there are two types of women with regard to a steady relationship: Type A is the woman who appeals to me visually, but lacks all depth. Someone who is effortless to conquer and who I start to be annoyed by rapidly. Lack of humor, arrogance or incompatible interests are among the reasons why this type of woman leaves me completely cold emotionally and there does not seem to be any special chemistry between us. A relationship is therefore out of the question from my side. At most an affair.

Then there is the woman in category B: Her, I find really adorable. I am totally taken, if not even head over heels in love. This type of woman has everything you can ask for in a potential girlfriend: Visually, she is scrumptious, and in terms of character, she is badass. She is educated and self-confident without being arrogant or acting untouchable. If I get to know such a woman, it always turns out to be a jinx. Most of the time she already has a boyfriend, which inevitably closes the door to any potential relationship. If this is not the case, the story ends regularly with: "Sorry, but ...." I just cannot understand why happiness is denied me every time. If it would have happened to me once or twice, I could live with it. Unfortunately, this has happened to me again and again over the last few years like a constantly recurring pattern.

The longer I am single, the more likely I am to consider simply getting into a relationship with anyone — for the simple reason that I no longer want to be alone. As a prospective graduate economist, this can be expressed as a formula as follows: Decreasing demands with increasing longing. Even category A women are now being considered as girlfriends. I do not expect to find the woman I want to spend my life with right away. I would be satisfied with a simple relationship in which I am reasonably happy, or at least not unhappy. How nice it would be to finally be able to show myself in public again with a girlfriend at my side. Simply to improve my self-esteem anew. To show that I belong. Or to finally feel real closeness again.

There were times when I practically kept myself away from the world of women. Especially during the time when my physical suffering dominated my everyday life, I lacked any strength to keep an eye out for women. I mean that in the truest and literal sense of the word. Because I avoided eye contact for a long time due to my zombie eyes. Instead, my gaze was always directed to the ground with my head bowed. And then there were the phases in which I felt totally blocked emotionally. This was usually the result of my feelings not being met with equal response from Type B women, leaving behind an emotional injury or two. Not only that. I had, in moments like these, lumped all females together and had a downright rage in my belly towards the entire female world. As a result, I could not open up to anyone, which in turn is another explanation for my continued status as single. Meanwhile, I ask myself the question, "Am I just by myself or am I already lonely?" The honest answer to myself rather indicates the second option.

Full of pain, even now, I look back at my previous relationships. There was the one who thought she had to cheat on me with my classmate. Or the other one, who lived in another city and from one day to the next, just ghosted me. Then there was the one who I sacrificed myself for and anticipated her every wish. I gave her everything: gifts and of course my full affection and love. But that was not good enough for her. With the words "I rather prefer assholes," she had given me the reason for us to go our separate ways. Considering this moronic reason for separation, in retrospect, I should actually consider myself lucky that we are no longer a couple. Yet, I cannot.

The pain I carried with me from all my previous relationships still lingers even years later. The feeling of not being good enough follows me, and I mourn the moments we shared. Or rather, the feelings of affection and love that were bestowed upon me within a steady relationship. The togetherness instead of loneliness.

My confidence with women has diminished over the years with each disappointing experience. The more I mentally return to these emotional hurts, the more insecure I am. The fear of being disappointed or rejected again is therefore my constant companion. To protect myself from being hurt again, I withdraw from women more and more. The scars inside me are too deep, and I suffer the pain anew every time I dwell on old memories of my relationships.

Although it is difficult for me, I try not to get stressed by my loneliness. Despite my best efforts, my surroundings often make this extremely difficult for me. The constant inquiries of my relatives, whether I finally have a girlfriend, is grist to the mill of my desires. One or the other of them probably already suspect that I secretly have a gay lover.

I have to admit to myself that I envy many of my friends their relationships. Meanwhile, I envy even those who have a real witch as a partner. This becomes clear to me again and again when we meet in our group of friends, and I am the only one without a girlfriend in tow. To be shown in such moments what others have, and I have been denied for so long, hurts immensely. When couples' nights are on the horizon, I put an end to the single stigma, at least in my circle of friends, by staying away more often. This emotional self-protection does indeed prove effective, but it also ensures that I often feel excluded. Furthermore, the hypersensitive among my friends do not miss the opportunity to make innuendos to me from their position of relationship superiority, such as: "Ah, is Tom again the only single among us tonight? Let me be your *wingman*, we'll find you one today."

I also have to answer the question of who and how many girls I am dating right now among the womanizers of my friends. In order not to look like a loser, I get involved in this ego battle and regularly use up my quota of lies for questions like this.

I am now twenty-five years old, and it has been almost five years since my last steady relationship. I virtually no longer know what it feels like to be loved at all. Considering my continuing loneliness, my longing for a steady relationship is growing incessantly. To complicate matters, the rules I have mentally established are still valid: "Without alcohol, you are short of something! You are not self-confident and easy-going enough! You just cannot land anyway!"

These assumptions are reinforced by the fact that I have not even come close to meeting anyone during my period of abstinence. I have not even struck up a conversation with a girl. Let alone have I flirted or made out. Not to mention a roll in the hay. Therefore, my decision is now firm to give in to my beliefs and to celebrate my return to the bottle: "I will break my celibacy! And I will do so as soon as possible!"

Looking back, I consider my period of abstinence a complete success, as I had never exhibited such discipline in all the years before, and had never been sober for more than a maximum of three weeks at a time. My improved health is just one of the positive results. At least now I know it has done something for me. In case I get worse again in the future. But now I simply have to put an end to my existence as a pious monk.

My buddies receive the news rapturously, and it quickly makes the rounds that the prodigal son is returning to the bar. They have all come to celebrate my rebirth in a Stuttgart disco. Without any doubts in the back of my mind, I just kick back and make sure I get the right amount of alcohol. Being resurrected probably makes me a bit too euphoric, which results in a complete crash, including a blackout. As punishment for this unreasonableness, I have to throw up violently both at night and in the morning, as well as at noon and even in the evening of the following day.

I had truly imagined this to be different. My summary of the evening is: no flirting, no affirmation, no possible relationship and no love. Instead, I abandoned my chosen path and broke my resolutions. Additionally, given my hangover, I lost an entire day and gained doubting thoughts as well as the reaffirming feeling of loneliness in return. Trapped in the depths of booze depression, I wonder how this will ever play out. Meanwhile, there is no success with the ladies, neither with alcohol nor without. I am confused and beg the world of women: "Why the hell don't any of you hot girls ever give me your love?

In addition to all the self-doubt, there are also voices that question whether being in a drunken state is really the right way to meet a woman. Or rather, as drunk as I usually am. Because, as has been confirmed once again, I simply cannot handle alcohol and regularly overdo it. In the past, it hardly ever happened that I was only tipsy rather than drunk as a skunk. What kind of woman can you meet in such a condition anyway? Either one who is just as drunk as I am (and therein lie all my hopes). Or, which is far more likely, one who has completely forfeited any ambitions and thus has nothing to offer. The party pictures, with which I see myself confronted more and more frequently due to an increase in digitalization, display a clear message and show me how I present myself to my environment when I am drunk. And that is really embarrassing at times.

6. Emotional problems

"If you do not know where you are going, you'll end up somewhere else."

[Mark Twain]

Almost exactly one and a half years have now passed since my semester abroad. Unfortunately, not much is left of my healthy lifestyle. My studies and work have taken over too much of my life again and have guided me down old paths. And the more I surrendered to everyday life, the more I strayed from the path I had taken in Bali. Meat and alcohol have once again become my companions. My healthy diet and Sami's breathing meditation are now only part of my life at irregular intervals. My body keeps telling me with slight back pain that I am no longer dwelling in my inner center.

Fortunately, I just handed in my diploma thesis, thus finally heralding the end of my six years of studies. My head is still pounding. Not from the strain on my brain, though, but because of the alcohol I used to close this dark chapter.

As a reward for the hardships of the last years, I am flying to Bali for five weeks with my study buddy Matt. To surf. And to party. To meet girls. To chill. To recharge my batteries. To forget my studies and all the pressure that came with it. And secretly I hope to meet the local healer Sami again. Too many fundamental questions in my life are still unresolved, and I am sure to find answers with him.

After a seemingly endless journey with a layover of several hours in Jakarta and a gin and tonic or two in between, we are back on our beloved Island of the Gods after such a long wait. It all feels so familiar, and somehow this daddy-is-home feeling overwhelms us both.

Bali shows us its most enchanting side. The sun shines from morning to night as beautifully as it can. Day after day, the waves offer us the best conditions for a perfect surfing vacation. Almost every evening we are out and about. Drinking, dancing, eating out, meeting people. A clove cigarette here, a local *Bintang* beer there. No matter how drunk we get in the evening, by midday the next day at the latest we find ourselves in *endless-summer* mode in one of the numerous *line-ups* hunting for waves. We visit several temples, take a trip to the most beautiful rice terraces of the island and climb the volcano *Batur* at sunrise. On days when we do nothing, we relax on the beach, listen to music, read a book or play table tennis in the compound of our little hostel.

I am the happiest person on earth right now. Actually, except for my recurring back pain, there is currently no urgent reason to schedule another treatment with Sami. Nevertheless, in some way I feel the inner urge to go and see him. Because even though I am perfectly happy at the moment, the uncertainty of my professional future as well as my continuing loneliness are problems that cause me a permanent headache. I am glad that I reach Sami by phone, and he grants me an appointment for this week. I look forward to his treatment and seeing him again.

Two days later, I set off early on my scooter in the direction of Kuta. Past all the tourist hustle and bustle and my memories of the last wild party nights, I find my way to his clinic. When I see him standing in front of the door from far away, I give him a friendly wave. He waves back amiably. We greet each other with a handshake, and I realize just by being in his presence that it is the right decision to consult him again.

He approaches me with his standard greeting phrase, "Hi I am Sami, please have a seat. What can I do for you? You come to me for what?" And it becomes clear to me that he does not remember our first two encounters during my semester abroad. I let him know that we already know each other and that he helped me with my back problems.

"Oh, yes, I remember," he tries to talk his way out of what is noticeably an awkward situation for him.

"Flat out lying! I do not believe a word you say, *Yoda*!" I am a little disappointed that I did not leave a lasting impression on him or remain in his memory. But with the number of patients Sami has had in treatment since then, I cannot blame him. I would have been pleased anyway.

Starting with his full-body massage, Sami addresses my needs. "With my massage, I can get information about what problems you have. Physically, mentally, emotionally, spiritually, whatever problems you have, your body tells me," he informs me. This time I am spared the thrashing of my back with his elbow, and so I can almost enjoy the massage. I am especially relaxed when he carefully stimulates my reflex zones on my hands and feet one after the other. Apart from that, I cannot really tell what else he is doing. All I know is that it feels good and that every touch is just right. When he is finished with the massage, he takes a seat at the head of the massage table, as he did during his other two treatments, and carefully places my head in his strong hands. This time, too, I feel a slight flowing of energy inside me, which is very soothing.

I have no logical explanation for what happens to me next. I am in a state of complete relaxation, and suddenly, as if out of nowhere, I have to start crying. I do not just shed a tiny little tear. No. I am compelled to begin weeping really loudly and with all my might. And somehow, it just will not stop. I am a little embarrassed. But Sami, with all his experience and empathy, obviously knows how to deal with a crybaby like me. Once I have regained control of my emotions, I immediately look for explanations for this. "How is that possible? I am happier right now than I have been in a long time! I have graduated and am once again having the time of my life here. So, why this emotional outburst with all the tears?" I cannot find any real answers. Perhaps the last of the burden that I had imposed on myself during the eleven semesters of my studies had finally dropped from my shoulders.

Following Sami's touch, I linger on the treatment table for a short while and take an inventory of my body. It feels as if some deep-rooted blockages in me have been released. It is truly liberating to simply let go of all the tension. The moment I gradually regain consciousness and gently open my eyes, Sami leans his head over me and smiles at me mischievously, "I think emotional problems you have."

"No way, psychic! What gave me away?" I think to myself and have to smile inwardly at the situation and myself at the same time.

We take a seat in his office. Now I finally have time to ask Sami my questions. He sits boss-like on the other side of the desk which he confidently conveys to me through his posture as he leans back in his chair: "Well then, starting you can!"

I pull out my travel diary, in which I have recorded all my findings, impressions, inspirations and questions since my semester abroad. Chronologically, I proceed through one after the other. I start with the most burning question for me:

1.) "How can I find a girlfriend?"

"Oh Thomas, my friend, do not think too much about the women. You are not ready yet. You need to look for yourself first. You need power first. Not strong enough you are," Sami replies. I find it hard to accept his answer because it means that I should continue to resign myself to loneliness. Yet, I long for nothing as much as I desire a steady girlfriend.

"And what can I do for myself? How can I be more attractive and self-confident?" I am not satisfied with his rather superficial answer and continue to probe.

"Mentally very weak you are. You make yourself stress a lot. And stress comes not from outside, it comes from inside. You need to learn more about yourself. You know everything already. Look inside for all answers. And do not be so strict. Life is very simple. Enjoy life. Use Sami's concept. You need to love yourself. Start from meditation!"

Diligently, I jot down everything and then decide to continue with the next question.

2.) "Sami, I finished my studies, but I do not know what kind of job to look for!? I studied something that I do not like. I really do not want to work in the job that I am now qualified for! I do not know which way to go. I do not know what I should do. I am not striving for a career. I just want to have a job where I can be happy."

Thereupon he answers me again without giving it much thought: "Start from economy. With what you studied. Still very young you are. You need some experience. You will find it. Happiness is a process."

Unfortunately, I cannot make a lot of sense out of this answer. As with my previous question, I was hoping for a bit more specific advice. Nevertheless, I am putting this on paper as well. Considering the unsatisfyingly vague answers, I decide to put my other questions aside for now. First, I need to let the advice I have received so far sink in.

7. Weightless

"There can be no doubt that all our
knowledge begins with experience."

[Immanuel Kant]

In the evening, we go out to the party of stronghold Kuta. I decide not to drink alcohol considering today's treatment. I feel well-balanced and, despite the somewhat confusing advice from Sami, nevertheless, invigorated again.

In front of *Greenbox*, a beverage stand and a popular meeting place for all students, we join a group of German newcomers. Just a few days ago, the new semester abroad has begun. The same one that positively changed our lives a year and a half before. As real insiders of the island, we do not miss the opportunity to make ourselves enormously indispensable with our local advice. Most of the people listen to us, and we try to answer all their questions about studying in Bali. But only those of the girls, of course. And one after the other, if you please. We tell them about our parties and present ourselves as cooler than we are with our stories about surfing life. We exaggerate the height of the waves as much as we otherwise would only exaggerate penis size. One could think that we are about to ascend to the Olympus of professional surfers.

Little by little, we've supplied information to all the new students and they turn away from us. Matt is completely immersed and continuously downs cheap rice schnapps. As luck would have it, standing all alone and somewhat apart from us is a charming girl who has so far been spared our tales. The two drinks in her hands suggest that she either is going wild today or is waiting for someone else. I take the chance and walk over to her uninhibited. "Hey, are you here to study, too?" I ask her in an entirely casual and natural way, without having a concrete plan in mind beforehand. She smiles at me and creates the impression that she is happy I approached her and she's enjoying my company. We then get into a rather superficial conversation. Of course, the numerous insights I gained during my study abroad in Bali once again provide an excellent basis for conversation. Her name is Martina. She is my most enchanting listener of the evening so far. I suppose she has always been the prettiest in class: Blonde hair, tan, with a gorgeous body, beautiful lips and a laid-back style. And moreover, she is badass cool. She is open and despite her beauty, not a bit arrogant.

As time goes by, we continually enjoy each other's company. My advice soon becomes superfluous, as we quickly move on to other topics. I feel very connected to her from the first moment, and sense the feeling is mutual. We laugh a lot, which I attribute to my incredibly great sense of humor. My easy-going nature is contagious. I am completely absorbed in the flow. Totally weightless. And all that without having to touch a drop of alcohol.

When Matt stumbles past me half an hour later with small red alcohol-infused eyes, I know that the little rascal has to be put to bed. Normally, I would celebrate him for this, as he is on the fast track once again. Today, though, I curse him for his unquenchable thirst. I ask Matt to wait for me for a short while. He's swaying, so I park him at the corner of a snack stand and return to the woman of my dreams. I cannot just leave it at this one conversation with her. After all the preparatory work I have done this evening, simply bidding farewell and leaving is not an option for me. Without further ado, I ask Martina: "Could I use your cell for a moment? My battery is dead, and I need to let a friend of ours know that we're about to go home."

She complies with my request, whips out her cell phone from her purse, and hands it to me. I type in a number and wait for it to ring. Since Martina is standing right next to me, she sees me pull my own cell phone out of my pants pocket, which starts ringing at the same moment. I have called myself on purpose, which has not escaped her notice. She looks at me in amazement.

"So, now I have your number, too," I announce confidently. With that, I put a beautiful smile on her face. We are both quite surprised at my ingenious pick-up skills. In fact, I am probably even more so than she is. I have no idea where I first picked up this trick. It really does not matter. What matters is that it worked. I save her number and find a few final words to flatter her about how much I enjoyed talking to her. With only two weeks left in Bali, I am not satisfied with the partial success of getting her number in a way that is both bold and charming. I want more. And now, just fully in the flow, I decide to seize the opportunity. For the desire to see her again is enormous. So, I ambush her again and ask: "Hey, what should Matt and I bring for breakfast tomorrow morning?"

Puzzled, she looks at me, but at the same time confirms my bold offer in a friendly tone, "Um, do you always treat every girl like that? This may come as a bit of a surprise, but just bring fresh fruit from the market. Is your buddy even up to it?"

"Do not worry about him! He has put up with a lot tougher stuff. He is used to it," I reassure her, and have the advantage of the element of surprise. There is only one winner tonight, and that is me. Unless, of course, the trophy of the Greatest Drunk of the Party is at stake, in which case the winner would certainly be standing within my reach at the corner of the snack bar. Finally, Martina gives me her address and describes the best way to get to where she's staying. Then she leaves with her friends, while we, on the other hand, make our way back to our hostel. Matt does not catch any of this, but just accompanies me like a scruffy street dog.

I cannot sleep the entire night. My thoughts of Martina keep me awake. I experienced the evening in a kind of natural intoxication. I am more than satisfied with my performance. I am fascinated and surprised by what is inside me. And I did all that even when sober. Somehow, I was completely being myself this evening. It is unclear to me how I was able to attain this feeling of elation. The session with Sami in the afternoon must have played its part.

In fact, Martina awaits us the next morning at her home with an extensive hangover breakfast. Of course, we forgot to bring the fruit. But that was to be expected. Martina and I continue smoothly right where we left off the night before.

Only that her roommates and my buddy Matt are involved in our conversations this time.

When we slowly leave after two hours to pick up our daily dose of sun and beach, I part from her with a heartfelt hug. Afterward, I point with my index finger to my right cheek and thus indicate to her that I expect a goodbye kiss right there. She complies with my request. The moment she moves her lips toward my cheek, I masterfully turn my head in her direction. Our lips meet, and I plant a kiss right on her lips. Her reaction suggests that this was not too intrusive and that she liked it. Somewhat embarrassed and with a bashful look on her face, she opens the gate for us and waves us off in the direction of the beach.

During the following days, we meet regularly. We do all kinds of things. Sometimes we meet in a restaurant for dinner. Sometimes we go to a concert. Sometimes we head to the beach together. However, there is always someone with us, which is why it is incredibly difficult to get physically closer to her in any way.

Our blossoming romance is somewhat thwarted by the five-day trip Matt and I are taking to the neighboring island of Lombok. But this trip cannot be cancelled because we have planned it for a long time. After our return, we only have one and a half meager days left to spend together.

Unfortunately, in life, all the good things go by much too quickly. And so, our last day has begun. The evening before our departure, to our delight, another student party is planned to conclude this unforgettable trip. Martina and I have arranged to meet there.

Matt and I do not miss the opportunity to pour a few beers before the party. Around 9 p.m., we enter the bar. We greet quite a few of our acquaintances, since we are well-known among the German students. Eventually, Martina's presence lights up the room and everything else fades into insignificance. Like a predator on the prowl, I approach her. When she smells me, she does not try to escape, but turns to me, beaming. I feel that we share the same affection for each other. I can tell by the way she talks to me, the way she acts toward me, and because she does not leave my side from the moment we meet. At some point, we are both quite affected by the booze. A serious conversation is becoming less and less likely. Even so, I do not harbor any hard feelings. The atmosphere is exuberant and while dancing, I openly seek physical closeness to her with my Latin hips and thighs. Finally, I have the opportunity to kiss her. I look deep into her eyes. She gives me a thumbs up and does not resist this perfect moment. I do as she wishes and kiss her. Floating on cloud nine with her across the dance floor, I feel like the most awesome guy in the world.

After a short break in the fresh air, the wild smooching continues. We sit down a little apart on a staircase and I advance very slowly to transition into light petting unnoticed. I hear initial shouts from passing and presumably jealous students: "Go get a room!" But these words do not bother me at all, much the same as my reaction to the words of my teachers. (No, of course, my teachers never shouted, "Go get a room!") But the vibe from Martina has seemed a little strange and slightly tense since we got outside. I do not attach too much importance to her behavior, and simply continue my smooth scanning of her hip region. In a brief moment when we are not kissing, she clears her throat and says completely unexpectedly with a subtly whiny voice in an unmistakably drunken tone: "I have to tell you something. After my semester abroad here in Bali, I will be traveling to Australia and New Zealand for another six months. I do not think it is going to work out with us. After all, I will be gone for another ten months, including my semester abroad. Please do not get me wrong, but we have only known each other for such a short time. I have the feeling that you are into me. I think you are really cute too. But honestly, please do not get your hopes up. I want to be unattached, both here and on my trip. I really do not want any obligations. I somehow have the feeling that you are expecting more."

I am at a complete loss for words. It feels like a real *Bud Spencer fist punch* in the face. Like a whiplash to the bare testicle. Like a stab in my heart. Of course, I had hoped for more! After all, one does not meet a woman like her every day. With the attempt to appear as self-confident as possible, I respond and give her the impression that she was only one of many: "Sure, I see it the same way. Do not worry, it is cool. Cheers!"

"Nothing is cool, you liar!" I clarify to myself. This is a setback I first have to cope with. How I should do so is a mystery to me at that moment, and I decide to deal with this situation in my usual manner. I head directly for the bar and booze myself completely to oblivion. The good mood on the dance floor is only superficial and faked. The crown of the party's biggest drunk clearly goes to me this evening. Although Matt is a great rival for me. My disappointment is simply too great. As a result, I am even too drunk to fully savor the affection on her part, at least on this evening. I leave the place in a semi-conscious state. I have completely forgotten how we said goodbye to each other.

I spend the night puking in the toilet. At least that is what Matt tries to tell me. I will probably never know if that is actually true. Because after my attempted suicide at the bar, my memory is almost wiped out. Booze depression kicks in as soon as I get up. This time it hits me harder than usual. Because in addition to all the physical pain and nausea I have inflicted on my body, there is also unbearable emotional pain. Again, it is the same pattern with the women. Again, I am being jinxed. Again, a girl from category B has crossed my path. Again, I was disappointed beyond measure. And again, I am lonely.

Yet, this rejection might not be permanent after all and there is a chance that she will suddenly feel a great longing for me when she returns to Germany in ten months' time. Accordingly, I see it only as a temporary setback and exercise optimism. The fact that we befriended each other on Facebook gives me hope that I have not seen the last of her.

c.) Encountering dreams

1. Flash of inspiration

> *"May your choices reflect your hopes, not your fears."*
>
> *[Nelson Mandela]*

The month on Bali has restored my spirits, quite apart from the emotional pain. I am totally motivated and full of energy, and I am now looking for a job. I follow Sami's advice and first apply in the world of business and finance. After all, this is my professional home. Or at least it should be. I do not have many other options to choose from anyway. Since I have no idea what other alternative route I could take right now, further studies are out of the question given my lack of professional orientation. An apprenticeship would be a step backwards for me. A career change would render all my studies useless and is therefore not really worth considering. Advanced training would be a possibility, but here, too, the question arises: "With regard to what?"

When I handed in my diploma thesis, I promised faithfully to myself that I would never study anything again. Or at least that I intend to take a break from it. My decision is therefore set in stone. Now the time has come to take my first steps into the world of work.

I am lucky that economists are needed in virtually every company and, thanks to the booming economy, are desperately in demand. Therefore, I have to admit that my parents were right when they suggested, for this very reason, that I should pursue this course of study in my earlier days of profound lack of goals and plans. There are more than enough open positions available in the market at the moment. I just have to choose where I want to start. These are the optimistic ideas I had about my start in professional life.

Unfortunately, reality tells quite a different story, and things are far from being as easy as expected. I applied for a wide variety of jobs in a wide variety of industries. Among them: assistant in a large bakery; commercial clerk with a car dealer; employee in patient management in a hospital; financial management in a retirement home; junior controller in a furniture store; sales manager with a radio station; and, of course, I have applied to all the well-known Stuttgart companies in the automobile industry. I make sure that the requirements of the job ads are not higher than I think I am capable of. And still this is not all that much. For fear of being overwhelmed and not being able to meet the requirements, I therefore apply almost exclusively for jobs that do not sound very demanding. My insecurity about my professional skills is frighteningly high. I do not feel thoroughly prepared for the professional world with my largely theoretical knowledge from my studies. Hands-on tools are still non-existent. I only have heard of PowerPoint, Excel and Word in stories and they remain unfamiliar to me. At the moment, I do not trust myself with a real career, and I am happy if anyone eventually hires me at all.

I send out one application after the other. Unfortunately, there is not a single job that I am even remotely interested in. I could not seriously envision gaining a foothold in any of them. But that is not the point. First and foremost, it is important to get started and earn some money.

The days go by, and my applications start to pile up. I am still waiting in vain for my first chance to appear in person somewhere. I find it disrespectful that some companies even have the audacity not to bother to send a rejection letter. They seem completely indifferent to the fact that a lot of work is involved in an application and that hopes are pinned on it.

As time goes by, I begin to reduce my already very low standards even further. I apply for every job offer that catches my eye that even remotely fits my profile.

After three months of unsuccessful applications, marked by plenty of disappointments, the time has finally come. I have received an invitation to an interview. As a medical controller in a hospital in Stuttgart. Now I have to find out what that actually means. At least I have a rough idea. I am meticulously preparing for my big performance and I am highly motivated to bring this unsatisfactory time to an end. My optimism grows with every hour of preparation. Similar to my studies, I tend to do too much preparation rather than too little, which I attribute to a lack of conviction in my own abilities.

A few days later, I put on my suit, tie, shove a stick up my butt, and go. Sitting across from me are the head of the medical controlling department and a consultant from the human resources department. After some initial nervousness, I manage to get into the conversation just fine. It goes pretty well. Despite that, the stiff atmosphere in the room does not at all make me feel at ease. Thanks to my excellent preparation, I am able to answer all the technical questions with flying colors. I rattle off my resume and let those present know how enthusiastic I am about the company and what great interest I have in the position — exactly what they want to hear from me. As if memorized, I spit out all my strengths and weaknesses. My greatest successes and failures. My motivation for the job and the benefits I bring to the employer. Much of this is outright lies. Everything is going smoothly so far, and I am increasingly sure of myself. Right up until the time when the head of the department asks me about my medical knowledge. I am a bit surprised, as this was not listed among the requirements in the job advertisement. As I have done throughout the entire interview, I answer in a carefully composed and rather stiff tone: "As you can see from my resume, I studied economics with a specialization in the management of social institutions, controlling and business ethics, and I have no special knowledge in the medical field. At the same time, I have no practical experience in this area to date."

When I finish my sentence, this also marks the end of the interview for my male interlocutor. In an unmistakable manner, he lets me know that I should not have high hopes for the job, since medical knowledge is a mandatory requirement. To be polite, he asks me one last final question before he dismisses me immediately following his interrogation.

As expected, I receive a rejection a few days later. Although this was not my fault, I take the rejection to heart and get extremely upset about this complete idiot of a medical controller. "If medical knowledge is an urgent requirement, why the hell does he not list it in the job posting too?" I call him numerous swear words. "Does he even know who he is dealing with?" I threaten him as if I were the Godfather himself.

"I couldn't give a shit! I would not have wanted the job anyway. And I am certainly not interested in this total douchebag." This round might go to me, but I am about to lose the fight. Meanwhile, my small doubts have been joined by the big ones. After this disappointment, I begin to imagine the worst scenarios. For example, I picture myself still not finding a job in a year and not finding anything after that because of this gap in my resume. I am extremely upset and harbor thoughts full of worry. There is no trace of patience and confidence anymore. The fear of being dropped at the edge of society puts me in a permanent state of tension. The feeling of not being able to measure up has wrapped around me like a veil. The same persistent questions in my head just will not go away. "How is it possible that I cannot find a job? I have a good degree in an important field of study. Have I gone through all the agony of my studies for nothing? Then I could have saved myself this crappy degree!"

Exactly in these moments, when my self-doubt is at its greatest, I additionally mourn my Bali acquaintance Martina and regret that everything would certainly go better with her at my side. Or at least would be more bearable.

My days are quite monotonous, and I have no real tasks besides the applications. After I graduated, I gave up my part-time job at the post office. A new part-time job is out of the question at the moment because I want to get started professionally and am focused on a permanent position. Unfortunately, I cannot really enjoy my spare time while looking for a job. What a pity. I would have had just enough time to devote myself to the pleasures of life. In my mind, though, everything revolves around getting a job, on which my future life is completely dependent, so to speak. My mental ballast is enormous.

In order to compensate for the stress of working on my job applications, I go jogging regularly. Exhausted from my everyday life as an unemployed person, I lace up my running shoes and set off in the direction of the fields. I need to get rid of my surplus energy and move almost at a sprint past the fields and woods. No trace of cars or other disturbing noises. I am completely at one with nature. The cool air nurtures my body with fresh oxygen. For a brief moment, I banish the worries and fears about my future from my mind. I could run endlessly. Mindlessly, I float across the fields. Despite my brisk movements, I am completely at peace inside. From deep inside me, an impulse unexpectedly emerges, creeping up on me like a string of individual words:

"...found a Healing Retreat..."

"...with Sami..."

"...in Bali..."

The more I give this thought space to unfold, the more specific it becomes. It is not so much an afterthought, as an emergence in bits and pieces that happens all by itself. One after the other, all my thoughts come together like pieces of a puzzle that finally form a coherent picture. In my mind's eye, I see a place where people can be accommodated and treated in a holistic way. Where personal growth takes place and people have time for themselves to recharge their batteries. A place where people can get help with all their mundane problems. Where physical, emotional and mental healing occurs. Where it is possible for them to rediscover their path. To get answers to their questions. All this with the professional support of Sami.

The more I reflect on this on a rational level, the more promising everything seems to me. I see so much in it. People would love this. I would love it. After all, the clinic where Sami currently is offering his treatments is really a dark hole, with lingering mold on the walls and stale air. Not to mention the location of the clinic. In the middle of Kuta on a rather busy side street, where the sound of motor scooters constantly stifles any sense of tranquility. This is not a suitable place to experience something as profound as his treatment. Often, for serious mental, emotional or physical problems, a single session with him is not enough. It would be ideal to have the opportunity to offer a program over several days and sessions.

I firmly believe that expanding his services could help many people and also prove to be very profitable. I refuse to let go of that idea. Or rather, the idea refuses to let go of me. I perceive how positively excited and happy I am about it. "Besides his treatment, there could be yoga and meditation. In addition, Ayurvedic kitchen with healthy food. Everything is aimed at healing," I mentally move a step further.

The day after my flash of inspiration, I can think of nothing else but my own retreat with Sami. The idea is further reinforced when I casually send off my application to work as a finance clerk for a no-name company. A stinking desk job with a fixed schedule of nine-to-five and the same activities every day has no chance in comparison to the vision of fulfilling myself professionally in the most beautiful place in the world. This gives me a crystal-clear idea of what I want to pursue professionally and what I do not want to do. I have never been faced with such a clearly defined goal. I have definitely found what I was never really prepared to look for when I was at school or during my studies. I finally have a precise idea of what I want my future to look like. This feels like the birth of a real dream. The attraction is not only the opportunity to pursue a career in a location where I and many others usually go on vacation. I also see it as an opportunity to express my creativity, to use my skills in interacting with other people, and to learn from Sami how to live a healthy and happy life. However, all this is and will remain only a daydream if I do not actively pursue this idea now.

It takes me a few days to get my thoughts in order and write down all the ideas on a notepad. But now the time has come. I summon up all my courage and sit down at my laptop to contact Sami via e-mail. With no strings attached, I just want to check in with him to see what he thinks of my vision:

"Dear Sami,

How are you? Around two years ago, I was studying in Bali. I came to you for two treatment sessions. You really helped me out a lot. Four months ago, I also visited you for another treatment with a lot of questions regarding love and my work. I hope you still remember me!

Last week I had an idea. I was thinking about starting a retreat center with you. To rent a house where people can stay and get treated by you. To offer a complete package: healing, sleeping, catering, transportation. A place of silence and harmony which is suitable for the kind of treatment you do. What do you think? Could this be something you'd be interested in? Could you imagine uprooting and changing locations from your clinic in Kuta?

I am really looking forward to hearing from you!

Kind regards,

Thomas from Germany"

I press send, and at the same moment, I feel a certain tension because I am not sure I'll get a response from him.

The days go by and unfortunately, there is no answer. "A favorable response from him also begins to seem too good to be true." I fear disappointment even in my most promising endeavor.

So, I go about my daily routine. In the morning, I write my applications, then I loiter in front of the TV. This is followed by my sports program. When I return to my room after cycling and turn on my laptop, there is an alert from my e-mail account, indicating that I have received a new message. Opening the inbox folder, I immediately register the new mail from **Balichyhealing@gmail.com** as a reply to my message with the subject *Healing Retreat*. My heart begins to beat faster. After all, my future is hanging by a thread. There is still the question whether I will have the opportunity to follow my heart, or if I will be doomed to dole out my life in a boring office job. This will be revealed right now with this e-mail. I go through the following words step-by-step in a most anxious state:

"Dear Thomas,
for my late answer very sorry I am. You know I do not lots of computer and social media. Good idea you have. I am very sorry, but I do not really remember you so well. Too many clients I have. Maybe we can talk in Skype about everything? God bless you,
Sami."

I am pleased about the generally rather positive attitude towards my request. I reply promptly, and we arrange to talk on *Skype*.

I am just as nervous as I would be at a job interview, but somehow in a pleasant way —and without a stick up my ass. I enter Sami's *Skype* name into my account and press the green button to video call him.

"Toooot...Toooot...Toooot...Hello Thomas my frrrrrr..." I receive another short greeting, until the audio dies away again and his video feed freezes to a still image. His Internet connection is inferior, as if he lives on the moon. Both picture and sound are very distorted much more of the time than they are working properly. This makes it impossible to have a proper conversation, simply for acoustic reasons. The situation is aggravated by his mediocre English with a Balinese accent, which causes additional problems of comprehension. In any case, we do not get off on the right foot, and even after several attempts I can only tell him in a very vague way what exactly I have in mind. At least I can hear that he is generally not averse, and we agree that we will both think about it again and that we will write to each other again in a few days. After less than five minutes, our conversation is already over. A few moments later, I receive the following e-mail from him:

"Dear Thomas,
very kind you are. Very good idea you have. But difficult for me to understand everything. Come to Bali. We need to know each other better and talk about it. Good opportunity for you! Sami"

2. Island of dreams

"Twenty years from now you will be
more disappointed by the things you did
not do than by the ones you did."

[*Mark Twain*]

A few emails later spent clarifying questions to Sami, my mind is made up to return to the Island of the Gods after such a short time. The dream of beginning a retreat center with Sami is alive and shall be initiated as thoroughly as possible during the next four weeks on site. There is a huge longing on my part to do something professionally that feels like a real purpose and not a societal stranglehold. Although I am determined to take this path and the mere thought of it causes me endless feelings of happiness, I am still ambivalent: "What kind of impression will this make on the people around me? After all, I still have no job and people will think that I am once again leaning back and taking a vacation! That I am avoiding my obligations, rebelling against the system. I hope not to disappoint my parents with this. After all, they have supported me financially very generously during my studies. Accordingly, I am obliged to keep applying diligently to get one step closer to professional life as soon as possible."

"But what the heck, I have nothing to lose. Even if Sami is not convinced and a joint Healing Retreat Center is out of the question for him, it certainly won't be a total loss for me because I can still enjoy the time as a vacation. Even if I then just end up letting another month pass and look the monster of lifelong unemployment deeper and deeper into the eye. Finding a job seems hopeless at the moment anyway," I justify myself to my own reservations.

I immediately book a flight to Bali and tell my entire circle of friends and acquaintances the same old story: "… a healer in Bali … who helped me with my back pain and eye inflammation … very popular with tourists from all over the world … want to open a retreat with him … a place in which his patients can sleep and where they receive intensive treatment from him … with an all-round carefree package … have already discussed this with him cursorily in advance … am now flying to meet with him and discuss this in detail … in the best-case scenario we will get started right away with the first preparations …"

In general, my intentions are met with an almost universally positive response. Especially my closest friends admire my courage for taking this step. Of course, I am also exposed to occasional critical voices. Mostly, their concerns revolve around whether it wouldn't be better to start working and earn money first. In doing so, they confirm the fears that I have already chewed over in my mind. It is not that I do not want to or have not tried. But so far, even with the greatest of efforts, it has simply not worked out to get a job.

The few days I have left until my departure are spent exclusively on my new project. I research the market online and find out which services of this kind already operate in Bali.

I compile my market analysis and all my ideas in a structured form and thereby accomplish the first preparatory steps for the creation of a business plan.

Then I turn my attention to Sami's homepage, which he sent me a link to upon my request. To put it this way: the only good thing about it is that he at least already has an online presence. Apart from that, I don't have much positive feedback about the overall presentation. There is neither a contact form on the website, nor the price for his treatment. Furthermore, there is no information about Sami on the website. His page only states that he offers massages and therapies and that he is a fifth-generation Balinese healer. Nothing more. Only the same text, written in terrible English, can be found under each of the different tabs. This is by no means the signature of a creative marketing genius. The design of the website is terribly dark and peppered with mystical images. There are hardly any appealing photos, or rather none at all. I do not find its online presentation very inviting. Quite the contrary, rather discouraging. I immediately realize: If something should really come out of this, the first task would inevitably be to breathe life into the homepage. It should be informative and visually appealing, with beautiful pictures of the Island of the Gods and of Sami. Furthermore, as many testimonials from former patients as possible should be included as social proof.

I start sketching out what the new homepage should look like, what information I need to gather and what pictures I need. Therefore, I must have my laptop and camera with me at all times. I am full of anticipation, as I am firmly convinced that with all the work ahead I will also discover a lot about Sami and learn a lot from him.

In Bali, I find myself in a now completely familiar environment. As with my last trip a few months ago, I moved into the same very basic hostel *Arnawa Inn*, which is located near the beach. But now, there is much more to this stay than intending to hit the road every night or spend the days hanging out on the beach. This is about making dreams come true. Specifically, I hope to earn a nice extra income with the business in the near future and to establish a second source of income. In the best case, I hope to be able to live off it at some point. That is why I do not waste a single day and despite my jet lag, I show up at Sami's practice in Kuta first thing in the morning the day after my arrival.

Unlike the last time we met, the greeting today is a bit more familiar and for the first time he does not welcome me with his Jedi Master standard phrase. He has kept the whole day free for me and postponed all his appointments. Finally, I have the opportunity to present my project in detail and without the permanent interruption due to challenges with technology. He follows my explanations attentively, even if they are only quite rudimentary with regard to the practical implementation.

Immediately thereafter, Sami gives an extensive answer. In fact, he has already played with an idea along those lines. He tells me about his mission as a healer. Bit by bit, he introduces me to his own visions. He lets me know that money has no great significance for him, and he is not eager to expand his business for profit. For him, wealth and luxury are not on the list of life goals. Specifically, he is interested in supporting other people on their journey through life with an open heart and a helping hand. Because that is exactly what he was born to do.

In order to pass on his knowledge not only in individual treatment sessions and one-on-one consultations, he would like to found an academy. More precisely, a training center. In order to finance this, he has established a foundation in addition to his work as a healer: The *Cahaya Hati Yogini Foundation* (which translates as from the heart of a Yogi Foundation). Through the foundation, he hopes to be able to generate enough donations to establish the academy. The idea of expanding his business as a healer has therefore been met with open ears. In his opinion, the additional income could be another step towards the completion of his much bigger plans. He tells me about the great popularity among his patients, which has been going on for years, and like me, he is well aware of the economic potential of the entire endeavor.

The training center is designed to give people with no prospects (physical or mental disabilities, no formal education, living in poverty, from broken families) the chance to train with Sami. The most talented graduates will then work in his clinic or have the opportunity to be sent to other countries as massage therapists. All others will be supported financially to be able to pursue their own path to self-employment.

He hands me his twenty-page foundation brochure to make his idea a little clearer. I skim the pages at high speed and, like reading a newspaper, am more concerned with looking at the pictures than reading the text. Still, I take the brochure with me and intend to review it in detail over the next few days. After all, it is important to be well-informed in this respect as well.

In order to give me an idea of the reality in Bali, Sami tells me about a young couple who, until a few years ago, had no prospects at all and had to live in poverty. Without financial support from their families. Without work. Without any formal education. Without a degree. And therefore without a future. He taught them the basics of massage therapy in a training course that lasted several months. He also provided the young couple with money to afford massage tables and the first month's rent for a treatment room. Today, the two run a massage studio that is frequented almost exclusively by locals. The two earn enough without having to worry about their future.

I sit there transfixed with visionary fascination. I had had no idea that Sami had plans of this magnitude. Until now, I had firmly assumed that he was just lining his own pockets with his treatments, and there was nothing wrong with that. Nor did I know that there is a small back room of about ten square meters in his clinic, which he calls his home. He lives there in a rather Spartan way, equipped only with a worn-out mattress and a small television set. Even though his income, which is quite high by local standards, would allow him to afford a much better standard of living. Instead, like most Balinese, he lives a thoroughly modest life. Together with his ideas, this adds to the credibility of his story.

I am haunted by doubts whether the business model for the retreat could really be a source of income for me. Somehow, I could not take my share of the profits to make my materially satisfying life even more complete, while Sami, through whose work all this is made possible in the first place, spends every cent to bring his selfless vision to fruition. With regard to his sensibly planned use of profits, I dare not even broach the subject of money.

In general, I like the idea of being part of something so grand and joining this heartfelt visionary. My deep desire for my life to be of help to other people is awakened like a dormant monster. This need originated in my early elementary school days. One of my best friends at the time was born with a disability that confined him to a wheelchair for the rest of his life, only allowing him to walk with crutches. He never let this handicap affect him, and so it was the most normal thing in the world for us children that one of us sometimes needed a little more support than others. He never let anyone talk him into not being able to do something. I have many fond memories of spending time with him, and he has become a great inspiration to me.

One moment in particular has stuck in my mind. Due to his disability, my buddy had to be accompanied to the bathroom regularly during breaks. We shared this task equally within our group of friends and were happy to do so for his sake. On that day, I was trusted with this task. I have no idea why two seven-year-olds would suddenly be talking about yearning dreams. Anyway, that was precisely what we were talking about at that time while walking to the toilet. I cannot remember what I said in the slightest. Somehow, dreams for me have always been subject to wild fluctuations anyway, and could change from one day to the next without persisting permanently. Even so, what my buddy told me when I asked him about his dreams still has a lasting effect on me today. In a deeply mournful voice, he told me at the time, "I would like to be able to run as fast as you one day!" This sentence has only revealed its true effect over the years. It made me think and made me realize many times how grateful I am for my life. In moments when I myself am in poor health, this mental retrospection provides me with support. It teaches me to be humble and to keep in mind what kind of lives other people have to face. Even today, this sentence from my friend regularly brings tears to my eyes. Over quite some time, I have developed the urge to contribute to improving the lives of others during my time on earth. Since then, I have seen it as my deep obligation to get involved socially in whatever way I can. Now, working with Sami offers me exactly this opportunity. Profit is becoming more and more secondary in my mind and must yield to my moral and social values.

Over the course of the next two days, Sami and I take our time talking through our ideas. We discuss our visions regarding the accommodations, the treatment program, the catering, the staff, a driving service and so forth. Since Sami has already worked as a therapist in another retreat program, he already has experience in this regard. Therefore, we do not have to reinvent the wheel.

We quickly arrive at the realization that all the work ahead can hardly be accomplished in the remaining three and a half weeks. Sami and I therefore agree that we will start our retreat with a new homepage and define this as our first intermediate goal. In my eyes, from a sales point of view, it is first of all important to increase his level of awareness and to make his treatment accessible to people beyond word of mouth. The foundation work around the academy should be pursued only secondarily at this time and give way to the project of the retreat, which should serve as a source of money and thus as a basis for the further foundation work.

Otherwise, our ideas are mostly in line with each other. In the creative process, promising ideas regarding the implementation are blossoming. We decide to place an ad in the local newspaper in order to look for potential lodgings together and to check whether our expectations are aligned here as well. Once the right facility is found, it can be quickly inhabited when the time of our retreat arrives. For the moment, the only option for us is to rent. Together, we have enough savings to pay for a five-bedroom house including a pool for three entire years in advance.

Since we have not prioritized the search for a house particularly highly, this is done only incidentally. We receive the first offers and take our time to visit each potential facility. So far, we just have not found the right one. Either the properties were too noisy or too small, too remote or too run-down, without a garden or simply too expensive.

Nevertheless, we keep our eyes and ears open, hoping to find the appropriate location during my stay.

3. Sami

"Sami's knowledge, care and skills as a
healer are truly valuable and rare."

[Sarah, former client]

My task in the next few days is limited to eliciting extensive information from Sami about himself and his work as a healer, in order to write appropriate content for our homepage. Therefore, I am a permanent guest at his clinic and use his small office as my workplace.

The focus of our website is entirely on him and his extraordinary abilities as a healer. After all, he is the main character and superhero around whom everything revolves. From a marketing strategy point of view, it is important to awaken people's needs in a visual way and with appealing content and information.

In order to be able to provide me with information about himself, Sami has kept this evening free for a short interview with me. We meet in a street *warung* and while we eat, he cheerfully starts talking. I write everything down in detail. Not only the surroundings, but I also capture the friendly interaction between us which makes me feel that this is not the kind of work I am used to. This is new territory for me, since my understanding of work has always been characterized by having to carry it out in an office and under a hierarchical relationship with the supervisor. I squeeze him like a girl on a first date. I ask the questions, he provides the answers. I ask him about every detail of his life as a healer. I want to find out everything about his career. I do this not only to provide the information on the homepage for others. Rather, I also have a personal interest in it.

It takes almost the entire evening to coax his life story out of him. Stunned by the multitude of information that has passed between us, Sami and I call an end to our time together for today. I return to my hostel and let it all sink in. I had already guessed that there was far more to his treatment than the talents of a simple massage therapist. But this level of experience, skill and knowledge he shared with me over the course of the evening is quite admirable. He has truly experienced life and has dedicated his entire existence to providing his patients with healing in full doses.

In the two days that followed, I compile my notes as follows:

"Chyrillus Ketut Samiratha, who goes by the nickname Sami, is a traditional Balinese healer (Balian Uut) and doctor. With his knowledge and years of practical experience on the harmony between body, mind and soul, he can identify the origin of misfortunes, diseases and ailments and find appropriate remedies for them. As usual for a Balian Uut, his treatment begins with devotion on the physical level. Or, in his case, with a massage of the whole body.

Sami was born in Bali in 1964. He has skills and knowledge that have been passed down to him as the fifth generation within his traditional Balian Uut family. At the age of thirteen, he discovered his extraordinary gift to heal people. The small miracles he performed at a young age led people from the village and surrounding areas to seek him out for help.

With the goal of becoming a monk one day, Sami studied at a university in Java for a total of six years after graduating from high school. First, he devoted himself to Christian spirituality. Then he studied Western philosophy.

The way he helped others at that time seemed more like magic than rational logic to most people. For this reason, Sami decided to study Ayurveda at a university in Bali and find out more about the human body. He studied Western medicine, naturopathy, reflexology, biology, physiotherapy, anatomy, pathology and nutrition. After four years, he graduated with top marks as an Ayurvedic doctor from the university.

But his quest was not over yet. He had more questions about understanding what makes for a happy life and how diseases develop, and he desperately wanted to understand them. Sami used his subsequent two-year study of Chinese culture (including Traditional Chinese Medicine) to acquire knowledge and techniques of another Far Eastern culture.

In order to broaden his horizons beyond the locally practiced healing methods, Sami also traveled to various countries around the world. As a student and teacher of numerous seminars, he has visited countries such as Australia, Hungary, the Netherlands and Germany since the beginning of the new millennium.

Sami has been using his extraordinary gift to heal people since 1977. Thereby he draws on his holistic healing concept, which he has developed over many years, and in which he combines teachings from Western medicine with Far Eastern as well as traditional Balinese healing."

I am quite satisfied with my text, even if it does not fully reflect what Sami shared with me. After all, it is crucial to just briefly list all of the important details in order not to scare off visitors to the homepage by offering a flood of information. I go through the text over and over again, to let it work on me from the point of view of a homepage visitor and thus future customer. Each time I read it, I become more aware of the importance of the information it contains, which increases my admiration for Sami.

4. The gift of a new life

> *"A healthy person has a thousand*
> *wishes, a sick person only one."*
>
> *[R. Berger]*

As part of my duties, I am trying to get in touch with as many of Sami's former patients as possible, asking them to provide me with a few lines about their experience with him. To my regret, he has neglected to maintain any real database in the past, which is why I can only fall back on a handful of e-mail addresses from his more than a thousand patients in recent years. I try my luck and write to each one in turn personally.

Just a few hours later, I receive an e-mail from Bob from the Netherlands, who happens to be in Bali right now and lives only two houses away from Sami. He invites me to meet him in person to compose his review together.

Pleased about the feedback, which is both fast and positive, I thankfully accept his invitation. Since I wanted to meet Sami in the afternoon anyway, this is the perfect opportunity.

His home looks very simple from the outside. As is customary in Bali, everything takes place outside of one's own four walls, which means that I get to see most of the neighbors. In his residential complex, there are apparently only locals apart from him. This makes it easier for me to immediately identify him as Bob. He has settled down with a cigarette and a beer on his veranda directly in front of his apartment. We say hello to each other, and he then gives me a tour of his empire. It is a rather short tour, since it is only a small room of about two-hundred square feet. As he explains to me, it completely meets his requirements and is large enough to accommodate the most important things such as a television, bed, air conditioning, refrigerator and closet.

He invites me out to the veranda to join him there. Kindly, he offers me a cigarette, but thankfully I decline. I also resist the temptation of an ice-cold beer. After all, I am focused on talking to him based on a mission of healing. I introduce myself to him in a few sentences and grant him insights into my own experiences with Sami. Then I tell him about our plans for a retreat center, what we need his help for, and where the information from him will be placed on our homepage. Subsequently, he tells me about his life. As it turns out, as a pensioner, Bob lives several months a year in Bali. The room and the veranda have become his second home. It is therefore no coincidence that I meet him here.

After some small talk about how much we both love the Island of the Gods, how delicious the food tastes and how nice the people here are, I quickly advance to the most important point. I ask him to tell me about his encounter with Sami in as much detail and with as much emotion as possible. I have no idea what to expect or for what problems he has sought Sami's help. It is unclear whether he just had a minor ache and Sami was able to magically make all his problems disappear into thin air with one firm blow and a children's healing spell like "kissing it better ..." or whether a terrible fate befell him.

Before he gets going, he lights up another cigarette. As far as smoking is concerned, he has certainly assimilated well in his second home. Fortunately, he has no further plans for tonight, which allows me enough time not only to jot down his story in keywords, but also for us to directly compose the content while we are together. Then he gets started. Sometimes I ask him questions in order to tease more details out of him. When we are finished after about one hour, I read out to him what I have written to make sure that he agrees with the overall result:

"In 2010, I spent several months in Bali. While visiting a friend at a local hospital, I had contracted bacteria that left marks all over my body in the form of red pustules and severe itching. The dermatologist I consulted diagnosed me with an allergy and prescribed medication. However, when there was no improvement, I went to a hospital for help.

But there, too, the only diagnosis was an allergy, which was to be remedied with medication. To no avail. On the contrary. Meanwhile, I had up to six hundred purulent and bloody pustules all over my body, and especially my arms and legs were completely covered. My strength had disappeared completely so that I could not even walk anymore and was bound to my bed.

When an acquaintance then admitted me to hospital, I was diagnosed with the hospital germ MRSA (methicillin-resistant Staphylococcus aureus), which was treated with antibiotics and several injections. After a five-day stay, I was discharged and a few days later my skin problems seemed to be over.

But only a few weeks later, the problems had completely returned, and I had another doctor help me, who also gave me antibiotics and several injections. Unfortunately, without improvement. In the eight weeks that I was confined to bed due to lack of strength, I had lost all my fingernails and any hope of improvement. It is an indescribably terrible feeling to be exposed to such an illness and to find no one who can help you. I had therefore already resigned any hope of a complete cure.

Word of my serious illness had spread throughout my neighborhood and one day a local resident, whom I was already familiar with by sight, stood in the doorway of my room. His name was Sami. He confidently told me that he could help me with my suffering. Since I had nothing to lose, I agreed to his treatment.

One day later, he treated my entire body with an extremely painful massage, thus reviving my weakened immune system. After the first session, he advised me to walk a little every day, despite my lack of strength, to boost my immune system in addition to continuing with treatment. On his recommendation, I also stopped taking medication to let my damaged liver and kidneys regenerate.

During the three weeks that I was treated with massages, natural herbs and leeches every two to three days, my condition improved continuously and a few more sessions later, my months of suffering were finally over.

Today I have no more problems and can enjoy my life as a pensioner here in Bali to the fullest. I sincerely thank Sami that he stood by me and offered his beneficial treatments in such a difficult time and gave me hope again. God bless you, my friend!"

Bob is visibly moved because of all the memories coming back to him as he recounts his experience. He agrees with the content I wrote and gives me his OK to publish it. Then he shows me his arm, where the last scars of the pathogen are evident. With moist eyes and a huge frog in his throat, he finally bursts out: "Sami has given me a new life."

When I bid him farewell, I myself am completely taken aback. I was so emotionally moved by his story. Our first testimonial is a real powerful shout-out that has secured its place on our homepage.

In the days that followed, I received further information by e-mail from various people all over the world. Each report is fascinating and unique. Among them is a stroke patient from Australia, for whom Sami was able to cure his hemiplegia, as well as a woman for whom the encounter with him brought about a profound spiritual change. In addition to my own testimonial and that of Bob, I select five others whose diverse stories are an excellent representation of the extraordinary healing Sami will be offering at our retreat center in the future.

Until recently, the question whether it was the right decision to return to Bali came to me continuously. I always found something that raised doubts in my mind. These became especially prominent whenever I felt the need to go surfing or just spend time on the beach, but was unable to do so because of all my responsibilities. In the back of my mind, I regularly had some sort of concern that doubted Sami's ability. Because honestly, I have to admit to myself, so far, he has not performed any real miracles for me and has not managed to fully relieve me of my health problems. Not to mention that his advice has so far not borne fruit in my hopes of finding a girlfriend. Therefore, somehow he owed me proof of his ingenuity to eliminate the last doubts.

But now, after all the information I have gathered about him in the past weeks, he has finally managed to do that. I feel encouraged in my intention to build a successful business with Sami and consider it a real privilege to be able to work alongside this man. And with everything I've learned, I am gaining more and more confidence in him and his constant suggestions regarding my own path in life.

5. Ego

"True change is within. Leave the
outside as it is."

[Dalai Lama]

During my stay, we go on excursions to the most beautiful places on the island. I have the unique opportunity to get to places that you normally do not have access to as a conventional tourist. The goal of our trips is to take appealing pictures of our superstar Sami for our homepage. We go to the mountains, to a water temple, to rice terraces and visit Sami's acquaintances in a traditional local village. It is hard to capture the magic of each setting in pictures, but I am happy with the results, all the same. Plus, we always have a lot of fun on each outing, and it is nice to become more familiar with my future partner along the way.

When we are not going on excursions, I am busy writing information for the homepage. Among the content is information about Sami's healing practices, a short summary of his healing concept, the course of a typical treatment and general information about the duration and cost of a session. Since there are constant communication issues with Sami — both in terms of contents and verbally — the job sometimes takes a lot of time. Furthermore, the texts have to be translated into flawless English, which poses a great challenge to me as a non-native speaker.

In the evenings, I devote most of my time to the post-processing of the images. I am still enjoying what I am doing very much. There is no one who tells me what to do. I can make my own decisions about what to do and how to do it. Sami grants me all freedoms and bestows upon me the utmost trust.

Tonight I have an appointment with Sami to present my preliminary results to him. I can legitimately say that I am proud of myself. After all, I have already achieved so much in such a short time. And all this by myself, entirely according to my own ideas. Only yesterday, we recorded Sami's therapy techniques and I spent half the night trying to edit them in time for my appointment with him.

When I arrive in Kuta, Sami is already waiting for me in our favorite *warung*. I have printed out everything on paper so that I can make handwritten corrections. We order some freshly barbecued fish and I start to present my results to him. Together, we go through the structure of the homepage and browse through the various short paragraphs and pictures I have taken. I explain to him with precision what I had in mind for each point. Sami follows me attentively without uttering a sound. He sits completely motionless next to me and glances at his documents, but never breaks eye contact with me. Before I have even presented half of what I have outlined, he bursts out unexpectedly in a loud and aggressive tone: "Is this everything? Already here in Bali for three weeks you are. Use my time every day. A lot of energy I spend. I think you are professional and do your best? This is nothing. No good. I do not like. Very angry I am. Big dreams you have, but no idea how to realize. For me it is enough. Stop it. I cannot do this anymore. Your spectacular project is over!"

He angrily slams a 100,000 Rupee bill on the table, stands up without even bidding me farewell, jumps on his scooter and speeds away.

"Sami wait," I try to stop him, at least to tell him my view of things. I glance after him and hear the engine of his scooter getting steadily quieter in the distance. The people in the restaurant are eyeing me. After all, Sami has caused quite a stir with his exit in the style of a real diva.

I stand there, crestfallen. My heart races, while my body seems paralyzed. Slowly, I return to our table and am distraught by what has just happened. Within a few seconds, my entire world has collapsed. I cannot even begin to explain his behavior. Especially not the way he announced his displeasure to me. This side of him is entirely new to me. I have never experienced him like this before. I have feelings of disappointment and failure. I feel nothing but inner emptiness. As if on their own, negative thoughts shoot through my head, reinforcing these feelings: "This cannot be true! I put all my effort into it. Surely, it is not that bad. Terrific, I cannot even get that shit together! No matter how much I do, I am just not good enough. What am I supposed to tell my parents and my friends now? I cannot find a job in Germany, and I failed miserably in my attempt to establish some social program here. I am sure they all think I am a failure. And that is precisely what I am!"

With the self-inflicted shit storm in my head, I sit at the small table in shock and motionless like I am paralyzed with fear. Thousands of thoughts come up. All jumbled together. None of them even remotely positive. Adrenaline and cortisol flood my body. My heart would not stop beating like mad. I begin to tremble slightly. Although my hunger is persistently huge, I cannot get another bite down.

I head for my hostel to be alone with my feelings. Once there, I throw myself onto my bed, as losers do. Since it is already evening, the day does not have much more to offer. I remain on my bed and find it difficult to sleep.

The next morning, I wake up still feeling like the biggest loser in the universe —no sign of improvement. I feel this heaviness inside me, unforgiving. I continue to be tormented by the same questions as the day before. In addition, there are general doubts about myself, if not about my entire existence. I doubt my character and question, as I have so many times before, why I have neither a job nor a girlfriend and why I seem unable to succeed at anything. Furthermore, I keep reminding myself of my past health problems and regret why something like this has to happen to me, of all people. My biggest concern is the idea of presenting myself as a failure in front of my friends and family. I would not fool myself. The project simply flopped, and I cannot deny that I failed. Of course, it is hard for me to admit that, and I try to blame Sami for the failure. I am furious with him. I doubt his abilities, and I am confident that such behavior is not worthy of a real healer. "Why did he let me go on like that? He could have provided feedback sooner that he did not agree. I would have changed it immediately. Then we would have been spared all this. All that work —all for nothing. I should have taken a nice vacation."

With all that anger in my belly, I grab my surfboard and head for the surf spot. I have nothing to lose, and I plunge into massive breakers. If it were not for this anger in me, I would certainly not have dared to go out on the water. The waves are bigger than they have been in a long time. I meet the walls of water without any feelings of fear —neither of skidding nor of hurting myself in any other way. To my own surprise, I am having one of my best sessions ever, right here and now. For the first time since almost an entire day of complete dejection, a small spark of happiness sets in again.

After almost two hours in the water, I grab my board and make myself comfortable in a nearby beach bar. I try to make the best of my remaining five days in Bali. My feelings go up and down like a roller coaster. At least they are now also minimally up again. Is this due to the many beers that I have had in the meantime? Nobody knows! But in any case, it does contribute to my improved mood.

With a dangerous mixture of disappointment, rage, defiance and alcohol in the blood, I stagger back to my hostel and fall into a deep sleep. The next morning, I feel considerably worse emotionally. Unfortunately, the high of the previous day was not a very lasting experience. The attempt to conserve the feeling of happiness from surfing with a few cold beers failed miserably. I give an extra-large hangover breakfast a chance, including Bali's best pancakes. Even so, my mood is and remains low.

I made myself comfortable on the veranda in front of my hostel room. While I immerse myself in self-pity again, I receive the following text message from Sami out of the blue:

"Do something best for yourself. I like you to make a project starting from yourself. Not for me. You need to learn more about yourself. Do not punish yourself doing bad. You need a process. The goal of your project is spiritual awareness."

I still feel enormous anger towards him because I have invested a lot of time, energy as well as money in the entire endeavor, and he has ruined everything in one fell swoop. "What is the man trying to tell me? Why has he suddenly come crawling back now? Why is he writing to me again? I thought everything was all over? I just don't understand!"

Over the course of the day, more messages from him arrive, all of which I can neither understand nor really frame. One of them reads:

"One day you will know what I did for you. One day you know what I want you to do. You need to listen to yourself. What you are doing for me is not for me, but for yourself. Do not worry. I never judge you bad. I know who you are. And what you need to do. You are not doing something special for yourself. I like you to do something for yourself. Help me doing best start from helping yourself. If you do the best for yourself means that you are doing the best for myself. I know what I am doing for you. Three weeks is enough for me to teach you. I want you to do self-introspection. Everything you know already. Ask yourself the question you need to know. I will never forget! All we still need you!"

I understand nothing. "What does this guy want from me? First, he bites my head off to no avail, and now he starts acting like a smart-ass again! He should first question his own behavior." I am undecided whether I should be angry or curious about what his messages are all about. I decide for the latter and write the following message:

"Sorry Sami, but I do not understand you. You left me alone with all my problems. You let me work on our project for quite a long time and made me feel like a loser! Why didn't you just tell me earlier that you did not like it?"

I think that says it all. I put my cell phone aside and pursue my temporary goal of enjoying life. So off to the beach. I dedicate myself to the supreme discipline of all spiritual exercises: chilling out. What more could you want? I also treat myself to four cold beers and an ice cream.

When I return to my hostel, slightly woozy, my cell phone's display shows three missed calls and a text message from "Sami Healer." I read through it carefully:

"YOU ARE NOT ALONE my lovely brother. I cannot always be with you physically. The principal project is not finished yet. Do not think too far. I do not like you forget the eminent project (awareness). Do not live under pressure. This is your project. You must be happy, positive, aware. I see you run away too far. And under target, make yourself stress. You need to learn more deeply perspective of life. You will not understand if you use your mind. Very kind you are."

I do not understand everything he wants to say, but emotionally I get the clear message that he still thinks highly of me. I carefully reread his messages from that day and decide not to answer him, but to go see him directly. I need clarity now.

When I arrive at the clinic, which he also calls home, he has a big smile on his face and I am completely relieved. His smile is infectious. It remains a mystery to me why he is so happy all of a sudden. Three days earlier, he had been furious and had left me standing there like a harbor whore, but now he welcomes me with a hug. I only have a brief moment to wonder before he gives me the answer to my still unasked questions: "You know, Thomas, what I did was for you. So hard sometimes to know you are sad. Excellent lesson for you! Very good for your process. I make you shock a lot. Good actor I am. If I tell you something not so effective. You need to experience. Experience is more strong than a lesson teaching you with words. What you learn from it is up to you. But one thing I will tell you: Your problem is, an ego you are!"

At first, I am still a bit suspicious about this sudden change of heart. We talk all evening. Only during the conversation do I realize that he has subjected me to a kind of shock therapy. Looking back, I do not find it quite as funny as Sami does because the last three days were really rather painful and associated with a lot of self-doubt. Sami lets me know that he loves what I have accomplished so far, which of course motivates me tremendously. I still cannot believe that the dream is alive again from one moment to the next.

In the last two days on Bali, I finish most of the pages for our website and focus almost exclusively on taking a vacation. So, the goal for this first stage has been accomplished. I have done everything I wanted to do. We just have not found a potential location for our project yet. Unfortunately, we never found the right one during all the visits. But that is okay because now it is first of all about creating the homepage and to beat the advertising drum for our future project. The path to the big dream is made up of baby steps. One thing after the other, all without stress. Just like Sami constantly preaches to me. For this reason, I will first make an effort to find a job in Germany and to gain a foothold professionally. After all, I also need an income. I can continue to work on the idea of the retreat center on the side. A good friend in Germany has already promised me that he will take over the programming of the website for us.

d.) Facing reality

> *"What a liberation to realize that the*
> *'voice in my head' is not who I am."*
>
> *[Eckhart Tolle]*

The intense time in Bali, in which I learned a lot about myself, has left deep marks. Especially Sami's accusation of being an ego raises many questions. I consider his allegation unjustified.

These days, on the Internet, it is relatively easy to obtain detailed and comprehensible information on all kinds of issues. For this reason, right away, I embark on a search to find out what constitutes an ego in the first place. As I learn in different sources, an ego according to the spiritual understanding is someone who identifies himself completely with his thoughts. This results in the most profound absence of consciousness. As a result, a misconception of oneself is established. For an ego, happiness can only be found on the outside, whether through a particular position in society, the possession of things, or the occurrence of certain events. If I apply this information to myself, it is quite justified to call myself an ego. I am a person who is completely identified with my thoughts. Or to put it even better, a human being infected by my own thoughts. They determine my reality, and I believe everything that this voice in my head tells me, without even beginning to question its validity.

The more I try to find out what is going on in my world of thoughts, the more obvious this becomes to me. To my horror, I realize that I almost systematically fall back on mostly the same thought patterns. It costs me a great deal of effort to identify and capture my predominant thoughts. Eventually, I feel like a child who is compelled to peek behind a closet door, where he suspects there are monsters stirring up trouble. During my introspection, I categorize myself into three key areas, 1.) Personality 2.) Relationships and Love and 3.) Job and Career, and jot down bullet points of what thoughts spontaneously come to mind in each area:

1. Personality:

"I am not good enough ..."

"The others are much better ..."

"I am not really good at anything ..."

"I am not confident ..."

"I cannot articulate myself well ..."

"This is way out of my league ..."

"I am so freaking forgetful ..."

2. Relationships and love:

"I am not good enough ..."

"I am not attractive enough for women ..."

"I cannot find a girlfriend anyway ..."

"In the end, I will be disappointed again anyway ..."

"When sober, I am too shy to approach anyone ..."

3. Job and career:

"I am not good enough ..."

"I am not smart enough for a career ..."

"I am not particularly confident ..."

"I shall be lucky if I get a job at all ..."

"I have to work hard for my money ..."

"With my skills, I will never really make much money ..."

"I am undecided about what I actually want ..."

"I lack a sense of purpose ..."

"I am afraid of failing and not meeting the

 requirements ..."

"The others have much more going for them than I do ..."

Good grief. Just imagine how it would feel to have such statements hurled at you by someone else? Surely, upon hearing them, one would not be brimming with self-confidence and love for oneself. Talking such crap about yourself in unconscious inner monologues is basically the same thing. Perhaps the sentences even have a much greater impact than coming from someone else. After all, there is no one whom you trust more than yourself. And you probably would not lie to yourself, which is why these statements must inevitably correspond to the truth.

Now I begin to understand a few things. I am gaining alarming insights into myself. Based on these thought patterns, it is no wonder why I have been quite dissatisfied with myself and my life for some time. It becomes clear to me that much of my life is a deceptive illusion that I initially created with my very own thoughts.

I try to understand the origin of these beliefs and where they come from. Thereby, I realize that a few of them have been with me since my early years. For most of them, though, I am unsure where I acquired them. I cannot explain whether they are due to my upbringing, were passed on to me by my parents or grandparents, or derive from people outside the family. Since I have repeated many beliefs in an endless loop, and they have been etched into my mind over the years, they have become a permanent component in my life. They feel like they have been there forever, which is why it is so plausible to actually think they are a part of me.

Quite a few of my prevailing thoughts seem to have been added in recent years. They have emerged from negative experiences. I have become a slave to my own past. This is particularly evident to me in thoughts that arose from a disappointing experience with a woman and that have been instilling in me the opposite of courage in order to ensure that I am spared such painful feelings in the future.

The more I look inside myself and ponder my mental fabrications, the more I recognize the origins of my own problems. I realize that my thoughts shape me into who I am. They create fears and set limits on what is possible in my life and what is not. They mold my character and forge my identity. The mental statement "I am ..." grants me attributes, while "I am not ..." denies them to me. Thus, when I say, "I am forgetful, unreliable, funny, empathetic, and so on" the thought bestows the corresponding attribute upon myself. It is entirely up to me whether these are negative or positive. So if I confidently claim that I am not good enough —well, that is equally true. Be it with regard to women, to my job, or to my own self-esteem. It is remarkable how a single thought or statement can completely change the course of a human being's life. "I am tall ... I am short ... I am stupid ... I am smart ... I am poor ... I am rich ... I am pretty ... I am ugly ... I am this ... I am that ... Compared to whom? Who determines what is the absolute variable to compare yourself with? Against what can we measure such statements? Who can assure me with all certainty that what I believe is true?"

In all my thinking, I realize that thoughts of any nature can be changed. It is entirely within our own power to decide whether we believe a thought to be true or untrue, whether we retain it or change it.

All these patterns have to be crushed in the future. But how I can bring about a change is a mystery to me. From now on, I will at least try to stop myself from following one of my patterns again. It would be best if I could recognize the thought even before it unfolds.

2. Welcome to the desk

> *"Everybody is a genius. But if you judge*
> *a fish by its ability to climb a tree, it*
> *will live its whole life believing that it is*
> *stupid."*
>
> *[Albert Einstein]*

A lot has changed in my life since I returned from Bali. I can hardly believe that in the past few days I have signed my first employment contract. Soon I will start working in a hospital as an assistant to the head of finance. At my job interview, I presented myself very well which included outlining my skills and how I meet their job requirements and was able to convince people across the board that I'm a great fit, both professionally and personally. I attribute this positive change largely to my time in Bali, from which I definitely emerged stronger and more self-confident.

In the next few days, I will be recharging my batteries as best I can and preparing myself for the upcoming tasks. Starting my career marks the beginning of an entirely new phase in my life. And somehow I am no longer afraid of it, I am even looking forward to it.

In the meantime, I have also moved into my own apartment. I have decided finally to turn my back on student life and no longer live in a shared flat. From now on, time after work belongs entirely to me. Only my own apartment can offer me the freedom I need. As luck would have it, an apartment has become available in my good friend's mother's house. The location is perfect, and I feel right at home there. It is not so much the bargain rent she has offered me for the large two-room apartment with a fireplace. Rather it is the garden, which is available for me to use and share with the mother herself, who being a spiritual person is concerned with the same issues as me. I have now found a real home here, and I feel prepared to face the daily work routine.

The first week of work starts off pretty exciting right away. I get to know my working environment and my immediate group of colleagues. I am also introduced to the organizational structures of the company and made familiar with my future tasks. As promising as the first week begins, the following weeks are disappointingly boring. I have to shadow my colleagues in accounting for three weeks. I cannot expect anything exciting from this. So, I just listen attentively —or at least make it look that way.

The weeks and months go by, and I quickly realize what role I have taken on with this job. As an assistant, I am more or less the go-to guy. My field of activity is topped off with tasks such as writing minutes, preparing presentations or taking on smaller projects within the company. I do not have the feeling that I will find the slightest bit of fulfillment in this job. None of my strengths really come into play here. In addition, I spend most of my time hanging around in front of the computer, which does not necessarily send me into a frenzy of joy. The largely very monotonous tasks do not arouse any euphoria in me, which increasingly has a demotivating effect on me. In addition, I often have very little to do, and it is enormously exhausting to always make it look as if I am working at maximum capacity, and I am always on the edge of my seat. This false appearance is also reflected in the working hours when I clock in and out. I am aware that managers analyze exactly which employee does how much overtime every month. With my numerous extra hours, I give them the unmistakable signal that I am pretty busy. Actually, the extra hours are accumulated through classic procrastination instead of actual hard work. Starting work early is not considered in any way significant, while leaving early —for whatever reason —is viewed critically. Therefore, I often stay longer without really accomplishing anything, and I am convinced that I am the only one doing so. After all, I have to prove myself and recommend myself for higher tasks. Working hours play a fundamental role in this respect. It is a never-ending game of cat and mouse that I simply play along with, even though it makes no sense in my eyes.

It was already clear to me during my studies that I would not want to work as a certified economist. Yet, at a certain point, there was simply no turning back. Now that I find myself in the middle of my professional life, it sucks even more than I thought it would. I find myself in exactly the kind of situation that I wanted to avoid by all means: I have a job and the security of a fixed income, but no joy in it whatsoever. I nevertheless try to accept the situation, as I have been looking for a job for quite some time, and it is now a satisfying feeling to finally be able to earn money and gain professional experience. At the same time, my patience is being tested and I long for a positive change, no matter how small.

Time flies by, and I feel trapped on the hamster wheel of professional life. Being in this grind of work sucks. There is no sign of a diverse and exciting life. The same rhythm every day: getting up in the morning, taking the train to work for almost sixty minutes, exercising patience in front of my computer screen for an average of nine hours until it finally starts getting a little enjoyable, and then going home. The next morning, the same thing starts all over again. My only glimmer of hope is the good relationship with my boss, who shares many common interests with me and makes the time at least somewhat bearable.

As I gain more experience, it becomes clear to me that not only do I not enjoy my work activities at all, but I am also exposed to common issues in our working world. I have to struggle the most with the constant pressure to perform. It is constantly a matter of having to prove one's abilities. You never perform well enough. As a lone fighter, you have to regularly extend your elbows, which is definitely not in my nature. What goes on in the professional world is absolutely crazy. I predict that many of my colleagues will, in due time, collapse under the enormous workload and suffer burnout. When I consider that sometimes I receive e-mails at three o'clock in the morning, I feel my suspicions are further confirmed. I have discussed this topic several times with my colleagues from Controlling over lunch in the cafeteria, who, along with my boss, are my closest confidants in the company. We wonder whether e-mails we receive at these ungodly hours really originate from the flow of work, or are merely prepared during working hours and then sent in the middle of the night when they get out of bed to use the toilet. I guess we will probably never discover the truth. What we did find out, though, is the hidden feature in our mail client that allows us to send emails at a delayed time. Since this discovery, it is not uncommon for my colleagues to receive my emails only after 7 p.m., and in this way, I send them an unmistakable indication that I am a real workaholic.

I would not claim that I am excellent at what I do. I undoubtedly lack professional competence. This is not due to my lack of intelligence, rather I am completely indifferent to most issues and lack all enthusiasm. Whether it is annual financial statements, inpatient and outpatient billing, contracts, insurance, the Association of Statutory Health Insurance Physicians, inpatient admissions, health insurance funds, the medical service of the health insurance fund or health policy —all these topics do not exactly make my heart beat faster, but rather trigger a gag reflex in me.

The hospital sector in general increasingly makes no impression on me, as I have noticed over time that it is less about healing than about the financial incentives that a hospital is exposed to within the legal framework. The health care system is a more or less well-oiled machinery that, due to the wrong incentives, is pushing the goal of improving people's health more and more out of sight. My goal of contributing to something good with my work is only achieved to a minimal extent, if at all, with my current job.

The fatigue at work has meanwhile also had an effect on my physical condition. For some time now, I have felt exhausted. This is noticeable by the fact that I no longer have any impulse for doing anything after work. I lack all energy and need more sleep than I prefer. Therefore, I usually spend my evenings in front of the television and let the light entertainment program wash over me, which means that I cannot even begin to find a real balance to my life. I have less and less time for my friends. I am miles away from a fulfilled life at the moment. A true vicious circle.

The dream of our healing retreat center in Bali has not been destroyed, but it has definitely lost momentum due to my time-consuming full-time job. Time simply does not allow me to dedicate myself to the tasks of our project in addition to work. Besides that challenge, I find it difficult to devote my energy to something that is so far away, and not just in terms of location. Maybe this is also due to the fact that my buddy just cannot seem to get going with the programming of the homepage. He has been telling me for several months that he will soon get to work on it. At the moment, everything depends only on him because the content of the homepage is finished, and he has already been instructed how things have to look. Since he does not want to accept any money for his assistance, I also have no means to put a little pressure on him. Finally, he has kindly agreed to do it. In reality, there is still so much work to be done on our project that it will take at least one to one and a half years before we can actually start earning money with it. Consequently, it is out of the question for me right now to put all my eggs in one basket and turn my back on my job in Germany. After all, I have to earn money in some way. So, I am practicing patience here as well.

3. Would you like yourself if you met yourself?

"It is not your job to like me —it is mine."

[Byron Katie]

The plan to observe myself with my restrictive thoughts, so far has succeeded only partly. Once or twice, I have been able to recognize a pattern and prevent the thought from arising. Most of the time, though, it is the same as always, and I only realize afterward that I have again been thinking and acting as usual. I just can't get a grip on how these thoughts are subconsciously ingrained in my mind. The same thoughts keep coming up in certain situations, almost automatically. At work, I often find myself doubting myself and the thought of not being good enough subtly resonates within me. This often leads to emotions of being overwhelmed, which in turn adds to my own stress. The constant inner reminder that my workplace is boring and that I am rotting away there is an additional factor of discontent.

Despite profound analysis of my beliefs in the different areas of my life and the first achievements in pursuing the gloomiest of them, I am currently far from being at peace with myself. Faith in myself has indeed returned since my time in Bali, and has since encouraged me to accomplish things that I would not have thought myself capable of before. Regardless, I still cannot claim that I think I am particularly outstanding.

I still do not have a girlfriend, despite the knowledge I have gained through Sami. I still feel emotionally blocked, and I just cannot get rid of the memories from the past that have caused this emotional pain. My broken heart is blind and, although my whole being longs for it, not ready to receive love. The loneliness really gets to me the most. It has been a full eight years since my last committed relationship. Some of my friends have already married. The first even have children. Others, on the other hand, have lived their lives to the fullest and have had fun all over town. And me? I do not even know how it feels to have a real relationship. I cannot even get someone excited about having a little affair with me at the moment.

It is not that I have not done anything to change my situation. Other people's lives are just drifting past me, and it seems as if I am the only one who is standing still. I finally want to know why love comes to others without any effort, while I strive for it unsuccessfully. "What are others getting right that I am doing wrong? What do others have that I do not? What have they discovered that I am blind to?"

For an in-depth analysis of my situation, I try to put myself in the shoes of the opposite sex and imagine meeting myself from the perspective of a woman. A visually attractive one with appropriate charms, of course, in order to make the setting as accurate as possible. I concentrate to immerse myself in the situation as deeply as possible. "What would I see? What would I feel? How would I behave and how would I react to myself?"

So, I imagine myself with imaginary breasts facing me and confronting reality: "The first impression is definitely a positive one. The athletic physique and his positive charisma make him likeable. His body language does not necessarily express the self-assurance that I hope for as a woman in the presence of a man. His gaze periodically drifts to the floor, and his hands are constantly moving uncontrollably.

I would engage in pleasant conversation with him, only to realize at some point that he is not really being authentic. It seems like he is obsessively trying to be funny and please me. Kind of a weird guy. I quickly realize that he wants to be with me at whatever cost. I could have him anytime. This makes him quite unattractive because as a woman, only the type of man who has self-confidence and is sure of himself and hard to conquer is of any interest.

I would consider the man in front of me nice, but he does not possess any real attraction for me. He just seems to be too preoccupied with himself. You can feel that clearly. I would slow him down in his attempts to conquer me at some point and put a stop to it. 'Sorry, but...'

Unfortunately, after this introspection, it is clear that I would have to answer NO to whether I would like myself if I met myself. This honest answer reveals to me in all clarity that this is probably also the reason why I search in vain for my counterpart in the female world. "Why should someone love me if I do not love myself? How am I supposed to expect anyone to actually recognize something lovable in me if I cannot see it myself?" The lack of affection for myself makes me think, and I would all too gladly do something about it if I knew what to do.

At least there is a small ray of hope in my life right now. I recently started messaging on Facebook with Martina, my charming date from Bali two and a half years ago. At the beginning, we had exchanged a few cursory messages from time to time. Understandably, my hopes were quickly ruined when she told me that she had met a German on her trip, with whom she has been together ever since. The joyful news that this German is now no longer her boyfriend set off emotional fireworks in me. I sensed my chance, however small. Since I have never been able to get her out of my mind, I have permanently clung to the idea that I might have her as a friend by my side at some point in the future. The moments we shared were too beautiful, and I remembered her too perfectly. Between us, there was something unique.

If I read the signals in her messages correctly, she is still interested in me. We would like to meet soon, but due to the distance between Munich and Stuttgart, her weekend job, and my full-time job, this has never been possible so far. Since she is originally from Stuttgart and her father still lives there, she was on a visit back home only recently. Nevertheless, a meeting still did not work out because I was in bed with the flu on that exact same weekend. It was a jinx as always, and probably just not meant to be. An old belief, which unfortunately is confirmed every time anew. Regardless of my thoughts —everything is still jinxed (and this is for real).

4. Disease as a mirror of the soul

"Before you heal someone, ask him if he is willing to give up the things that make him sick."

[Hippocrates]

My physical condition has deteriorated considerably in the last few weeks. In addition to fatigue and lack of strength, I have also been suffering from severe abdominal pain for the past few days. My family doctor has therefore put me on sick leave for the rest of the week. According to his expert diagnosis, it is a gastrointestinal infection. Unfortunately, the medication he prescribed is still not having any effect even after a few days. Specifically, my pain is a dull twinge in the lower region of my abdomen where my appendix once was. The pain is so severe that I can barely manage to stand. Therefore, I spend the days almost exclusively in a lying position and eat soup and bread as much as possible.

The same situation presents itself in the second week. I am still in bad shape. When I come home from my family doctor for the third time, I am not only physically exhausted to the maximum, but also extremely disappointed. He does not seem to be able to help me, and every visit to his office is extremely time-consuming: Arrival by public transport, quite considerable waiting time, treatment, trip back by public transport. And all of this in severe pain. My blood work does not allow any conclusions to be drawn. Instead of giving me sick leave for one or at best even two weeks, he has me come in every three to four days, only to be unable to tell me what is actually wrong with me.

I use the time at home to read as much as possible. I also meditate whenever I can. If my stomach permits, I go for a walk in the fresh air from time to time. I hardly watch any TV. I try not to let these depressing days get to me and to stay as positive as possible despite the circumstances. There is something good about being able to just take a breath and allow yourself the time to rest.

In the meantime, I also had an MRI and a sonography in hospital, which unfortunately or fortunately didn't result in any diagnosis.

After four weeks of being sick at home, I decide to undergo a gastroscopy and colonoscopy. I can hardly remember anything from the examination. The only thing that remains in my memory because of the anesthesia is the mischievous smirk of the head physician, who leans over me and asks, "Well, is it the first time?" Generally, I would cheer him for such a flippant remark. But, having been affected by it myself, he has been at the top of the list of my enemies ever since.

The results of the gastroscopy and colonoscopy yield no findings. Two days of hospitalization and the loss of my anal virginity for nothing.

Even after the fifth week at home, there is no improvement and so, on the advice of a surgeon, I have no choice but to undergo surgery to determine the cause of my pain.

I am depressed about the helplessness with which I am exposed to my suffering. I have been struggling for five weeks now and cannot really enjoy anything. My pain is all-consuming and will not let go of me, even at night. I spend my days on the couch lying on my back like a bug, hoping to be healed soon. Completely isolated from my outside world and unable to participate in social life.

In the meantime I have been to my family doctor at least six times, had several blood tests done and gone to the hospital twice. And nothing has even begun to provide any kind of explanation, let alone any relief. Quite the opposite. If I had saved myself all the trouble and stayed at home, I would most likely have recovered better. Therefore, my decision to undergo this surgery as a last resort and to allow the intrusion into my closed circulatory system remains firm.

During the weeks at home, I had a lot of time for reflection and I believe that my pain is psychosomatic in nature. After all, past days at work have felt as if my whole being is resistant to the job. Every time I picked up the computer mouse, my arm started to hurt. I experienced a mental block that continually intensified over several weeks. Pondering on my dominant thoughts at the time, I realized that they were exclusively negative in nature: "What am I actually doing here? What kind of shit is this again? I am not enjoying this at all! This stresses me out endlessly. I just cannot and will not do this anymore!"

The fact that my body is now expressing to me that I have been fighting something I do not want for quite some time, does not surprise me. On top of the general dissatisfaction at work, I had been under enormous pressure for some time. The managing director of our hospital himself had made me the project manager of an important project with an economic scope of several million Euros. The expectations for me were extremely high. Results had to be delivered quickly. The pressure was beyond words. Not only from management, but also above all from myself. After all, this was a huge opportunity to recommend myself for bigger tasks and to prove my skills. Nonetheless, I had to realize quite early on that the project was doomed to failure. Not least because of the short-term targets. My shortcomings in this area, the lack of support from IT, and the incompetence of the subproject managers involved gave me a feeling of being overwhelmed right from the start. The fact that my body is now fighting back against this stress, which has been going on for weeks, is entirely reasonable.

And in addition to all the difficulties at work, I have not been able to get rid of the constant feeling of a lack of love for several months. The loneliness and the desire for a girlfriend have had a negative effect on my emotional state. I do not want to rule out the possibility that this is one of the reasons for my stomachache. After all, just before I got sick, I had to go through another extremely painful experience with a category B woman.

After my previous health problems in the hip and back area that continued for years and my long-lasting eye inflammation, I'm now experiencing once again that my health issues aren't being resolved in Germany and I'm not getting any help. Healing only takes place when it is already too late and the physical body expresses the disease. Instead of treating the human being as a whole, only the symptoms are treated instead of searching for the cause.

The surgeon does his job extremely well, but after the operation, he could not give me any reason for the pain. He could only find some minimal scars around my former appendix surgery site. After three days in the hospital, I am discharged. Because of the severe pain caused by the wound, I do not feel prepared yet to go home. Despite that, the economic constraints of the hospital do not allow me to stay another night, and I am dependent on the help of my friends and family at home.

I have had physical discomfort for almost eight years now. While I've had to struggle with different issues each time, I was never really fit and healthy for very long. Furthermore, I have been living in solitude and with my persistent self-doubt for the past eight years. And finally, I have done nothing really fulfilling career-wise for the last eight years. First, I spent six years studying, which I almost did not enjoy at all. And now, for fourteen months, I have been trapped in a job that picks up exactly where my studies left off.

No matter how negative the last weeks have been for me, somehow I am deeply grateful for this phase and especially for the spare time I had for myself. I used it extensively to question myself and to draw up plans for a happy life. In doing so, I gained a lot of insights. The question regarding the meaning of my life became my constant companion during those days. I am now firmly convinced that none of this happened to me, I caused it myself. For many years, I had struggled with the question of why I of all people was exposed to such problems. Today I see it differently. I now understand that all this is my responsibility and that only I can bring about change. I have reached a point where I simply cannot go on as before. The years behind me have cost me a lot of energy, and I have lost a lot of zest for life. Now I have had enough. Therefore, I want to put an end to my old life. It is time to bring about a fundamental change. Not only in the outside world, but rather within. I am tired of being sick and weak all the time. I am no longer willing to continue living my life this way. The experiences of the last weeks have finally been the straw that broke the camel's back.

5. No growth without resistance

"When everything seems to be going against you, remember that the airplane takes off against the wind, not with it."

[Henry Ford]

During my absence from work due to my illness, I made the decision to rekindle my fire of enthusiasm for life: I will resign from my job, travel to Bali and make my dream of a joint retreat center with Sami come true. I see this not only as an opportunity to bring my vision to life, but also as a unique chance to undergo profound change with Sami's help.

It must be fate that Sami contacted me by email during this very time and asked if I would be willing to travel to Bali to help him set up the retreat, both financially and with my business skills. He had no way of knowing that I was home on medical leave with severe abdominal cramps at that very time. I had not told him, despite keeping in regular touch with him. It was as if he had sensed it. Just at the right time. In the course of this, Sami informed me that he owns a ten-acre piece of land, which is perfectly situated and offers ideal conditions to build a retreat facility according to our very own ideas. He had never said a word about this before. In the end, this information was decisive, which is why I made this decision with such conviction.

The decision to start something new is usually accompanied by the challenge of ending something old. This is especially true in my job, where my resignation is imminent. It gives me a headache to think about how to break it to my boss gently that his very best sailor is about to leave the ship. In the end, I decide to follow the band-aid tactic and end everything quickly and painlessly. I wait for the perfect moment, but there is no such thing. So, I close my eyes and go through with it. It is anything but easy for me, as I have always had a good relationship with my boss. In a way, it feels like having to end a love affair. Saying "It is not you ..." would certainly add an extra touch to this feeling.

What was planned to be a short process turns into a long, agonizing endeavor. I experience incredible appreciation as he tries everything to prevent my imminent departure. To stay in relationship lingo, he practically begs me to give him another chance. He even offers me half a year of unpaid leave. Despite his efforts, I remain strong and want to take on this new phase of my life with full determination. If I were to return after only six months, I would go straight back into the old vicious circle and would not be able to have the freedom to pursue what my heart has been longing for so long. My desire for a fundamental change is my greatest impetus right now.

Due to my long period of advance notice, I am still tied to the company for another six weeks. We agree that I will ensure a flawless handover over the next few weeks and otherwise not spend much more time at the office than necessary. After all, I am still struggling with the consequences of my surgery and even after the days off over Christmas and New Year's Eve, I am still not relieved of my abdominal pain.

There is one last hurdle to my trip to Bali now —talking to my parents. For days, I can only sleep restlessly because of the tension. I constantly play out the scenario of how they will react to my confession. Because my plan not only takes me out of my comfort zone, it also takes me out of my parents' comfort zone. After all, parents have a clear idea of what life should look like and how it should proceed. Quitting my job and traveling to Bali to build a retreat center with my savings together with a stranger, sounds in their world a bit like wanting to fly to the moon in a self-built spaceship. I am terrified of this conversation because I do not want to disappoint my parents. On the other hand, I am no longer willing to put this burden in front of me. I want to finally put it behind me to ultimately pave my way to Bali. Therefore, I muster up my courage and call my parents bright and early on Saturday morning: "Hi, it is me, are you home for the next hour? I would love to talk to you!"

Unsure and with concern in her voice, my mom replies to me, "Um yeah, oh God what's wrong?"

"I will tell you right away, I will be there in fifteen minutes."

We take a seat in my parents' living room. I start the conversation as follows: "Well, you know I have been home on sick leave for quite some time now. I have questioned many things and realized that I no longer want to live like this. I have lost so much zest for life through all the health issues of the last few years. Looking at it matter-of-factly, I can say that I have not been really happy or healthy for the last eight years. Besides, I honestly do not enjoy my job. I will crumble if I keep going the way I am living currently. This is not the life I want to live! I have therefore decided to bring about fundamental change and do something that I really want to do. You know that I have been working on the idea of opening a retreat center with Sami in Bali for quite a while. Sami has now written to me and asked if I would collaborate to establish such a facility. I have finally decided to do so. So, I quit my job and will live in Bali for the next ten months to set up the project with Sami. I already have a ticket for the return flight. I will live off my savings for now and also invest money in the project. This is my dream. For the first time in my life, I have a clear idea of what I want to do. Never before have I been as determined as I am now. So, I ask for your understanding and wish nothing more than for you to believe in me and support me on this path."

As I finish my explanation, I look into the stunned faces of my parents. I can tell they are both struggling with the situation. I was aware that this would not produce immediate approval from my parents, and had tried to prepare myself mentally for this situation. I had certainly misjudged their response, and my wish for support unfortunately does not come true. On the contrary, I have to justify myself for making this decision.

"What are you going to do for a living? Now you have a degree in economics. You could have saved yourself the trouble. Do you not want to work in your profession for a while? Do not let that Sami rip you off! I am terrified that once you leave, you will be cut off from the system and will no longer be able to find a real job when you return home. Just imagine that. In the end, you might find yourself on welfare. I know what I am talking about, I worked in the social welfare office for twenty-five years. Things can happen damn fast. This is living on the brink of poverty. You need money to feed a family someday," my mother prophesizes my own personal apocalypse.

I try to present the situation to her a little more realistically and to appease her:

"You cannot always assume the worst. I will only be gone for ten months and will then return to a normal job. I promise. Meaning that this can easily be justified in any application for a new job. Especially since it is also something in the social sector that can be passed off as development aid. I just see so much incredible potential there, why should this not become a successful venture? I can now apply everything I learned in my studies. So, my studies were anything but useless. I simply long to be happy and healthy. I have been offered a unique opportunity, which I will seize now. As I said, you can no longer change my mind. The only thing I want from you is moral support and faith in me. I will not take any rash action. Quite the opposite. I have thought everything through carefully. I know that money is important. But if I am unhappy and unhealthy, this will do me no good. I just need to take this step now."

After two hours, our conversation ends. I am sorry to see my mother so downcast, and I interpret her reaction as an expression of her love, worries, doubts and fears for her son. To a certain extent, I can certainly understand that.

6. Realignment

*"We cannot direct the wind. But we can
adjust the sails."*

[Aristoteles]

A few days ago, I started to work intensively on the completion of the website for *Bali Chy Healing*. In the meantime, I found a more reliable friend to program it for me, after the one who originally promised to do it, still has not shown any inclination to work on it after more than a year. We spend a lot of time together in front of the computer and make excellent progress. From day to day, my project takes on a more concrete form. The homepage is about to be finished.

In the remaining time at work, I feel free and detached. Considering my still open activities and projects, an insane amount of dead weight falls off me. Finally, I am rid of the shit. Hallelujah. For the foreseeable future, not being exposed to any pressure or having to extend my elbows gives me the sweet feeling of freedom. Finally, I am rid of my monotonous desk job at the computer. Never again do I have to wear clothes that make me feel like a nerd.

Inwardly, I let out a loud cry of "Freeeeeeeeedom" at every opportunity with the persistence of a *William Wallace* from the movie *Braveheart*.

Despite my euphoria and immense anticipation of Bali, I am a little melancholic because it is quite difficult for me to leave behind my accustomed environment and no longer have my loved ones within reach. You probably only appreciate what you have when it's no longer there. Or, as in my case, when it is foreseeable that I will soon no longer have it.

I enjoy the time so close to the home stretch to the fullest because everyone wants to see me again and spend some time with me. In addition, my abdominal pain is as good as over. There is still a little residual pain, but it is rarely noticeable in everyday life.

I have the feeling that since I resigned from my job and talked to my parents, I have regained the ease I lost years ago. The enormous anticipation also plays a significant part in this. And suddenly, it seems that I'm getting back into the swing of things even with the world of women. I received a message from Martina. I consider it a rather pleasant one:

"Hey Tom, I will be visiting my father in Stuttgart next weekend. Do you have time and want to catch up with me? Kisses Martina."

"Woohhhoooo," I scream from within me. "I am back. She wants Tom!"

We arrange to meet in Stuttgart at the bar where I usually hang out with girls to date —I have not been there in a long time. My heart rate is at its peak when I see her walking towards me coming from the train. She is almost prettier than I remembered. Three years have passed since our last meeting in Bali. It seems like an eternity.

We make ourselves comfortable in the bar and talk as if we had seen each other only yesterday. Most of the time we laugh. We never break eye contact. Thus, many times throughout our conversations, I look deeply into her eyes and our souls touch each other. There is an indescribable feeling between us. Such attraction. My heart is dancing. There is an army of butterflies in my stomach — or rather, they are enormous dragons creating mischief. I wish the evening would last forever.

Shortly before one o'clock, she finally has to leave to catch her last train. And she has to leave pretty fast because otherwise she would not be able to get home where her father is already waiting for her. So spending the night at my place is not an option. At full sprint, she just gets a foot in the already closing door of the train. There is just a quick and superficial embrace. We wave briefly at each other, and then she is gone again. I could kick myself for having had multiple chances to kiss her the entire evening, but I never took the opportunity to do so. If only we had had a moment longer, I would have dared. However, this train has now literally left.

From now on, hardly a day goes by without any contact between us. I can clearly feel her affection towards me. The fact that I adore her like a goddess will certainly not have escaped her notice. In the last three weeks before my departure, we definitely want to see each other again. Even better: we play with the idea of going on a trip together for a weekend. There cannot be a more obvious signal of her interest in me because

I think it is impossible to share a bed with her without becoming intimate. Since I am already booked up with various farewell dinners and celebrations on two out of three weekends due to my imminent departure, we agree on the second to last weekend before my departure.

As the weekend is imminent, and my anticipation is almost causing physical pain, I experience a bitter disappointment arriving in a text message from Martina:

"Hi Tom, I hope your preparations are going well so far!?? Unfortunately, I have to disappoint you. I got the results of my statistics exam, and I did not pass. The next chance to retake the exam is already in four weeks. If I fail it, there goes my studies. Please do not be angry with me, but I have to study the entire next weeks and have to cancel our weekend together. I hope you understand! What a shame.
Big kiss. Yours, Martina"

I now really have a thick skin when it comes to being disappointed by women. Unfortunately, it does not seem to be thick enough yet. My frustration is gigantic. Nevertheless, I do not give myself too much time to feel gloomy. After all, my time in Bali is just around the corner. And if I regard the situation matter-of-factly, maybe the change in plans is for the best. It is hard to imagine how emotionally tricky it would have been for me if we had spent an intimate weekend together and developed real feelings for each other, only to find ourselves separated a short time later being in different parts of the world. I would certainly have constantly regretted my decision to go to Bali. Surely, I would have missed her dearly and then longed for an early return to Germany. Now I can devote myself to my dreams and my personal change on Bali completely unattached. That has top priority for me from now on.

PART 2

e.) Living dreams

1. Heart work instead of hard work

"In all beginnings dwells a magic force.
For guarding us and helping us to live."

[Hermann Hesse]

My attempt at the check-in counter at Frankfurt airport to convince the lady to upgrade me to business class due to my ongoing mild abdominal discomfort (which is not even a lie) fails. With a little more sensitivity on her part, this would certainly have been possible. Instead, I run the serious risk of being allowed to fly at all. In return, she asks me whether I am fit to fly at all with my complaints. For a brief moment, I curse German narrow-mindedness before I meekly settle for the lower class in economy, into which I fit much better with my upturned cap on my head anyway.

The journey to Bali has become a routine for me after all these years. The total of more than twenty-four hours from my parents' apartment door to entering the door to my room at the hostel pass by smoothly. Even the traffic chaos around the airport cannot even begin to throw me off my game. Despite my planned stay of ten months, I have not taken more luggage than usual. Only my travel backpack which is filled to the top with t-shirts, underpants, board shorts and one or two treats from home. My carry-on luggage is a small backpack in which I transport my laptop. And finally, of course, my surfboard is a must. It is a truly liberating feeling to travel light because it makes me realize that I do not need any major possessions to live. This independence from property allows for maximum mobility as well as flexibility.

The Island of the Gods welcomes me as usual with open arms and embraces me with all its beauty. There is not a cloud in the sky. I am greeted with a warm smile at every corner, as if people know I have just arrived. Perhaps it is my pasty white skin that gives it away. After all, it is mid-March and the past winter has robbed me of any sun on my skin in the last four months.

I have known the Balinese owner of the inn where I stay in Seminyak and most of his staff for several years. In the past, a few heated table tennis duels were fought here and a few liters of beer were consumed. The *Arnawa Inn* has felt like a second home every time I have visited the Island of the Gods. So, it shall be my safe haven this time as well. I could not imagine a better place to stay, given the central, yet quiet location. It is only a few minutes' walk to the beach, which is one of my favorite surf spots. The rooms are furnished with just the necessities of air conditioning, a king-size bed, a closet and a bathroom, but they are reasonably well-maintained. Generally, I do not plan to spend too much time in my room anyway. My palace for dropout expats is topped off with a small veranda in front of the room. Since I see myself as a regular by now and the manager agrees, he offers me a special price for the rent. At least, he claims that vehemently: "Best price for you, my friend."

Considering my longer stay and my lack of income during this time, the equivalent of $180 dollars per month is actually an excellent price that I can live with perfectly well. The deal, instead of sealing it with spit and a handshake like real men, is brought to a close with a freshly prepared Papaya Mango Juice. As a thank you for the many years of trust, he also provides me with a small refrigerator for my room. A nice gesture, with which my small cabin ascends to the equivalent of the presidential suite of the resort.

I do not have much time to get settled because Sami asks me to be present at the ceremony for the blessing of his property, which is already planned for the first day after my arrival. Only then can the construction work begin. He has deliberately waited for me.

Sami picks me up from my hostel in his car. When I see him driving up from a distance, the corners of my mouth go up all by themselves. As soon as he sees me, he starts to honk like crazy. He stops right in front of my feet, gets out of his car and embraces me with a loud laugh. At this moment, my anticipation becomes immeasurable, as our project now truly becomes tangible. After this very warm welcome, we set off in the direction of his property in the southwest of the island. To Canggu to be exact. We travel through the streets of the region popular for all surfers, yogis, hipsters, hippies and expats and turn left in a small side street. I am enthusiastic about the location already because it is located in the middle of a very traditional neighborhood, where tourism has not yet taken hold. Nevertheless, the location is very central. It is only a few minutes by scooter to the trendy cafés, bars, stores, restaurants and yoga studios. The beach is also close by and can be reached in about five to ten minutes, depending on traffic.

When we stop, and I get out of the car, I am struck by the beauty of the property. Large shade trees open up above the grounds. The land is overgrown with grasses and shrubs. There is a small river running alongside the property. On the opposite side, there is a scene of indescribably beautiful rice terraces. There are almost no disruptive noises from scooters or the like. A perfect place for peace and harmony. The location for our retreat center could not be better.

I get to know our Balinese architect Pak Tude, who is very likeable to me from the very beginning. Although he speaks only very little English and my Indonesian is definitely in need of improvement, we understand each other at once. For the ceremony, we called in a local priest. He lights incense sticks and recites some kind of prayer or mantra in the various corners of the property. He also constantly drops blessed water on the ground. Sami, Pak Tude and I sit by the offerings that have been set up and watch the entire ceremony from a distance. We meditate and pray for the blessing of our endeavor. After fifteen minutes, the entire procedure is finished and the place is energetically cleansed.

We then talk in detail about the construction project. Pak Tude and Sami explain the construction plans to me for the two-story main house, which will have five rooms, a living room area, and a kitchen with a dining area. Furthermore, they plan to have a large balcony that will provide ample space for yoga practice. They ask me for my opinion and if I agreed with the current plans.

I had no opportunity to deal with this issue before because I had no idea how much money we would have available to build the facility in the first place. The main house is already largely covered, Sami informs me. I like what I see on the plans and approve. In return, I experience enormous appreciation, not least because my opinion is being asked for here. The groundbreaking ceremony takes place on the same day.

Immediately after my approval, the excavators start rolling. Or rather, the construction workers start swinging their shovels. They begin to prepare the ground for the construction of the house. I get the first spatial idea of what our facility will look like. Our project begins and I am overjoyed. Although, I am also a little exhausted due to the absolute sensory overload that I have been exposed to for several hours. Countless thoughts buzz through my head, and I am completely agitated due to the restlessness of my mind. I realize that the strain of the long flight and the partly emotional farewell from Germany have left their mark, and ask Sami to first give me time to slow down and settle in. This is precisely what he would have recommended me to do anyway, as I need to work on the project only with positive energy, passion and love.

The following week I spend a lot of time on the beach. I read a lot and treat myself to some well-deserved time off. Thanks to Sami's treatment, my stomach pains are now completely a thing of the past. According to his assessment, my *iliopsoas* muscle was inflamed, caused by stress and over-acidification of the body. He recommends that I avoid sweets and spicy foods until further notice. In addition, I should avoid acidic food and eat more green vegetables. It is also important to become physically active again. That means going jogging or surfing again to give my body new stimuli.

With each additional day of vacation, I become more relaxed and the ballast of the last few months disappears. I have defined resolutions for myself for my time in Bali, which I would like to implement. According to the principle "radical changes require radical measures," I am sometimes very strict with myself and eager to incorporate many things into my goal, namely to bring about a fundamental and positive change in my life. I have defined the following rules for myself, which I will follow to the best of my ability and conscience from now on:

- No alcohol
- No cigarettes (one or two clove cigarettes are okay)
- Healthy diet
- Plenty of sports
- Daily yoga and meditation
- No thoughts/eyes for women
- Focus inwards

- No bad and limiting thoughts
- Learn as much as possible from Sami

Since I am full of energy, I can no longer stand wasting my time on vacation. My dream is waiting to become a reality.

I am starting to take on our business plan with everything that will contribute to the success of our Bali Chy Healing Retreat Center: Product description, SWOT analysis (Strengths, Weaknesses, Opportunities, Threats), market analysis, target group analysis, market entry barriers, pricing, distribution channels, promotional activities, financing, business organization, short, medium and long-term goals, mission and vision and much more. From now on, the business plan will serve as a guideline for our project. And there you go, my studies were good for something after all. I have come full circle.

2. Panca Mayakosha Healing Concept

"Don't worry, be HAPPY."

[Sami]

Since the beginning of my stay, Sami and I have made it a habit to meet for dinner on the days we do not get our own fingers dirty on the construction site. This is something we both want. On the one hand, it gives us the opportunity to discuss our project and discuss further steps. On the other hand, these meetings allow me to soak up his valuable knowledge. I gain profound insights into his healing concept and his concept of a happy life, everything that can contribute to bring about a corresponding change in me and in my world.

In order to better understand myself and the origin of my problems, over time he introduces me to, among other things, the omnipresent natural laws of the universe. He teaches me how we manipulate ourselves with our minds, that everything is made of energy, what yoga and meditation do to us and how we can come closer to our true nature. Furthermore, he shares his own experiences with me and gives me clues about what he is getting at through anecdotes. It is up to me to interpret, question and put these into practice. Never before, has Sami told me specifically what to do and what is right for me. And I do not expect that to change in the future. The most important advice he gave me for my personal development during my time in Bali is: "You learn from what you are doing. From the experience you make. And most important: My concept you should use."

I cannot really use this advice yet, as we are only at the beginning of our project. In any case, I am keeping it in mind. The wise man, who often seems like a teenager with his playful manner, will somehow be right again.

Once again, I remind myself what it means to apply his concept. He already conveyed it to me when we met for the first time during my semester abroad. On each subsequent visit, he has provided me with additional details. Since then, it has assembled for me like a mosaic and has shed more and more light on my darkness. Sami's *Panca Mayakosha Healing Concept* is a holistic healing concept that he has developed over several decades and in which he combines teachings from Western medicine with both Far Eastern and traditional Balinese healing knowledge. It includes, among other things, the knowledge of traditional Chinese medicine, yoga philosophy, Ayurveda and the teachings of various world religions and all philosophers. He has acquired this knowledge in years of study as well as through in-depth personal experience. The connections between all this, which are decisive for his concept and therefore make it unique, were revealed to him during deep meditations. It is used as a theoretical construct to identify, classify and treat problems of various different types. In this way, it allows for a holistic view of the origin of problems.

According to this theory, the human being is composed of five (*Panca*) levels (*Mayakosha*), which are in constant interaction with each other. The five levels include:

1.) **The spiritual level**: happiness, consciousness, divinity

2.) **The intellectual level:** mind, beliefs, worldview, values

3.) **The emotional level:** feelings, temperament, sensitivity

4.) **The vital level:** life energy, chakras

5.) **The physical level:** anatomy, pathology, physiology

These levels are related to each other in a pyramid-like hierarchy. While the physical level is at the bottom, the spiritual level is at the top of the pyramid. All levels are directly connected to each other. Disharmonies within and between the various levels can manifest as disease by expressing themselves on the material (physical) level. This is the only level that is "tangible" in the sense of the real world, as the other levels are not visible and operate on a subtle level. Viewed in this context according to Sami's concept, unlike the approach of classical Western medicine, the body plays a partially subordinate role. Problems arise predominantly on a higher level. In his healing concept, problems are never seen as isolated, but are always viewed holistically. Illnesses or indispositions are therefore always a sign that something is wrong within us, which is why they should be taken as a warning signal to pay more attention to our personal well-being. By addressing the upper levels therapeutically,

156

problems on the lower levels can be remedied. At the same time, the concept offers starting points for how we can succeed in developing harmony and happiness in our lives. They are as follows:

How to be happy — Be HAPPY!

H: Healthy (physical level)

A: Aware (vital level)

P: Present (emotional level)

P: Positive (intellectual level)

Y: Yourself (spiritual level)

"**Be Healthy**" refers to the physical level. This is about achieving and maintaining the health of one's body, which is a vessel for our being. Among other things, a healthy diet, regular exercise or adequate sleep can contribute to this. Health on a physical level is essential for a happy life.

"**Be Aware**" refers to the energetic (vital) level and states that it is up to us to choose what we focus our attention on. It means that we can nourish our energy when we focus on something positive and weaken it when we direct our attention to something negative. Therefore, it is important to free one's energy more and more from all negativity and focus on what makes us feel better.

"Be Present" refers to the emotional level and tells us not to dwell mentally in the future or past, but to let our lives unfold with peace in the present moment. It teaches us to let go of negative experiences and practice forgiveness. Also, we should not worry about future matters because that will not relieve us of tomorrow's problems, but will only rob us of our peace in the present. Giving space to allow all emotions to unfold in the here and now, and feeling them consciously without trying to suppress anything, has a healing effect on our entire system. This is because fighting something only causes it to continue, while consciously feeling it causes it to dissolve and disappear.

"Be Positive" refers to the intellectual level and states that we always attract into our lives what we mentally send out. Therefore, a fundamental positive attitude is of great importance. Life never happens in opposition to us, but in support of us. It always takes place in cycles in a wave-like manner. Negativity is therefore part of our life. Seemingly negative experiences can help us to grow. It is up to us how we deal with them. In addition to practicing acceptance, it is equally important to be fully confident that everything has its justification and everything happens at the right time in the right place.

"Be Yourself" refers to the spiritual level —our true nature, our soul, our higher self. It says that we are created after God's image and therefore are nothing less than divine. As part of this divine consciousness, we can co-create our own lives with the creative power of our thoughts, feelings and actions, and are therefore no less responsible for our own lives. The key to a happy life is to recognize and embrace life as this divine self, and not to be deceived and thus diminished by one's limiting mind or the outside world.

On a basic level, I understood the concept. It has always all made a lot of sense to me when Sami has contextualized my problems, whether physical, mental or emotional, using this framework of understanding. Yet, as long as I still have questions and my problems continue to be stubborn companions, I will not follow all of this in good faith, but will continue to question it using common sense. Especially the part "Be Yourself —be your divine self" sometimes still seems to me like the prophecy of a drugged-up guru from a mysterious sect. But also in this respect, my teacher demonstrates sensitivity and always serves me only as much as I am currently able to tolerate. He lets me gain my own experiences and leaves it entirely up to me whether I believe something or not, without trying to forcefully convince me of it.

Understanding the concept is one thing. Internalizing it and integrating it into one's daily life is another. Only in the evening in bed, when I find the peace to look back on my day, do I notice that I have gone through the day once again as if on auto pilot and without the slightest spark of awareness. But at least I am aware of this in the meantime, even if it usually only happens in retrospect.

In order to better follow my mentor's advice in the future and incorporate the concept into my daily life, I have started reciting HAPPY to myself as a mantra and emotionally placing myself in the respective state of each component: "I am healthy (Health), I am aware (Awareness), I am present (Presence), I am positive (Positivity), I am divine in nature (Yourself)."

At first, I just recite it to myself a few times. With a little practice, though, I get better and better at it. I repeat it whenever I have the opportunity. Whether in a traffic jam on the scooter or while regularly waiting for one of the invariably late locals, while sitting on the toilet, while eating, as a short break at work, or at the beginning of my regularly scheduled meditations: "I am healthy (Health), I am aware (Awareness), I am present (Presence), I am positive (Positivity), I am divine in nature (Yourself)."

3. Bali Chy Healing Retreat

*"The people who are crazy enough to
think they can change the world are the
ones who do."*

[Steve Jobs]

The history and culture of Bali includes a wealth of knowledge about healing, spirituality and philosophy no less profound than India, but it is not nearly as well known for it. It has thousands of years of tradition, and is born of a civilization based on the simplicity of the spirit as well as respect for nature. This along with its exceptional energy contributes to why Bali is called the Island of the Gods and offers refuge to spiritual seekers from all over the world. There are only a few books in Western languages, in which this knowledge is compiled.

Sami's holistic treatment is unique in its form. Through his studies of Western culture, especially the philosophy and Christian spirituality prevalent there, he understands like no other how to integrate and therapize the Western mind and the problems caused by it, in his treatment. This greatly sets him apart from the other traditional healers on the island, who are largely limited to their own culture and have little, if any, understanding of the particularities of other cultures.

In terms of life coaching and groundbreaking advice on how to shape your own future, we have a real unique selling proposition in the market with *Bali Chy Healing*. This uniqueness is our great strength, but the downside is that with Sami we are dependent on only one person.

Our retreat package is designed to meet Sami's holistic approach and cover all five levels of his healing concept and philosophy (HAPPY). Sami's unique skills as a healer are the cornerstone of our retreat center. After a small traditional cleansing ceremony, in which guests' bodies and minds are attuned to promote optimal benefits during their stay, Sami begins individual therapy on the first day of the retreat program. This is based on his intuitive and diagnostic massage, in which he identifies the origin and nature of the problems and diagnoses whether they are physical, energetic, emotional, mental or spiritual. Based on his diagnosis, he designs an individualized treatment plan for the remainder of the guest's stay, which includes a wide variety of therapies to achieve maximum success. The package includes, apart from Sami's initial treatment, another massage and two other healing treatments, which will be provided by Sami and members of our team of highly trained therapists and specialists. In addition to the initial treatment, there will also be a final treatment with Sami, where individual problems can be addressed and questions can be asked.

Twice a week, a yoga instructor will offer classes at the facility. On one evening of the week, there will also be a meditation session, in which the guests will be taught meditation techniques. The therapy program is topped off with an excursion, including a traditional ceremony, to a special cultural and spiritual place to which conventional tourists have no access. In this way, guests are provided an insight into the culture as well as a spiritual cleansing.

In order to make our guests' stay as pleasant and unforgettable as possible, we offer an all-inclusive package in addition to the main focus of healing and well-being. For the transportation to and from the clinic, which is included in the retreat package, we have established a partnership with a business owner who has a fleet of vehicles of all sizes as well as a large team of drivers. He will also offer private cab service to our guests in the future.

The complete package includes a quiet guestroom, three meals a day, daily housekeeping services, pool, air conditioning, internet, small library, walks in the nearby rice fields and the caring hospitality of our staff. At least that is our plan.

4. Rumah Bapak Sami

*"Only those who know their goal
will find their way."*

[*Laotse*]

The name of our facility will be *Rumah Bapak Sami*. With this name, we want to express explicitly that this is a homestay and not a conventional vacation home. Translated into English, the name means "Sami's home." However, it is intended to be a home not only for him, but also for all those who seek his guidance and healing. We already have a clear idea of how we want to design the facility. In addition to the main house, which has five rooms and can accommodate up to ten people, we also plan to add a small annex where treatments will take place on the lower floor and Sami's new home will be on the upper floor. The pool will be located right next to it, with a large Buddha statue and a fountain towering above it. Furthermore, a traditional Balinese *lumbung* is planned, which can be described as a kind of open pavilion. Finally, a small temple area is envisioned for the entrance area, where meditations and ceremonies can be conducted.

According to the Balinese *Feng-Shui* concept, each component of the facility is to be aligned in a specific cardinal direction. Each structural element is thus assigned its designated place in the system and fulfills its purpose. Any objection on my part questioning this arrangement is immediately disregarded. There is no room for disputing this way of setting up the buildings and areas on the ground. "In Bali must be like that," as Sami always says so beautifully.

The beautiful garden has been planned to offer enough space for yoga, for meditation and for relaxation. Among other things, we plan to grow our own medicinal herbs, spices, vegetables and fruits there. These will become the basis for the healthy food, juice therapy and our herbal natural healing treatments that we will offer to our guests in the future. For this purpose, a variety of different types of meals with a variety of healthy ingredients is planned, which can be used to treat specific diseases, accommodate different diets, to detoxify or simply to increase overall well-being.

With our ambitious plans, it is obvious that even with lower costs in Bali, a lot of money will be required to transform our ideas into reality. I am willing to allocate a large part of my savings for this purpose and to make it available to Sami as the future owner of the facility. Fortunately, I have always lived a very frugal and modest life, putting aside as much money as possible. I have never felt the need for expensive things that many people consider necessities, rather I have relied on my gut feeling and continued to save my money with the thought that I may need it for something important at some point. That moment has now come.

Sami, in addition to my financial support, has one or two acquaintances from whom he can borrow the rest of the money. And in the end, there is also the possibility of taking out a loan from the bank.

Our architect Pak Tude will do the construction of the main and secondary house. The construction of our planned *lumbung* and the pool were commissioned to two separate specialists in their respective fields. We will get the Buddha statue for free from an artist friend who wants to show his gratitude to Sami with this gift for the help he received from him a few years ago.

I am in charge of the interior design. This includes the design of the rooms with furniture, plants, pictures and colors, as well as the layout of the dining and living room area, and especially the acquisition of all the necessary furniture.

While I am free to let my imagination run wild when it comes to furnishing the interior, Sami takes over the planning and implementation of the exterior. This includes the construction of the sewage and water system, a small temple, a wall around the compound, construction of the park area, paths and paving outside the main house, the management of the garden, the construction of the entrance area and similar things. So, in addition to the conceptual work, there is also a lot of manual work waiting for us to do, which will demand a lot from us in the coming months.

For the construction work on the exterior, which we carry out independently under the direction of Sami, we have access to a group of construction workers that we can fall back on and with whom we roll up our sleeves side by side. This group is made up of family members, acquaintances, as well as Pak Tude's construction workers who are available to us for extra money after their regular shifts on the main and secondary houses. We often put in extra shifts and work with lights on until late in the evening. It is probably the case that the construction workers —or simply "the workers" —as I affectionately refer to them, have never seen a Westerner work as hard as me before. They've also probably never seen anyone who requires treatment of one kind or another as often. A scratch here, another bump somewhere there, a tenth-degree sunburn, and so on. I simply do not miss out on any of the aches and pains that can happen while working on a construction site. But what can I do? After all, my skin is not like an elephant's. If they lack any Western safety standards and trample all the rules of occupational safety with their flip-flops instead of safety shoes and baseball caps instead of helmets, I will certainly not be the only one to break ranks. The consequence is that a lot of my blood is spilled. Fortunately, I always have an experienced healer in my immediate vicinity and luckily, we can get started immediately in our efforts to test the power of existing medicinal plants for their treatment effectiveness.

With all my authority, I declare an absolute ban on smoking for our entire facility and to express my will I even hang up a sign at the entrance with the same message: "No smoking! Dilarang merokok!" After all, we are about to establish a Healing Center. Therefore, I consider inhaling the carcinogenic substance on our premises to be extremely inappropriate. But who am I kidding? Indonesia is probably the world's worst nation when it comes to smoking, and with costs of less than one dollar per pack, a veritable smoker's paradise. Seemingly everyone here is addicted to the blue haze.

After only a few hours, my authority is undermined and the first employees begin to light up one cigarette after another, with great pleasure. And without any respect, right in front of my eyes. It was worth a try. But not any longer. I resignedly give in to the invitation of one of the workers and secretly light a cigarette with him behind the shell of the main building.

"But don't tell the boss ...," I whisper to him with a fat grin and a raised index finger in front of my mouth. He knows I am referring to myself, which triggers a loud burst of laughter from both of us at our mutual rule-breaking.

f.) Whenever the student is ready, the teacher appears

1. Loneliness in paradise

> *"Paradise is not a place, it is a state of consciousness."*
>
> [Sri Chinmoy]

Working on our project brings me tremendous joy. I am at our construction site almost every day. On the one hand, to keep an eye on the workers, on the other hand, I am fascinated by the progress we are making every day and how we are getting closer to our dream step by step. It is indescribably exciting to follow how, for example, a staircase is built, the water system is installed, or a scaffold is erected from bamboo. Furthermore, I had no idea how the construction of a swimming pool works. Let alone an almost fifteen foot tall Buddha statue with a fountain on top of it. And all of this was done with the most rudimentary tools and aids, which felt like they dated back to the Stone Age.

As an amateur craftsman with all thumbs, a completely new world of admiration and fascination, if not magic, is revealed to me here. Technical skill is matched here with painstaking labor (at least as long as one of the bosses is present). Our project not only gives me the chance to learn something from Sami, but also to expand my craftsmanship to at least beginner level. Ultimately, though, I am more of a thinker.

The business plan has been completed after many hours of professional pondering, and I am busy promoting our project. For this purpose, I have revamped our Facebook presence and launched an Instagram profile, which I regularly feed with appealing content. For some time now, Sami has also been collecting the email addresses of his patients, who are kept up to date by us at regular intervals through newsletters. I write to lifestyle and health magazines in Australia, Indonesia, the USA and parts of Europe to draw their attention to our extraordinary retreat center. In the meantime, we have also received the first excellent reviews on the platform *TripAdvisor*, which I consider crucial for our upcoming success. I am already in touch with a number of bloggers and influencers, who, I hope, will write one or two articles about us.

I am completely absorbed and approach my tasks with great enthusiasm. Nevertheless, there is something that keeps me from fully enjoying my time: I am not really happy. I have been here for three months now and unlike my previous vacations, this time I have not yet met any people. No friends with whom I can surf, jog or meet for a drink. If I do not have an appointment with Sami, I sit almost exclusively alone in the restaurant and eat my meal without any company. I sit there like a lonely cowboy in a saloon. It is simply dreary and often embarrassing to show myself as a social outsider in public. While at the other tables, people are having the time of their lives in their little groups, I sit there alone and just gaze into space. All I need is someone to come over and ask me, "Excuse me, don't you have any friends?" Although I think it is pretty unlikely that something like that will ever happen to me. But just the thought of it makes me feel uncomfortable. At the moment, there is no one except Sami with whom I can share my joy or even my sorrows. No one to whom I can confide all my experiences. This is completely unfamiliar to me. I go to bed alone and wake up alone in the morning. Instead of meeting friends and going out every night as I did on my previous vacations in Bali, I usually find myself isolated in my room or on my terrace, working on our project, meditating, watching movies or reading. Every day I run into the same people. Mostly locals who are involved with the construction of our facility. It seems impossible for me to make new acquaintances right now. After all, I spend a lot of time on the construction site and thus make myself scarce. I am aware that friends could be made quickly if I changed my focus and opened up to the world of parties and vacations. Because in the past, I have proven that I can always make friends quickly. Nevertheless, I am not ready for that. After all, time is supposed to bring about a fundamental change here. Apparently, it is just necessary for me to experience this social isolation at the moment because even the friends I already have on the island are not really available right now and obviously do not want any contact with me.

I have to admit to myself that I have conditioned myself over the years to only be happy in the presence of others. Since childhood, I have always had a huge network of friends and the company of at least one friend around me regularly. The same goes for my family, who I have always been close to. But here, I have no one by my side. Being alone is completely unfamiliar and is a source of great difficulty for me. Consequently, I make my happiness completely dependent on my fellow human beings and place the responsibility for it in their hands.

It is quite remarkable. I find myself in the middle of paradise and I've been living my dream. Every outsider envies me for this, and it is obvious that I should be happy because of these circumstances. Nevertheless, I am not! It is not only the lack of social life that causes me problems. My everyday life is also extremely monotonous. Every day is the same. Often, even the weekends pass by without me perceiving them as such. Every day is just like any other. My cravings right now could inspire a mantra characterized by "maximum fun, friends, joy, laughter, shenanigans, boozing" or the like. Instead, I continue to diligently recite to myself, "I am healthy (Health), I am aware (Awareness), I am present (Presence), I am positive (Positivity), I am divine in nature (Yourself)." Even so, I am slowly losing faith that this will really get me anywhere.

A typical day looks like this: Yoga in the morning, then surfing, jogging or walking on the beach. Then to the construction site to see how things are going. Followed by the daily strategic work on the computer and a long siesta. One usually merges seamlessly into the other. Afterward, I am busy with the procurement of all the items for our house until the evening, when we roll up our sleeves together with the workers. Eat, shower, sleep and repeat. I've been repeating that day after day and week after week. In general, I would immediately subscribe to this way of life because it is the lifestyle I have always longed for. It offers me all the freedom I need to let the day unfold and move at my own pace. And all this in the immediate vicinity of the beach and in bright sunshine.

But what good is all this if I feel empty and unsatisfied inside? I am fed up with the monotony of everyday life in paradise. I do not even appreciate surfing or time on the beach at the moment, and because of my indifference it is only mediocre fun. I search in vain for things I can do to spend my days in such a way that I happily collapse in bed in the evening. Or to at least experience a little variety and thus moments of happiness during the day. With all my might, I fight the unhappiness and succumb to blind actionism: I travel for two days to the north of Bali. There I visit an impressive temple, go snorkeling in the sea and enjoy myself. When I return, I immediately fall back into my routine. The short feeling of happiness is blown away. I buy new clothes and feel insanely cool for a few short days. Still, feelings of happiness occur only very superficially and the effects are quickly gone.

I treat myself to an absolute feast in one of the hottest restaurants, which leaves only rudimentary traces of joy (not least because I am sitting around there as a lonely cowboy again). I get a massage and am physically relaxed. The inner emptiness still remains. I treat myself to a yoga class in a beautiful facility, but even this momentary harmony only lasts until the end of the day. The next morning, all the benefits have faded away.

I go through all the options in my mind of what else I could do to finally get to the place where I would like to be emotionally and finally get my life started. Something subconsciously always makes me hope that the next moment or the next day will bring me happiness and fulfillment. This conflict tears me apart inside and drains a lot of energy. And this circumstance is beginning to seriously distress me. Not to mention the disappointment that my expectations of the time here in Bali, with the hope for attaining inner peace, love, joy, fulfillment and bliss seem to come to no fruition. Lack of understanding sets in, and I simply cannot explain to myself why my feelings are currently at such a low. Or rather, why they do not shoot through the roof despite my life in the midst of paradise. Thoughts like, "You cannot even manage to be happy here," cause my old self-doubts to resurface. "Was it the right decision to come here to Bali? Why cannot Sami, as a healer and life coach, make me happy or at least show me a way to do it myself? How the hell am I going to be able to compete in the shark tank of professional life when I am so vulnerable to stress? How do I manage to stress myself out here in paradise?"

My inner conflict continues for the days that follow. Despite all the doubts and the absence of real feelings of happiness, inside I have faith, even if only very subliminal, that in this phase of my journey there is a chance to learn something and grow that way.

As with any problem, I seek advice on this from Sami. However, he cannot recommend anything better to me than to continue to trust in his concept and to follow it. This is somewhat sobering, and I feel abandoned by him. Therefore, I practice patience and admit to myself that the grass does not grow faster if you pull it. Or rather, that happiness is not something that can be forced. I simply give myself permission not to be happy sometimes.

I find it a real liberation to let go of my efforts and surrender to the process without resistance. This small readjustment seems to have an effect after a short time. Sometime later, when I recite the HAPPY mantra to myself as usual and put myself emotionally into the respective state of the individual words, I have an unexpected inspiration with "I am present (Presence)." I realize that in the last few weeks I have been constantly thinking about the future without allowing even a glimmer of presence. Figuratively, I see myself —like a donkey with a stick holding a carrot in front of its nose —running after happiness. I run and run and run, but never reach my goal, no matter how close it may seem. In my mind, I had understood what the spiritual teaching of the here and now is all about. But at this moment, I am experiencing firsthand what it means to actually enter the archway of the present. The mindfulness with which I experience this moment is a breakthrough on my chosen spiritual path. It is so vivid, so full of energy. With my anchor in the here and now, I can observe what the thoughts are that

I am pondering: Most of them revolve around the future or come from the past. None of them have even the slightest relevance to the present moment. I therefore let them go, which leads to me becoming even calmer, even more centered. I no longer feel any impulse to want to bring about a change. There is only the here and now. And it feels so damn good. It is a eureka moment that finally makes me truly understand this simple, yet groundbreaking teaching.

The present has always been a means to an end for me. I am constantly striving to be somewhere other than where I am right now. And I am constantly longing to be doing something other than what I am doing right now. I pay little attention to the now. And I do so continuously. As a result, the present experiences a constant rejection. Therefore, it is no wonder that I am constantly stressed and powerless. Because this way of living is actually connected with a lot of resistance and restlessness. The last weeks here in Bali are emblematic of my entire suffering in the last years. My way out is an unconditional acceptance of the present moment —no matter how undesirable it may be. Thereby, peace sets in and energies are released because I no longer am fighting against something. If I succeed in this and I am present with full awareness, happiness follows me like my own shadow. I am firmly convinced of that.

An ambivalent feeling of mixed relief as well as regret arises. On the one hand, I am incredibly grateful that this inspiration has come to me at exactly the right time, so to speak. On the other hand, I could kick myself for having overlooked so many beautiful things in the darkness of unconsciousness with my previous lifestyle. In order to leave my path of "running after the carrot" as soon as possible, my full attention shall be completely directed inward again. For this reason, from now on, I will do heart meditations in the morning, at noon and in the evening. They shall help me to center myself even more and to move from the mind to the heart. My unattended mind, which has determined my life until now, whenever I was not present, will now be brought to an end. I am no longer willing to constantly play the same record in my head and let the same experiences become my reality. It is time for something groovy: a record I can dance to, with new vibes and fat beats.

2. The river of life

> *"My commitment is to truth not*
> *consistency."*
>
> *[Mahatma Gandhi]*

I experience the effectiveness of the method of acceptance when, early in the morning, the neighbor's cats begin a wild rampage on my terrace, as they do every morning. They yip at each other, tear at things lying around, throw things off the table and are just incredibly annoying in view of its effects on my very light sleep. Every morning I get upset about their fuss and noise because I hate to be woken up for no reason. Especially since I usually wake up very early anyway. When I begin to stop paying attention to the damn cats with their annoying meowing and their stupid behavior, but just accept them in their existence without judging them negatively, suddenly inner peace returns. I let go of my resistance, which leads to no more resonance. And without the appropriate resonance, the conflict with the cats loses its reason for existence. From then on, the cats no longer have any influence on my thoughts, and certainly not on how I feel. I made peace with the situation, and to be honest, I am uncertain if they came back at all afterward or if I simply stopped noticing them from that moment on. How nice to be able to internalize what I learned with such a great experience. Even though this feline controversy does not exactly equate to the importance of a diplomatic solution to avoid a nuclear war, it still represents an absolute benchmark experience for me. Actually, experiencing something has yet another very different learning effect than just reading about it. It reminds me of Sami's shock therapy a few years ago.

The more I accept my presence with all that it holds for me just as it is, without the desire to change it, the more silence and satisfaction returns. Increasingly, I succeed in identifying the thinker and critic voice in my head as such. In the state of being present, I am surprised at how often I am able to identify my thoughts. My feelings regarding my loneliness have turned around 180 degrees. I believe that the reason for an increasing peace of mind lies in the fact I am not exposed to the distraction of others. I now understand that my social isolation has its justification and gives me the space to be more with myself. My inner balance is certainly also due to my heart meditations, which are becoming more intense every day in light of my decreasing mental activities. I feel I am on the right path, and I am proud that I found it on my own and without the help of Sami.

When I tell him about my inner breakthrough and the experiences of the last few days, he just smiles to himself, as if he knows exactly at which point I am currently within my growth process. "Happiness is a process," is the only thing he has to say to me.

It is a sunny day. I got up with the first rays of the sun, as I do every morning, and went to the beach for a casual walk. Afterward, I prepared a fresh fruit salad for breakfast and went straight to our construction site. Now I am sitting by the small river that separates our property from the beautiful rice field opposite. The birds on our big shady trees are chirping as beautifully as they can. A light breeze picks up now and then, adding comfort to the warm temperatures. I take a seat on a small wall right at the edge of the water and follow the hustle and bustle of the small river with great anticipation. It is as if I am hypnotized by the continuous movement of the water, and the longer I observe the flow, the more I fall into a trance-like state. My full attention is focused on the water. With the stream, there is no beginning and no end. It is literally all a flowing transition. I could sit here all my life. The river would never stop flowing without outside influence. From where I am sitting right now, I cannot see and therefore cannot know where it comes from and where it leads. The water does not adhere to anything, but takes its course naturally. There are no obstacles that stop it in its flow. There is something very calming about the sound of the water, and it puts me further into a meditative state. As I increasingly become one with the element of water, a feeling arises that inexplicably forms into a thought and seems to me like a profound revelation about life:

The river is life. Every human being goes through life in exactly this way. Life happens on its own and always steers us in the right direction. Our task is to let ourselves drift. If you accept this river and surrender to the flow, everything continues by itself. This river has no destination. The goal is reached when we understand that we will be on the way continuously. Everything to the right and left of the riverbank is impermanent (material world, fellow human beings, money). Clinging to a section of the river is associated with pain. For life is in a constant state of change. If we hold on to one section for too long, it drains our energy because the river wants to carry us along (growth, new experiences) and we have to muster strength to hold on.

If we expect something special (expectations, desire) from one of the upcoming sections (future), this can lead to disappointment. Because often something entirely different occurs. Even if we get what we hope for, pain will occur because this section is also transient and must be left behind again at some point. Every thought, every wish that does not correspond to what is, goes against this current and provides resistance.

We always have influence only on the area in which we are at the moment (presence). Constantly wanting to go somewhere else while still in the here and now is associated with restlessness. We know where the flow has taken us (past). If one tries to return to a past shore (change or return to the past), it only costs strength to swim against the current. Even so, a change is hopeless, since we have no more influence on it. It is time to leave the sections (past conditioning) behind and be open for what is yet to come (positivity, trust).

To surrender to the flow of the river, to let oneself drift (accept, let go, trust) and to enjoy this process is what it means to really live it (happiness, fulfillment).

I cannot estimate how long I have been sitting by the river in this state of being. At some point, I feel the natural urge to move again. Therefore, I leave my spot and look for Sami, who is just doing his inspection rounds on the construction site like a sheriff. I proudly tell him about my new knowledge. And yet, his response is simply to ask whether I have now joined the ranks of the philosophers. As usual, he cannot help saying "Haha, so funny!"

3. Back to who I really am

> *"The secret of change is to focus all of*
> *your energy not on the fighting the old,*
> *but on building the new."*
>
> *[Socrates]*

I had hoped that Sami would have supported me a little more in my development. Somehow, I expect that from my teacher and even more from a good friend. I confront him with this while we are having dinner together in a *warung*: "Sami, why didn't you tell me that I was going in the wrong direction? You know, I have been quite confused the last weeks. You could have just told me what I needed to do!"

"You learn from what you do. From what you experience. Not from the books. Your own experiences you need to make. If I just teach you by telling, there is no big result. You have not been ready yet. Now some good experiences you have. Start with them. What I can now tell you: More about yoga you should learn! A teacher training in Denpasar you can do. I know a place where you can learn," he replies.

Without giving it a second thought, I express my interest right away. I see no reason why I should not follow his recommendations. Although I have been practicing yoga regularly at the lowest beginner level for some time, training to become a teacher has never crossed my mind. Delving deeper into the subject would be beneficial. After all, I feel insanely energized, balanced and relaxed even when I am practicing just for myself. And that, even though I only have some basic knowledge and do not always bend my body in a healthy way. "Sounds great. How much is it? How long will it take? Is it also for beginners? Where does the yoga teacher training take place? Do you think I am ready for it? I fear that I am not flexible enough to become a teacher! Especially, my hips. They're tight."

I notice from his reaction that it was too many questions at once because he only answers with a short: "If you want, we can drive to the *Bali-India-Foundation* in Denpasar tomorrow. There we can ask what you need to know. And whatever you do, please don't worry, be HAPPY!"

The next morning, Sami picks me up from my hostel, and we ride on his scooter into the depths of Denpasar. Away from all the tourists, on the way to the center of Bali's capital, a traffic jumble awaits us, the extent of which I have never experienced before. Around us is an army of scooters and cars. Even the most basic laws of road traffic seem to have been abolished here. To my misfortune, my driver is a local who is in no way inferior to the other road users. All around me is war. There is no right and left, only full speed ahead. The horn is only used to greet someone or to signal the other road users to make way immediately. The intended use and actual purpose of this warning signal is obviously completely foreign to the people here. I shout to the person in front of me. "Saaaami, I want to live!" He feels confirmed in his driving style and pushes the accelerator even more for no reason at all. Unfortunately, all scooters here are tuned to allow speeds well over 50 mph. The traffic light has already turned red, which does not cause him to slow down significantly. Passing all the competitors, he cleverly places himself in the first row at the traffic light, turns to face me in the back and confidently announces: "*Bali Chy Healing* number one."

Considering my mortal fears, I find it hard to celebrate him for this. I do it anyway because somehow I am also grateful to have a real player as a teacher.

Fortunately, we reach the Bali-India-Foundation largely unscathed, apart from the vast amounts of unnecessarily released stress hormones. We are welcomed by a local at the reception area. There, I get all my questions answered. The universe seems to support me in this new venture and in some way, I cannot ignore the impression that Sami has already planned my yoga teacher training long ago. Because, as luck would have it, the next trainer training starts in just five days. After a short consultation with Sami, in order to confirm my absence won't have a negative effect on our project, I decide to sign up. Four weeks of intensive training to become an *Asthanga* Yoga teacher lay ahead of me. The classes take place six days a week, with five to seven hours per day. The only drawback is that I am the only foreigner and therefore will be the Western center of attention.

Five days later, the day has come. Like a caring mother, Sami kindly accompanies me to the first training session. Without him, the capital city hell with all its traffic would probably have swallowed me up. Fortunately, there are several participants who work in the tourism industry and are therefore proficient in English. With the rest of my fellow participants, I communicate using a mix of Indonesian, English and hands and feet. I am surprised at how well this works in the meantime. Even if there are any communication problems, there is always someone from the group available to act as a translator. The course takes place on weekdays from three in the afternoon until nine in the evening. One third of the time is devoted to *yoga sutras* (yoga philosophy), while the rest is spent studying and practicing *pranayama* (breathing exercises), *asanas* (physical exercises) or meditation. On Saturdays, we travel together to the north of the island for classes in a yoga facility in the jungle. Sundays are our only free days.

In addition to the daily classes, we have been given a yoga lifestyle schedule to follow on our own. It includes getting up at 4:30 in the morning, brushing our teeth and cleaning our mouths with coconut oil, drinking a glass of warm water and then going for a walk for half an hour. Immediately afterward, yoga should be practiced for one to one and a half hours. Eating is allowed only at certain times of the day. At lunchtime, one should drink a juice, made from two tomatoes, a carrot, a piece of ginger and salt. Sleep is forbidden during the day, so as not to expose the body to the effort of first going down and then going up again. To further focus inward, surfing the internet and especially social media distractions are off limits during this time.

I am highly motivated and strictly follow the lifestyle recommendations of my Indian guru. For a total of three days. Then I have had enough. I am forced to modify the daily routine a little according to my individual circumstances. My afternoon nap was firmly established in my school days and also became a fixed part of my life during my studies. It is indispensable. Furthermore, I have to skip my morning walk. At this ungodly hour, it is unfortunately not possible for me to go for an undisturbed walk. On each of the three mornings, I was constantly molested by drunks on their way to bed, pointedly asked by prostitutes for paid sex or sexually harassed by some fake Marilyn Monroes with an Adam's apple. This is all due to the proximity of my hostel to the gay bars and red-light establishments of the island. Otherwise, I follow the rest of the guidelines stringently. The time during the training is fantastic. As part of a group consisting exclusively of locals, I get to know the culture and the way of life from an entirely different side once again. Balinese people are characterized by their openness. I can feel that myself because during this experience, I have a sense of belonging to the group. Somehow, everyone approaches each other as if they have known each other for several years and are good friends. We laugh a lot. Everyone demonstrates great sympathy for each other. Since we are all dressed in simple white, no social differences can be identified. I am aware that there are very wealthy group members, while others are struggling financially and live near the poverty line. In our interactions with each other, this is not noticeable. On the mat, we are all equal.

Apart from these interpersonal encounters, which have an enormous impact on me, I learn a lot about the whole philosophy of yoga. I can draw numerous conclusions for myself from this. The practical classes and my yoga lifestyle complete the training.

All this together, though, is quite exhausting because in addition to my yoga journey, I am also regularly at work on the construction site and spend every free minute promoting our marketing efforts. Despite all the exterior struggles, I am still noticing a tremendous change. I am once again much more balanced. My evening meditations are getting deeper and deeper and almost every night I have very energetic, almost enlightening dreams. My mind apparatus has come to a standstill as far as possible. Currently, my inner peace makes me an extremely happy person. I have almost exclusively positive thoughts, in particular towards myself. I could say that I have accepted myself as I am. This is probably a first taste of real self-love.

Physically, I am healthier than I have been for a long time: completely pain-free and without any discomfort. Furthermore, I am as full of energy as a Duracell bunny. I don't recall ever experiencing such a state of inner balance in my life. A feeling of anything-is-possible has set in, and I can already envision the success of our retreat center in my mind. I see and feel rewarded for all the agony of the past years. For all the health problems, for all the powerlessness, dejection and loneliness.

After four weeks, my yoga teacher training comes to an end with a beautiful ceremony. As exhausting as the training was, the warm feeling that I experienced during this time and the pride of being able to call myself a real yoga teacher outweighs it all.

The honor of having made it into the Balinese daily newspaper with a picture of my yoga teacher training graduation group is of course something I cannot withhold from my friends and acquaintances back home in Germany. I receive the first feedback with congratulations from my old colleague and head of the controlling department of the hospital where I worked before my time in Bali. Since we have maintained contact, but I have not heard from him for a long time, I naturally take this opportunity to inquire how things are going at work, how he is doing and general news. He answers me immediately: "Things are really haywire right now. Two of my employees quit unexpectedly. Now I have to distribute everything among the remaining heads. You know how much work we have. So, you can imagine that things are pretty stressful right now."

I answer him without even the slightest ulterior motive in my mind: "Oh, that is bad news, of course. I would love to help! Unfortunately, I will not be available to the German job market until December."

"Seriously?" he asks me.

"You know that I am going back to Germany in mid-December and will then start looking for a job. In that respect, yes, seriously!"

Sounding slightly irritated, he asks me to give him a few days so that he can consult the managing director. That same evening, I receive a *WhatsApp* message from him with the following content: "Would you have time to Skype tomorrow? I would love to talk to you face to face!"

I am surprised at the unexpected opportunity that presents itself to me. After all, I am in the process of blowing all my savings on building our facility. Despite all the dreaming, I have not lost my sense of reality and realize that when I return, I will definitely have to rehabilitate myself financially and look for a job.

The next day I have the interview with him. Admittedly, I am not the least bit excited. I am counting on him to sound me out, since I had very little to do with controlling at my previous job, and he knows that. Nevertheless, I have no intention of preparing myself for the interview. I am dressed accordingly: He should be glad that I put on a t-shirt at all. Plus my board shorts. My sunglasses on my nose top it all off.

Our conversation lasts about twenty minutes. There is not a trace of any technical details. Instead, he asks me what my expectations are and lets me know what tasks are planned for me. Furthermore, we talk about my salary and all the other necessary parameters. "Do you have any other questions? Otherwise, if this all works out for you, I would email you the employment contract within the next few days," he concludes.

"I got the job. Awesome! Just unbelievable. The opportunity fell into my lap. Without any effort at all. Now I can enjoy my time here completely relaxed, with the certainty that I will be able to establish myself again when I return to Germany."

In addition to the promise of the job, I am rather overwhelmed by the fact that what Sami has always preached to me is actually true: When I am at peace with myself and have a clear focus, everything runs smoothly by itself. Everything I need on my path comes when it is needed. I dance and sing my way to my scooter in a winner's pose with my arms stretched up and head towards the sea with the rhythm of "We Are the Champions" from Queen in my head. I run across the beach down to the water and dive into the lukewarm water. As I do so, I celebrate myself. How beautiful life is all of a sudden.

4. Spiritual burn-out on Nusa Penida

"Life begins at the end of your comfort zone."

[Neale Donald Walsch]

My parents immediately receive the good news about my new job in Germany. They are immensely happy for me. In fact, I notice that their worries about their son, who is stranded on an island far away from the society at home, have dramatically decreased as well.

Since Sami is still my only real confidant around, I also tell him this news that is absolutely outstanding for me. He is full of encouragement and frankly lets me know: "Congratulations. You really deserve it. Very hard you work since long time already. A lot of energy for your yoga teacher training you invest. Now it is time for some holiday. Tomorrow is full moon. We go to Nusa Penida for two days. Very special for you. I pick you up from your hostel. This time we go by car. I do not want you to worry about your life again."

At nine o'clock, the next morning, he picks me up on time. I am relieved that he has acquired the habit of punctuality from his patients over the years. Otherwise, I would have spent half my stay in Bali waiting for him. In the car, Sami is joined by two local acquaintances of his whom I already know. In addition, a *Pak Mangku*, as the native priests are called in this country, joins our travel group. He is waiting with a chef-like turban on his head and extraordinary smoking habits.

During the one-and-a-half-hour drive to the port of Padangbai, located in the west of Bali, I learn that the small island below Bali is a pilgrimage site for Hindus. After arriving in Padangbai, we charter a small fishing boat and cross over in the direction of Nusa Penida.

After a thirty-minute ride, we reach our destination. We arrange for a driver on the spot, who, Sami lets me know, will drive us from one temple to the next. I start to realize that I am about to partake in a veritable ceremonial marathon.

The first stop we make is at a small temple halfway up a mountain. We leave our driver at the car and go to our first meeting with the Gods for the day, heavily packed with offerings, incense sticks and all other accessories that must not be missing in a ceremony. We take our seats next to each other on the concrete floor of the open temple, warmed by the sun. All the Balinese members of our spiritual gang sit casually cross-legged, while all the Westerners, on the other hand, stubbornly try to make themselves comfortable in a similarly upright position, despite their stiff hips. In view of my hunched and constantly changing posture, though, this seems to me to be a rather futile endeavor. The priest, dressed in what looks like a chef's uniform, sits facing us on a small platform, similar to a church service. While we mortals meditate, the priest recites the most outlandish mantras and rings his very special priest bell like crazy. I find it somewhat disruptive as I drift off into the silence of my meditation. Just what that is supposed to achieve is a mystery to me. But I just allow myself to be drawn into it. Following the procedure, which lasts about eight to ten minutes, we are purified with the water blessed by him and are given a few drops of it in our folded hands. The offerings are then distributed to many different spots in the temple and incense sticks are lit before the I hear the following announcement, "Now we enter the cave through this little hole."

I pay no real attention to the words until one by one they disappear into the dark hole at the side of the temple. I comply with the request and am the last to climb down. What awaits me inside is pure magic: a huge underground temple in a cave of enormous proportions. The cave is about 500 feet long, if not longer. The light from the ceiling lamps show us the way from one small temple to the next, of which there are many. In the cave, we hold a total of five ceremonies, always with the same procedure. I am struck by the atmosphere of this place. At the end of the tunnel, at some point, there is light and we hold one last concluding session. This one turns out to be much shorter than the previous ones, which is due to the fact that our priest has to pee quite urgently. The rest of us join him, and so we form a chain of five in our holy looking robes at the bushes right next to the exit of the cave temple. This moment is a clear demonstration that we men are all somehow alike regardless of origin and race.

The master of ceremonies of our group gives the order to move on again after the short stop at the bushes. His agenda is obviously subject to a strict schedule. And so, we move on —

mindful and yet feeling a little time pressure—at a *Zen* gallop back to our driver, who is waiting for us in the immediate vicinity. There is no time to waste, so we set off on a direct route to head for the next temple. This time we visit a temple near the beach. We experience a ceremony there that is similar to what we have practiced a few times before. Only now under the open sky in the twilight of the beautiful evening sun. Furthermore, everything is a little shorter. The decisive factor is that our priest as well as the rest of the troop suffers from great hunger. We refresh ourselves only with a few bites of fruit and then move directly to the next temple, as it should be for a real ceremonial marathon.

It is already dark when we reach the top of the mountain, stretching over Nusa Penida. The full moon is clearly visible by now, illuminating the island in its light. I already have tired little eyes, which is due to the fact that I am about to suffer a ceremonial burn-out. The situation also seems to be getting close to escalating, as I am about to go berserk in light of my ravenous hunger. Everyone who knows me is aware that hunger, even in its early stages, is a real instrument of torture for me and turns me into an unpredictable monster. Since it is not foreseeable, when we get something to eat next time, we decide to consume some offerings for our own needs. Bananas, cookies and sweets have never tasted so good as at this moment.

The ceremonies under the full moon sky fortunately only last half an eternity, and so we reach the harbor around eight p.m., where some *warungs* are still open. We stuff our bellies, and I can hardly keep my eyes open after the extensive meal. Therefore, I lie down on the floor next to the table and directly fall asleep, regardless of the noise and dirt around me. The others remain sitting at the table and fool around heartily. The main occupation is to light one cigarette after the other, as if their survival depended on keeping a fire burning. Sami, of course, is exempt from this, as he is a non-smoker, contrary to the customs of the country. Our priest is clearly the chieftain of smokers. When, at some point during our trip, I confront him with whether smoking does not contradict spirituality, he demonstratively takes a pleasurable drag from his cigarette and lets the smoke rise into the air with his exhalation. While he follows the haze full of fascination with his eyes, he casually explains to me, "This is all *Prana*. I know how to use it." Still, I cannot really make heads or tails of it.

An hour, a few cigarettes and a power nap on my part later, we set up camp for the night at the next temple, directly on the beach. But before we finally go to bed, we hold a small final ceremony —and another and another. Until we finally make ourselves comfortable in our sleeping bags in the middle of the sand and sleep.

The next morning before sunrise, we hold a last final ceremony before we go back by boat towards our Balinese home. I am mentally and physically exhausted. With a mixture of too little sleep and too much information to process, I offer Sami a mental thank you full of irony for the really relaxing trip. The hardships of the return trip do not ease my state of exhaustion, and I do not reach my hostel until late afternoon.

Right away, I lay down on my bed without any major detours. Several hours later, I wake up again. It is already dark, and I briefly go to eat something before I finally put an end to the day.

The following morning, I wake up as if reborn. I cannot remember what exactly I dreamed. I only know that it was another very energetic dream. Even more energetic than usual. I really have no idea what this unusual trip triggered in me, but I feel a definite change. A positive one. I have taken another big step forward in my spiritual development. I feel a deep connection to my fellow human beings. All of a sudden, I can meet everyone around me with great openness, as if we have been good friends for several years. Just like a real Balinese. I had always wished for that. This is me! This is the real me. This is how I want to be from now on. The feeling of we-are-all-one envelops me. Until now, I have only read about this in spiritual books.

I enjoy this state and dedicate myself to my tasks as an entrepreneur. I pursue my administrative activities, which are still on my to-do list according to our business plan. I pay no attention whatsoever to the noise of the renovation work that began yesterday on the property next to my hostel. Even though I am normally overly sensitive when it comes to being disturbed by loud background noises. But today I am more focused than ever. My thoughts are razor sharp. I can focus all my energy on my work. This feeling is not at all familiar to me.

In the evening, I get together with Sami for our evening meeting at the construction site and talk with him to try to find out what is going on with me at the moment. I am confident that I will find answers to the inexplicable events and the changes that have occurred in me. He informs me: "You opened your *3rd Eye Chakra*. A high state of energy you reached, I can see in your aura. I cannot tell you, what the priest did with you while the ceremonies. You will not understand with your mind. It is not logical. Not rational. Enjoy this state, my lovely brother. Try to open your heart more!"

As I have been involved in holistic healing for several years now, I am aware, not least through my yoga teacher training, that the *chakras* are energy centers between the material (physical) and subtle bodies of the human being, through which energy is circulated to keep the mental, emotional and physical health of the human being in balance. The *Third Eye Chakra* is spiritually very significant because it represents qualities such as concentration, inner clarity, spiritual cognition, visualization and imagination. The knowledge about the *chakras*, which until then sounded very unworldly to me, and to which I did not really give much credence, now takes on a completely new meaning through this personal experience, which makes me believe in much more than just our material world.

5. Revelation-Ketut

"You do not have a soul. You are a soul. You have a body."

[C.S. Lewis]

All that has happened during the last few weeks has shaped me into the person I constantly wanted to be. Or rather, made me become again the person I have always been. I feel as if I have long forgotten who I really am and have now rediscovered myself again. I no longer have any fears about the future, and I have freed myself from the chains of my past as much as possible. Energetically, I am on a level that I have never been on before. Contributing to maintaining this state is certainly that I am doing something that fills me with joy. Something that I put my full passion into. Equally, my lifestyle on the beach and my rituals around yoga, meditation and reciting mantras play a big part in this. The fact that I still have no real friends here in Bali and still no partner hardly bothers me anymore. On the contrary, I have the opportunity to evolve completely independently, without getting lost in the distraction of other people. So, the focus remains fully on my spiritual metamorphosis and our retreat project.

I am just on my way to the construction site on my scooter when my cell phone rings. The name Scooter-Ketut appears on the display. Since on Bali all fourth-born Hindus are called Ketut, quite a lot of people are called by this name. To avoid misunderstandings in advance and to be able to distinguish one from the other, I have given each Ketut an additional name in my cell phone contacts. So, for example, in my list of contacts, in addition to the Scooter-Ketut, there is also a Furniture-Ketut, a Landlord-Ketut, Tailor-Ketut, Garden-Ketut and a Technology-Ketut.

To my dismay, Scooter-Ketut is a rather unpleasant acquaintance, who could be nicknamed Unreliable-Ketut, Rip-off-Ketut or Annoying-Ketut. The last times I was in touch with him, he always wanted something from me, which really pissed me off: Exchange my good scooter for a worse one, money for a maintenance, money for new papers and so on. I notice myself already wondering, "Whoa, what does this pain in the ass want now?" This reflection, which emerges spontaneously in me, has a direct influence on how I feel. I feel a little threatened, go into a defensive posture, and am slightly afraid of what he might want from me this time. My feelings are also immediately expressed on a physical level. My heartbeat picks up, and my blood gets pumping. I get slightly anxious. My body might even pour out a few stress hormones. At the same moment, however, I perceive that it is a thought that originates in my conditioned mind from experiences with him in the past. Therefore, before accepting the call, I reflect and observe while focusing on what is going on right now. I consider everything that the mere display of his name on my cell phone is capable of triggering in me. From the perspective of the observer, I let go of the negative thought and give Scooter-Ketut an unbiased chance. Reframing my thought to "maybe he just has a little question or something," puts me back into a state of neutrality. I remain completely tuned into myself and try to be as aware as possible during our phone call.

"Hi Ketut," I greet him.

"Hi boss," I get back.

"I just want to ask how long you rent the bike? Till December? I am not sure. I just want to check!"

I confirm that I will be renting the scooter from him for another five months. Immediately afterward, the conversation is over. I am happily relieved that he did not really want anything from me other than to ask this trivial question. Above all, though, this is a real breakthrough experience for me. Because this time I managed not to experience the situation as if in autopilot, only to realize afterward that I had lost my focus and awareness. I managed to put myself in a mindful state without further submitting to the patterns of my mind. I have been able to gain the valuable experience of how Sami's *Panca Mayakosha* (five levels healing concept) works in reality. My thought triggered feelings in me from a higher level that had a direct impact on my energy and physical body. I finally understand how body and mind correlate in direct interaction. But more importantly: I have even internalized in the experience the meantime. I am proud of the fact that I am now learning my own lessons, and I am able to understand them.

While the connection between body and mind is now fully understandable to me, I have been asking myself for quite some time what connection the two have with the soul. To me, body, mind and soul are terms that are commonly talked about together. One commonly hears about ways of bringing body, mind and soul into harmony. But that brings up the question, what is a soul anyway?

When I arrive at our construction site in the late afternoon with fresh insights to share, Sami is hard at work. Heavily armed with shovel and spade, he is about to lay a sewer system in our outdoor area. Nevertheless, I dare to interrupt him briefly to ask my burning questions. But instead of letting the work wait for a moment and taking a break, he casually explains to me without even making eye contact, as if I had just asked him about his bowel movement this morning: "When the mind is silent, completely quiet, access to your soul you have. This silence is not depending on the absence of external noise, but on the absence of your thoughts. Your soul is the emptiness, the true essence of your being. It is divine. It is who you really are. The answer to most of your problems is: be the observer behind your thoughts and feelings! The highest awareness is the state of your soul. Be aware what and how you think, talk, feel, eat, drink, act. You cannot sit in meditation and do yoga all day and all the times. Someday you maybe go back to an office job, without any space and time for yourself. Your awareness you have to keep in the daily life."

His eagerness to get back to work indicates that the explanation is over, and he offers me no room for further inquiry. Having gained enough wisdom for today, I settle for that and join him for the rest of the day, providing my physical assistance.

6. Self-love

"Love is the great miracle cure. Loving ourselves works miracles in our lives."

[Louise L. Hay]

Unlike a few short years ago when I humiliated myself with rejection, I can now look into the mirror of my small hostel room full of love for myself. What I see is a person bursting with joie de vivre and optimism. The bright blue eyes shine and show a deep sense of satisfaction. They express both modesty and gratitude. The body language suggests that the broad shoulders and broad chest are not only signs of physical strength, but also reflect the inner world. The high forehead and receding hairline are there, but do not catch the eye, as they are a perfect fit for this nice face and type of person. I love them and would not want to change anything about them under any circumstances. Even though they made me a very unhappy person just a while ago. I love every part of my body.

"After all, I only have this one life! So, why should I waste so much precious time and energy trying to be someone else, to be more perfect? What does it actually mean to be perfect? Is it not just something that is predefined for us by the media and our society anyway? Through advertising, which with its products and beauty standards stimulates the need in us to conform to an ideal and to be someone else? The constant desire to be more beautiful, slimmer or more toned makes us live in permanent dissatisfaction with ourselves. Who decides whether something is beautiful or not? In the end, is it not up to us? How is it possible that we are subjected to an ideal of beauty that is the standard for being pretty or ugly, and by which we are judged whether we are good enough or not good enough? Why do I have to conform to this image before I can consider myself perfect and accept myself as I am?"

Actually, it is not just my outward appearance that I have made peace with. I am full of love for myself. There are so many qualities about me that I distinctly like. I love my humor, my optimism, my empathy, my openness, my honesty, my courage, my reliability, my sensitivity, my perseverance, my determination, my ambition, my creativity, my vision and my dreams. I love being who I am. I am not perfect by any means. I am perfect in my imperfection. Just the way I am. I love my life. And most importantly: I love myself! Fully and completely with all my weaknesses and shortcomings. I am unique the way I am. A unique specimen. Created by God in His image. I therefore say yes to myself and yes to my life.

From now on, I celebrate at my very own party, in which I choose the playlist. I no longer depend on the presence of others to be able to dance and be happy. What others think about me no longer affects how I see myself. I no longer depend on their validation. I will not please everyone I meet. I no longer want or need that at all.

Just as I have learned to accept myself in my imperfection, I must also learn to accept and love my fellow human beings as they are and not just once they have become the way I would like them to be.

True self-love, accepting myself as I am, that is what I have been missing in the last years. Only now I realize that this is the only way to bring happiness and peace into my life. Constantly criticizing myself for things that I do not feel are good enough and that I cannot change either, does not bring about any improvement and does not change anything except ruining my peace at that very moment. I now understand what that well-known Bible passage means, "Love your neighbor as thyself." It means, first and foremost, to give love to yourself as well. Too often, we remain stuck in the belief that we do not deserve love or that we are not good enough. Consequently, giving love is as important as receiving it. Without love for ourselves, love for others is not genuine.

My energetic state, which is characterized by the highest vibration of love, projects directly to my outer world. Whereas in the weeks before I had fought many stubborn conflicts regarding wrongly delivered furniture, nasty rip-offs or screw-ups in construction, my encounters are currently characterized by absolute harmony. I perceive for myself how I, as a radiant personality, carry my light to the outside world. My love for myself seems to have a transformative effect on my outer world. Whereas in recent years I have been incessantly looking for love on the outside, it is now the women who seem to find something in me. I have to be cautious because hot flirtations are lurking at every corner right now, whether through eye contact or from short chats. Although, I still pay little attention to the ladies and do not invest any energy.

On the beach, I am addressed by a beautiful girl, after she has already almost sexually harassed me with her eyes in passing. "How are the waves today?" she somewhat clumsily entangles me in a conversation. Completely at peace with myself and without a hint of excitement, I reply to her curtly, "Pretty good."

After some brief small talk, I realize that she has never been surfing and was simply looking for an excuse to strike up a conversation with me, this dreamy man from the beach. She asks me if I will meet with her in the afternoon in a café in Canggu. Somewhat defiantly, I think to myself, "Interesting! All of a sudden, I am good enough for you girls again." I agree anyway, but then, without being able to contact her, I unfortunately have to cancel, as I am urgently needed on the construction site due to the upcoming construction of our water tank. I simply have my priorities, and this sweet girl does not change that. I do not regret not meeting her for a moment, as I am confident that it was not the last encounter with such a beach beauty and those new opportunities will present themselves soon. Besides, I no longer need the confirmation from the outside. Not even after my long period of isolation from womankind here in Bali. I feel great. I just do not lack for anything. "You arrogant bastard. Look at you with your new confidence," I say to myself in my mind. "Bali Chy Healing number one," I continue.

My optimism is to be rewarded because when I return from the construction site to my hostel late in the evening, a message on Facebook awaits me that thrills me. The message is from Martina. Since I left, we had only written to each other very rarely. What she writes to me now is completely unexpected and makes me gasp with excitement, despite my everything-is-possible attitude:

"Hi Tom,

I assume that you are still doing well in Bali? I would like to come and visit you. You know how much I love and miss the island! I already have a flight in three weeks and would stay twelve days. Would it be okay for me to book a room with you in the hostel?

Xoxo Martina."

"Abso-fucking-lutely," I let her know, first mentally and then later via Facebook.

g.) An encounter with love

1. Love in action

"Some people come in our life as blessings. Some come in your life as lessons."

[Mother Teresa]

The three weeks until Martina's arrival just do not want to go by. Never before have I looked forward to anything as much as spending time with her. For me, the situation is more than obvious: She comes to visit me because she feels a great desire for me. She wants Tom. On the Island of the Gods, that is. After our meeting last year shortly before Christmas, the desire to see each other again as soon as possible was enormous. Due to unfortunate circumstances, it was not meant to be then. I will now make up for it and settle our outstanding account. I am ready for it, since I am exactly in the condition in which I find myself irresistible. My hard work on myself and my giving up so much has paid off. I have brought about the exact change to finally be ready for the woman of my dreams. I am confident that there will be sparks between us. Not only that, I am even firmly convinced that she will become my "Martinacita." My feelings for her are as strong as ever.

I remember exactly what was happening and how I felt during the time immediately after I met her in Bali. I was frustrated and could not understand why it just does not work with women. I looked at the stars and begged the universe to make this charming girl my girlfriend. Resignedly, I wrote it off as an experience with a category B woman.

So three and a half years and a few frustrating stories about encounters with the world of women later, the time has come. During my time here in Bali, I have become extremely more mature and no longer run after a relationship as longingly as I did in the past. Nevertheless, as a miserable romantic, I am slowly longing for a storybook-like happy ending. For a woman by my side — for just this woman by my side.

My preparations for her visit are limited to telling the guys at my hostel the dates when I am expecting a lady visitor. With a twinkle in my eye and the expression "Knick-Knacking," which proves to be understood internationally at this point, I let them know that there will soon be excessive banging in the hostel in the near future. I am joyfully excited and count the days that remain. Screw my live-in-the-moment wisdom. I just want the days to pass as quickly as possible. I have made the arrangement with Sami that I will only visit the construction site every three to four days during her visit and that I will only be available to a limited extent. As expected, he fully understands this. He knows how I feel about her because, like a best friend, I have told him about our love story more than once.

The days before her arrival, I lie on the beach for several hours like a real tourist and work on my tan. There is no shade, instead I expose my body to the blazing sun. I do everything I can to be looking good. The perfect sun-kissed surfer boy look. My hair has already been bleached blond by the sun and the salt water. In the evening, as in the days before, I diligently do push-ups and sit-ups. Plus biceps and triceps exercises. I train very hard and am always on the verge of dizziness during my workouts. I have arms like the *Hulk*, and due to regular surfing, I already have four-pack abs. All my muscles ready to show off to finally get rid of the last remaining doubts. Not that I am questioning my newly regained self-love with these efforts. I just want to be on the safe side. Because in the end I am not quite as evolved past worrying about what others think of me as I believe I am. Of course, I want to please her. And of course, it is important to me that I also meet her visual expectations.

The extensive wait has finally come to an end. The day of our long-awaited reunion has arrived. According to plan, she should have arrived at the *Arnawa Inn* one hour ago by cab. However, nothing goes according to plan here, but rather according to the principle of chance. I curse the unpunctuality that is so common in this country but then just remind myself of the fact that the mills on Bali just grind a little slower.

Then it is time at last. It is already late afternoon as a cab with a blonde passenger stops in front of the hostel. The door opens, and I finally welcome the woman of my dreams as I am embracing her in my arms. We look deep into each other's eyes before we hug once more. Hard to believe, but true. Life is just unbelievably good to me right now. The sacrifices I have had to make for it are crazy. I had to travel to the other end of the world to come clean with myself. To love myself. And now this self-love is the magnet that manifests itself in the love of the outer world in the human form of a blonde angel in front of me.

She quickly stores her things in her room and freshens up, then says a brief hello to the sea. The sunset is more beautiful this evening than it has been for a long time, and the light of the evening glow could be interpreted as a reflection of my feelings. I take her out for a delicious meal right on the beach. We are still so wonderfully familiar with each other and have so much to tell each other. Not only the last rays of the sun create a warmth between us. She is so beautiful with her blonde hair, blue eyes, athletic physique and impeccable style. I am attracted to her, not only visually. We laugh a lot and given the heightened mood, within moments I break my alcohol celibacy with her, which I had followed with strict discipline for the previous five and a half months. We down one *Bintang* after the other. Unfortunately, the evening still comes to an end much too quickly, as she urgently longs for a bed in view of her jet lag.

She sleeps in the room next door. I lie down to sleep soaked in happiness and with a huge bulge in my pants in my trusted bed. After all, they say, the penis is the antenna of the heart. And this one seems to have received clear signals in the last few hours. I do not want to believe it and feel the situation of

212

having Martina near me now is completely surreal. Once again, my feelings confirm the fact that everything in my life falls into place when I am at peace with myself and live according to my heart.

The next morning begins just as beautifully as last night ended. We go to the beach together for a round of surfing. We laugh and joke around. Surfing is only secondary. Rather, we enjoy our togetherness like two teenagers in love. Right on the beach, a breakfast of pancakes, fruit salad and fresh papaya juice awaits us. Full of enjoyment, we stuff our stomachs to gather enough energy for the day ahead.

After a short stopover at our hostel, we then head to our construction site in Canggu. There she gets an exclusive guided tour and a detailed overview of our project. For every stone, no matter how small, I have an entertaining story to share, which she, of course, finds impressive. How could she not, in view of the now well-established complex? "*Rumah Bapak Sami* —The Home of Sami" or as I call it, "The Perfect Penis Extension."

We are on the road all day and have the best time of our lives. We wind down the evening comfortably in a fancy fish restaurant. Today has made it clear to me once again that she is my dream woman. Her outer beauty is only secondary. It is rather her inner beauty that makes my heart beat faster. She is open, humorous, deep, intelligent, self-confident without a hint of arrogance, modest and all her character traits are perfect as if she was made for me.

Still, just like the night before, she again goes to her room alone. So far, there has simply been no suitable opportunity to get physically closer to her than just to take her in my arms. I do not want to rush anything and just let the right moment happen naturally. Her affection towards me is clearly noticeable, yet I just do not want to mess it up. I want it to be perfect. As perfect as she just is. As perfect as I simply am. As perfect as we are perfect for each other.

The next day, too, we explore the island together. After a long walk on the beach, we go to a café to be pampered again with fresh fruit, pancakes and coffee. The time we spend together passes in no time, and it is already afternoon when we return to our hostel. To make the day of wellness perfect, we then treat ourselves to a relaxing full-body massage in a beautiful massage parlor.

We let the day end with a relaxing sunset surf. After our dinner in a simple street-*warung*, it becomes apparent in the hostel that our paths to bed will be separate again. Still unkissed and without having exchanged any intimacies so far, I am no longer willing to let her go. I can no longer bear to have her lying untouched in the next room while my antenna is continually receiving signals. I do not want her to think that I do not dare to make a move or that I lack self-confidence. I have to send out a signal! Here and now! I courageously seize the moment and knock on the door of her room to invite her out to her terrace. We had already wished each other a good night and said goodbye before we left for our rooms. Slightly overwhelmed in the moment and with no real master plan up my sleeve, I abruptly ask her to close her eyes. She complies with my request and stands before me with closed eyes in all her beauty. Determined, I walk up to her and place a big smack in the middle of her mouth. Admittedly, the kiss is brief, but the effect is by no means unnoticed. I have expressed to her with only one kiss delivered in a   kindergarten manner, unmistakably what I feel for her and indicated to her that I want her. Now there is no more room for interpretation. Now it is her turn. She flashes me a sweet smile and then, embarrassed, retreats into her den. I grin to myself and look forward to what the next day has in store for us in view of this progress. I am in irrepressible anticipation of the long-awaited super-expat-dropout-does-his-own-thing sex.

Before I go to sleep, I briefly check my Facebook account. Sami, who is otherwise rarely active on social media, posted the following quote on his wall. "If you love somebody, let her go. For if she returns, she was always yours. If she does not, she never was."

I have no idea if this post has any relevance to me. Nonetheless, the words resonate with me and make me think.

2. Back on Go

"Experience is the hardest kind of teacher. It gives you the test first and the lesson afterward."

[Oscar Wilde]

When I wake up early the next morning as the sun is coming out, Martina is already sitting on her terrace. It does not take much effort to perceive that there is a strange mood in the air. "Tom, can we have a few serious words with each other for a moment?" she asks me apprehensively.

"Yeah sure, what's up?" I reply a bit perplexed in view of her uncertain question. I have no idea what is bothering her, and I purely dislike hearing her talk in that tone of voice.

"So last night, that was a little unexpected for me, to be honest. Your kiss, that is. I did not know how to handle the situation at all. I could not sleep all night because I have to tell you something that is been bothering me since the beginning. I really, really like you. You are a great guy. A really good friend! And I hate to disappoint you. Unfortunately, nothing can come of this now. I started dating a boy from my university shortly before I left for Bali. We were hiking together in a group for a few days and there was a spark between us. I am head over heels in love with him. I am really sorry that I have given you any kind of hope. That is why I want to tell you this openly, so as not to hurt you."

Inside, it feels like my heart stops beating for a moment. But in truth, it beats like the rhythm at an electro-rave. My entire body is a pipeline of a wild cocktail of emotions. Feelings of disappointment, of incomprehension, of anger, of failure spill out inside me. My thoughts shoot through my head as if fired with a machine gun: "What the fuck!? Are you kidding me? Given me hope? We spend two and a half days like a newlywed couple on their honeymoon, and then you want to tell me that all this is not real?! You travel several thousand miles to visit me and just before you leave you start dating someone else? That is a joke! A pretty bad one at that! It took you two and a half days to tell me that!? You do not want to hurt me? Are you serious? Just admit to yourself that you enjoy your time with me to the fullest and that you have feelings for me. You heartless bitch!"

Since Martina bursts into tears right on her terrace in the midst of my heartbreak in reaction to her heartless confession, I keep those thoughts to myself for now. When I see her like this, I somehow feel sorry for her, too. Possibly because I just cannot see a girl crying and not immediately feel sympathy. Completely shaken up and struck by disappointment, I light an Indonesian clove cigarette. I attempt to handle the situation with some maturity and not lash out in a counterattack, which is why I strike soothing tones against my feelings. "Yeah, sure, I can understand that! After all, I cannot force anything! I am of course already very disappointed. I am sure you have noticed that I have a crush on you. And to be honest, I was one hundred percent sure that you felt the same way about me."

She has a huge lump in her throat, and the fact that she has no answer for me only confirms my belief. A few tears later, she moans again, "I am really so sorry! I hope you understand and we can still be friends. I really like you a lot."

"Yeah, right," I let her know, being as dishonest with her as she is with me. Never again do I want to have contact with this Satan with angel wings. Let alone remain friends. It is somehow unfair that she manages to play the victim with her crying. At the same time, I am the one who is hurt and deserves to cry. I would have liked to have confronted her a bit more with my perception of us and blamed her for her misbehavior. Instead, I shut up and comfort her.

"Is it OK with you if I stay here in the hostel for the rest of my vacation?" she wants to know meekly.

Finally, I find words that honestly express my emotional state: "I am really pretty down right now. I think it is better if we do not see each other again!"

After the heartbreaker has calmed down and is once again in control of her tears, I immediately say goodbye to her. With a tight hug, I pull her close to my body. I secretly hope that she will come to her senses, dump her clown in Germany and run away with me. But nothing of the sort seems about to happen. Not even when I press her even tighter against me. I wish her all the best on her future journey, but choose my words in such a way that conveys that I do not intend to see her again for the moment. Without a last glance at her, I turn away from her and shuffle to my room with my head down, to grab my surfboard and to leave the hostel as soon as possible. I make my way towards the ocean to throw myself into the waves on my board. I consider this the best way to distract myself and take my mind off things. Because surfing is like meditation. Letting go of my thoughts and just being completely with the beauty of nature and connecting with the waves regularly triggers happy hormones in me. It is a cure for many things, but as it turns out after just a few minutes, I realize it is not a cure for everything. I am trapped in my universe of disappointment, pain and anger. I discharge my energy into the sea. In return, I am given one washing machine spin cycle after the other. I stay in the water until I am completely exhausted and go for a walk on the beach with pudding in my arms and salt water in my ears. My thoughts do whatever they want with me and are completely out of control —my feelings too. I could not be further away from inner peace, tranquility and equilibrium.

When I return to the *Arnawa Inn* after a few hours, Martina is no longer there. Her towels and bathing suits have been removed. Her shoes are also no longer on the terrace. The room door is half open. The bitch has indeed disappeared. Her room is empty. And so am I. It is all over and done with. Instead of living the perfect life with her by my side, I find myself in a nightmare. No more hope of realizing that I am the better choice and that she will choose me after all. No laughter, no familiarity, no love, and certainly no happy ending. Instead, nothing remains but emptiness, incomprehension, powerlessness, anger and pain. I take a seat in the recliner on my little porch. Continuously, these self-doubts resurface in me. Thoughts of not being good enough, from which I could free myself as far as possible up to now, are suddenly there again. I no longer feel love. And even worse, I have lost faith in ever really encountering the love of a woman. Completely overwhelmed with the overall situation, I light the next clove cigarette. For the umpteenth time, I rebel on the inside and let my dejection turn into defiance.

"She is going to pay for this bitch move!" I swear to myself, hatefully. With the maturity of a 14-year-old, I first bitterly unfriend her on Facebook. I delete her number and thus remove the last traces of our only briefly flared up love. By the way, this should serve as a protective measure, so that I no longer have any contact data for her, in case I get my hopes up again in a few days and try to follow her around like a remorseful dog. Flashing her my symbolic finger by unfriending her on Facebook is my very last stand because let us not fool ourselves: There is only one loser in the entire story, and that is ME!

After another clove cigarette, I retreat into my darkened room. Caught in the headlock of my gloomy thoughts, I drop onto my bed. I am heartbroken. And yet, there is not enough for tears. Normally, all I have to do is listen to the theme of a sad movie (Forrest Gump, for example) and tears start rolling down my face. But at this moment, these are not feelings of sadness, happiness, emotion or compassion. Here, all the negative feelings are just having a wild party at the same time at my expense. I would like to cry and vent my emotions. Despite how I am feeling, somehow that does not want to happen. I swallow my heartbreak, as I have always done with disappointments with women. Only this time it is different. This time, apart from the disappointment, I ask myself the fundamental question of whether there is a suitable match for me at all or whether I simply have to resign myself to my loneliness forever and ever. I have serious doubts about Cupid's accuracy. Because I've done all the work to love and accept myself. I have reached the point where I have said yes to myself, accepted myself, and begun to love myself. I have not only cherished thoughts of love in my mind, but my feelings have constantly sent out the vibration of love. I renounced alcohol and devoted myself to yoga. I traveled to the other side of the world and let a wise man guide and shape me. I left everything behind. Family, friends, job, and illnesses. Parts of my personality have also been left behind. Beliefs, feelings and habits. Part of my motivation for doing all of this has also been to find a partner and to no longer have to go through life by myself. But even after all these sacrifices, I have not succeeded. It is jinxed as always. Yet, this time, from the results are not from one of my patterns, but from real witchcraft, according to my conviction.

I was firmly convinced that love would appear in the outside world as soon as I felt it inside. I let that become my own truth. I based my expectations on that. These are the teachings found in all spiritual books, and also what Sami taught me.

My emotional pain has also been manifesting itself on a physical level since daybreak. Initial pinching in the abdominal area, which I already noticed while sleeping, has turned into serious abdominal pain. Despite my emotional low and physical pain, I maintain my morning rituals. I make myself do an hour of yoga, followed by about twenty minutes of meditation. Never before have I felt as bad during and after this as I do today. Therefore, I lie down in my bed again and bathe myself in self-pity. I regret that I am denied what I have been longing for so long. While outside, the life of my dreams is waiting to be lived in the midst of paradise, I lie curled up on my bed with stomach cramps and am far from happy. I question what motivated Sami to quote, of all things, "If you love somebody, let her go. For if she returns, she was always yours. If she does not, she never was" on his wall the night before I fell out of love, which fits my situation like a glove. "How the hell could Sami have known that? Was he referring to me? Or rather, did he mean her? Will she maybe come to her senses and find her way to me after all? Possibly, she'll realize she misses me and have some insight after all after a few days apart!"

A spark of hope emerges. Even if it is only minimal. It is good that I've denied myself any chance of contacting her by my foresighted protective measures. The remorseful dachshund in me would already be standing by.

I need Sami, my friend and healer now as urgently as never before and ask him to make time for me. I am not willing to waste any more of my precious time on the island in my current emotional state. The period of social isolation has really taken its toll on me and now my broken heart will not let me enjoy my time here to any degree and will not allow that to happen anytime soon. Sami has time to lend me his ear. He is there for me. As he has always been. As he probably always will.

As we sit down to talk at the construction site in our already completed *lumbung*, I tell him in the detail of a storyteller what has happened to me in the last few days. How my thoughts have been going crazy ever since, how my emotions have been overwhelming me, how I have been struggling with severe stomachaches and how I have been missing any feelings of happiness. I ask him to enlighten me on what is happening to me right now and why I got this ass kicking of cosmic proportions with karmic significance. Just at the moment I have started to love myself and live according to my true self. He shows me how much compassion he has for me by the way he lets me finish, the patience and body language he uses to listen to my words. He clearly lets me know that he is aware of the gravity and importance of this event for me.

"Forgive her! That is your way out! You know, sometimes people have to be bad to be good. Fuck the morality. Come and join me all day at our construction. Release the bad energy by doing physical work. A lot of things we still have to do. Even you have stomach pain. Continue. You remember what I tell you in the beginning: You learn from what you are doing, from the experience you make. You know everything already. Listen to yourself to get answers." Then he leaves me behind and goes about his business in the garden with the workers. I let his words resonate and, against his advice, decide to temporarily return to my hostel room to be alone with my thoughts and feelings. However, the time and free space I want to use for reflection only leads me to mentally return to Martina and once again bathe myself in self-pity. My inner restlessness is almost unbearable, which is why I decide to listen to Sami's advice after lying in bed for only half an hour.

Back at the construction site, he welcomes me with some surprise, but without inquiring about the reasons for my quick return. In view of my long since bare upper body, I just roll up my sleeves figuratively. It is time to work! I already have the *Hulk* arms, even though I have exercised them for a different purpose.

The next few days continue to be marked by stomachaches. I notice them, but they do not prevent me from working hard on the construction site. "My mind is stronger than my body!" This is what I tell myself with full conviction when I consciously perceive the pain. "My mind is stronger than my body! My mind is stronger than my body!"

I continue to feel like crap emotionally. There is at least light visible in the tunnel. Occasionally, I can even manage a little laugh for myself. This happens exclusively in the moments when my thoughts do not revolve around Martina. This seemingly meaningless experience becomes a real game changer: At every moment, I have the choice of where to direct my focus. Attention is neither positive nor negative. It is neutral. Whatever I put my focus on will expand. Whether it is something positive or negative, it gains power and is fed with energy. It is like sitting in a completely darkened sauna and being the only one among the naked people holding a spotlight in my hand: It is up to me whether I direct the focus of the light beam on an aesthetically pleasing female body or a hairy sweaty beer belly. Do I remain mentally with Martina (in this case the hairy sweaty beer belly) and thus decide to feel bad? Or do I focus on what the present moment has in store for me —in all its perfection, wonder and beauty —and thus resolve to make myself accessible to happiness? Or at least not to be unhappy.

I finally realize what it means to be aware. Until now, the A for Awareness in Sami's mantra "Be HAPPY" had only been attributed a very minor meaning. Only now do I understand its depth. I am experiencing in my own body what it means to focus on something perceived as negative in order to thereby surrender to its low vibration. Whenever I find myself in situations where I feel bad or think negatively, from now on, I redirect my attention to something positive. On something that I can influence. I turn my focus to work. On my dream of our retreat center. On this oasis of beauty that is being created here.

Subsequently, I spend a lot of time on the construction site and lose myself in the work, just as Sami recommended. At times, I am on the construction site for more than twelve hours. The result is bloody fingers, several scrapes as well as emotional rays of hope to leave this devastating experience behind me. As construction progresses, so does my ability to laugh again. Or at least to stop crying inside.

3. Learning to forgive

"Nothing ever goes away until it has
taught us what we need to know."

[Pema Chadron]

Although I am finding it downright difficult at present, I continue to have faith in the path I have chosen. The pain still runs deep. I try to focus on the present instead of dwelling on the past. Time heals all wounds. I do not know whether this saying is generally valid. It certainly applies to me right now. With each passing day, I am able to let go a little more. This shows me that I have matured personally. A few years ago, the experience with Martina would have felt like the end of the world, and it would have taken years to get over it.

Just at the right time, I get a visit from my Bali companion Matt from Germany. It is soothing for my broken heart, but poison for my liver. Although he stays only for ten days, these days mean the world to me. It is the positive energy from a close friend and bon vivant that is now providing the distraction I need. I find just the right balance between work and enjoying the time with him like a vacation on the island. He completely takes my mind off things and lets me experience again what it means to enjoy life and absorb the beautiful things. We have enough time to talk about everything in detail. From afar, it was not possible for me to confide in someone else with all my profound insights. I let him know about my transformations so far, sparing him no detail. When asked how many women I have already nailed, I honestly have to answer "not a single one." But unlike before, this no longer makes me feel like I am being held accountable to prove my worth. I have risen above it. I am confident even without being able to show success with women, and I see myself as a thoroughly fantastic person.

We have a few awesome days, even if they are much quieter with senior-like outings than they were when I was a student. This is an entirely different stage of life. One that is characterized by profound changes and a journey to myself. The focus is no longer wild party nights and the relentless pursuit of women.

The joy in me has largely returned with Matt's visit. I am insanely grateful for friendships like this. Nevertheless, I am glad when the day of his departure has come. Now I can devote myself fully to my work again. And more importantly, I finally have time to get to the root of what has happened in the last few weeks and come to terms with it. This is only possible if I have enough time for myself.

Immediately after his departure, I set to work, confronting myself with the right questions. I feel ready for the answers as I regain access to myself. "Why could this have thrown me off track so much? Why did this happen to me with Martina? Why did it come to such an awful and unexpected end?"

My answers come to me either in my sleep or during meditation. They come over several days and are full of clarity. My inner silence provides the space to be receptive to the answers that come from the depth of my soul. My inner truth speaks to me. In my travel diary, I record everything as follows:

"Why could all this throw me off track like this?"
Counter question: "Why are you not solid enough?"

"Why did this happen to me with Martina? Why did it come to such an awful and unexpected end?"
Answer: "You are not at the end of your journey yet. You are only at the beginning. Your love for yourself must be unconditional. Solidify it. Let it become your foundation in life. It gives you stability. Learn to stand firmly in life. Life will always go in cycles. There will always be ups and downs. That is natural. That is the polarity of life. That is why you need a firm stand, inner strength, faith and love for yourself. You are still making your happiness dependent on others. Only you are responsible for your own happiness. Stop looking for it on the outside. You will find it only inside. As you noticed from Martina's tears, it was not her intention to hurt you. She had to do it. For your sake. She was the tool to give you the right experience that you desperately need for your growth. You will not find a logical explanation for it. Be grateful to Martina for letting you have this experience. Let her go. Forgive her. Love her. This is a milestone in your development. She promised you nothing, and yet, you had expectations of her. Learn to accept life. Learn not to manipulate it with your expectations and desires. You will ultimately lose. You will be disappointed. Give yourself to life. Learn to trust. Practice

228

patience. Everything comes at the right time. Let go of the past and be optimistic about what lies ahead. Surrender to the flow of life without resistance!"

"Thank you life! Thank you, silence! Thank you, wisdom within me. And finally: Thank you, Martina. But now I have to let you go. I forgive you. No, I even thank you for this precious lesson, even if it was quite painful and partly still is. I thank you for every moment of our wonderful time that we were allowed to spend together. But I no longer mourn you; I just enjoy the beautiful memories of you."

With some distance from all the incidents, it is possible for me to recognize that for years I have perceived Martina through rose-tinted glasses. This inaccurate image of her has been created from the perspective of my loneliness and desire to have a beautiful woman by my side. And now, with the current clarity in my mind and heart, I realize that Martina is not as great as I have always thought she was. It seems that I only wanted to be aware of her quirks in a subliminal way. Without my rose-tinted glasses, many of them become apparent. I was blind to recognize them. I glossed over everything about her. My mind kept making me think she was the one. That it was love that I felt for her. Yet it was nothing but desire. Desire for external validation. Desire to compensate for something that is not there —namely love. Her outer beauty has bedazzled me time and again and kept me stuck in this belief.

Regardless, the feeling of love is not a mental construct. Love must be felt. Now, with my head at rest and feeling the truth of my heart, I can certainly say that I am glad that nothing happened between us. Too many negative qualities and behaviors on her part reveal themselves to me. I would never have been happy with her by my side.

"What an incredible experience —painful and extremely instructive at the same time. What's going to throw me off track now that I have been through something like this?" Not only have I mastered overcoming my crisis once and for all, I have also emerged from it truly strengthened. For a brief moment, I feel unstoppable.

My final resurrection from being emotionally impaired has not escaped Sami's notice. Whether he perceived it in my changed posture or read it in my aura, we can only guess. But perhaps my returned continuous singing and whistling at our construction site has given me away. I proudly share my conclusions with him and ask him if I have understood everything correctly. Thereupon, he informs me: "Yes, you are right. Like I always say to you: Don't worry, be HAPPY. That is the way out. Your future is always a reflection of the vibrations you send to the universe with your thoughts and feelings in the present moment. Do not worry brother. You got HER already."

I wonder what he is trying to tell me with that last sentence. "You got HER already?!" In any case, he does not give me an answer to my question, but only gives me the reassuring look of a father who tells his son not to worry.

230

4. My concept of love

> *"Your task is not to seek for love,*
> *but merely to seek and find all the*
> *barriers within yourself that you have*
> *built against it."*
>
> *[Rumi]*

Seemingly incidentally, Germany becomes soccer world champion. I am so busy and focused on myself that this event becomes a complete side issue for me. Quite in contrast to the World Championships in the years before, where I followed the games so emotionally that I even shed a tear or two. Here, watching the games is entirely different, and not just because of the seven-hour time difference.

I watch the final against Argentina in the middle of the night in *MAMA's*, a German pub in Kuta, which has set up several screens and is full to bursting with almost three hundred guests. Even so, I am not in the proper mood, which is partly due to my fatigue. In addition, I am here all alone and without friends, which makes me miss any sense of togetherness despite the numerous compatriots in the bar. All my life, I have longed for the German team to become world champions again. And now that the time has come, it affects me only to a limited extent. I realize that happiness is only real when shared. In a one-man scooter convoy, I drive back to my hostel shortly after sunrise after the end of the award ceremony and scare away the last of the alcoholics who are on their way to bed after celebrating with my honking.

My quite low-key celebration of the world championship also has a silver lining to it, as I can start the day clear-headed and without a hangover at lunchtime. I gossip briefly with the guys from my hostel, who are thrilled for me and the success of the German team. Then I take my small travel diary and ride my scooter in the direction of the beach. I settle down in the shade of a large palm tree and observe the movement of the waves in the sea. The soccer events of last night fade away with every deep breath I take.

Here on Bali, I have learned so much about myself and love, which I now want to write down (there has been so much gathered in the meantime, I am even seriously toying with the idea of writing a book someday). I would like to reflect on everything that is wildly buzzing around in my head, compile it and give it a structure. Because only in this way, I can also draw my conclusions from it and learn how to establish love as a permanent part of my life. What I would like to explain to myself is not love for good food, a pastime, friends or parents, but love in the sense of romance. As it is presented to me as a need on television, in movies, books, songs, or through my environment. I reach for my little bible of insights and get started:

"We all long to have someone by our side to experience love and affirmation. To experience the feeling of closeness and intimacy and to have a best friend by our side with whom we can share tenderness

and through whom our desire for sexual satisfaction is fulfilled. To have a person who stands behind us and supports us unconditionally as we master the challenges of life. We want a partner who gives us support in crises. Someone with whom we can share our happiness and sorrow, and with whom we can develop personally with full enthusiasm as we pursue our passions in life. Love is an integral part of a happy life. A life without love leaves you lonely and, as we all know, sick.

In our imaginations, we have often conditioned ourselves to believe that we can only be happy if we have a partner by our side. Particularly often, the reason why we long for love is simply that we no longer want to be alone.

The expectations we have of our partner are tremendously high. We have the belief that we are not sufficient by ourselves. Therefore, we expect the other person to fill a gap that we ourselves cannot fill. Instead of loving the other person as they are and finding them perfect in their own way, there are permanent shortcomings that do not correspond to our own ideas. On the other hand, one strives to develop one's own personality in order to meet the demands of one's partner.

Whoever tries to compensate for their inner emptiness, due to a lack of self-love, through love from others, will be bitterly disappointed at some point. True love is a selfless thing. You do not ask what the other person can do for you, but what you yourself can give to the other person. And you can only give what you yourself have at your disposal. Love is not selfish because it is primarily about giving and not about getting. It does not mean that your partner's happiness is *more important than your own. Rather, it means that your partner's happiness is your own.*

Many people make the mistake of seeking love for oneself through love for another —I myself have done this for most of my life.

Love for ourselves is the source that causes love to manifest in the external world. When we love ourselves without needing an outside influence to do so, we are within love's vibration. Thus, we must first accept ourselves as we are and love ourselves completely in order to radiate love in this way. We must let the search for love and the associated deficiency that we radiate turn into abundance. We must stop sending out the desire for love to the universe which invites this state of lacking love to continue in our lives. Instead, we must send out the signal to the universe that we already possess love. If we do this and think, feel and act out of the abundance of love, love will appear in our lives. Love for ourselves is the magnet that attracts that love. Like a flower that blossoms, it attracts bees to itself.

However, the problem in our lives (where our minds constantly dictate to us what is logically explainable and what is not) is that we must first experience something in the external world in order to find it mentally and emotionally believable within. In order to be able to love oneself, one needs the right experiences from the outside, such as the affirmation of a woman. If you have conquered several girls, or they all fall in love with you right away, it is easy to believe you are an outstanding womanizer. This confirmation from the outside environment endows you with the thoughts and feelings on the inside. The confirmation moves from the outside to the inside. Only, what if the confirmations from others fail to materialize? In my early twenties, I had excellent success rates with women and was confident about my attractiveness to the female sex. But with each rejection, I lost faith in myself. Each subsequent negative experience fed my self-doubt and produced thoughts on the lowest frequency, such as, "I am not good enough. I have nothing to offer. I will not find one anyway. She is not interested anyway. There are better guys than me. It is jinxed. It is just not meant to be." Finally, I protected myself from being hurt any longer and therefore avoided the world of women as much as possible. As a result, the affirmations continued to fail, and I continued to lose self-love. With increasing times of loneliness, this feeling of lack continued to grow deeper. There was no trace of love for myself. Instead, self-confidence was at its lowest level. And what could be more unattractive than a partner who has no self-confidence whatsoever and virtually begs for love? Everyone knows how annoying people are who are absolutely and compulsively looking for a partner. They are trapped in exactly this situation. They radiate nothing but sheer lack. The lack of love.

This will continue until we learn our lessons. There is no other way out of this vicious circle than the way within. We have to start with ourselves. We must, instead of longing for the emotion of love, achieve a state of being in love. We can only do that within ourselves. We get there through meditation, the best place to focus is on the heart. Through visualizations. Through mental reprogramming. For example, we can recite affirmations to ourselves. These are like little seeds that we plant in our subconscious mind. We keep telling ourselves something until we firmly believe in it, act on it, and ultimately experience it in our reality. In the same way that we

*constantly do this with negative matters, we can also do this in a
positive sense.*

*We must learn to forgive and let go of our negative feelings from the
past that have become our own prison. We must fill our feelings,
thoughts, words and deeds with love and send them out to the
universe. We must be love itself.*

*All my life, I have searched for love, believing that I could find it in
women in the outside world. Although I found love for myself during
my time in Bali, the experience with Martina showed me that I am
still under the strong influence of my outside world, or rather the
world of women. First of all, the love and trust for myself has to
solidify. Otherwise, I will continue to call such painful experiences
into my life as my teachers."*

But all of this sounds easier in theory than it is to put into
practice. Through my self-reflection, I am quite aware of my
situation, yet my heart is still broken. It will take some more
time on the yoga mat or on my meditation seat to heal. All the
same, I now know the state I was in before this emotional
setback. I know what it feels like to be completely in tune with
oneself and one's environment. And I know how to reach that
state again. I need to make peace with the past. Instead of
judging the people who broke my heart, I feel gratitude for
them. Especially because they allowed me to grow so much
inside with these experiences. I see what I experienced with
Martina as one step back in order to be able to take two more
steps forward. I will not continue to search for love. Instead, I

am strengthening the relationship with myself by forgiving myself and accepting myself as I am, full of love. I am certain that love will find its way to me all by itself, without any effort. I am attentive to resisting loneliness. However, not with expectations in my head, but with an open heart. I allow myself time and practice patience. I know that I have already sent out love. I give credence to the words of my teacher Sami, "You got HER already." I have already sent out the frequency of love. On my path to manifestation, just one experience intervened, which was indispensable and of elementary importance for my life's journey.

h.) Lessons for life

1. Made in Germany, not!

"Life is 10 percent what happens to you and ninety percent how you respond to it."

[Lou Holtz]

It is quite fascinating what kind of spiritual springboard Bali has been for me in the last seven months and what kind of growth I have achieved. Undoubtedly, the place that teaches me the most at times is our construction site. Much like Sami prophesied to me at the beginning of my journey, "You learn from what you are doing."

One of the most important lessons I learn on the construction site is to exercise patience. A lot of patience. Endless patience. Patience that almost causes me physical pain. One of the characteristics that distinguishes me as a person and that I cannot imagine being without is my strict punctuality. My mother always says that you can set the clock by me. And she is right about that. In order to be able to guarantee my punctuality, I usually even prefer to arrive a little too early for my appointments. And that is only to avoid making the other person wait for me. In my view, punctuality is a sign of respect. Respect for the precious time of the other person. If they have to wait for me, I rob them of their time. In my own personal rules of life, the highest of all commandments is therefore: "Thou shalt not be late!," which means nothing other than I expect the same reliability from my fellow human beings.

My threshold of tolerance is a maximum of ten minutes waiting time. Anything more than that is unacceptable and can cause me to emotionally derail as a result of my high standards with regard to being on time. Not infrequently, this results in me being totally pissed off. I knew from the start that the clocks here in Indonesia tick a little slower. But that they sometimes stop ticking entirely was not to be expected.

The two people I deal with most here —our architect Pak Tude and Sami —are fortunately experienced in dealing with Westerners and know that punctuality and reliability are more or less an integral part of our culture. Everyone else has a more relaxed approach to time. I do not want to rule out that this has its origin in the Hindu religion, which says that we will all be reborn, which makes time infinite and devalues its preciousness. This is, of course, completely ignorant towards us Christians. Almost no one here is on time, even when I allow for the leeway of being ten minutes late. Thirty minutes late is, in fact, standard. One to two hours is not uncommon. But the fact that people are delayed by days is beyond imagination and makes me turn into the *Hulk*. Furious with rage, I instruct the people afterward that they should stick to their time agreements. But the plan to educate them in this way is as promising as teaching a dog to do mental arithmetic.

In order not to waste my time senselessly waiting, I have recently made it a rule to schedule my time accordingly to allow for the typical 30-minute delay. So if I have an appointment at 2 p.m., I plan to be there at 2:30 p.m. at the earliest, and I do not even have a guilty conscience about it, even though this is a violation of one of my most sacred commandments. After all, this is part of adapting to the culture of the host country. And I do nothing else. I am simply turning the tables.

The one thing I can really draw from is the patience of the locals when it comes to time. In cases when they themselves have to wait for someone, it would never occur to them to reproach the other person for being late. Let alone get angry about it. Instead, they casually hang out somewhere, take a nap, or simply joke around with the other people present (they all seem to know each other somehow anyway). In their view, the time is not wasted unnecessarily with waiting, but exploited to the fullest for their own well-being.

I could certainly be a bit more relaxed about the issue of punctuality if we had not set December 13 as the date for our official opening ceremony, and thus we only had two months left until the final completion. Unfortunately, this unpunctuality is omnipresent and affects not only appointments, but also deliveries and the completion of jobs. I am under a bit of pressure because I am directly dependent on the reliability of some partners.

Apparently, in addition to the different understanding of punctuality in this country, there is also a different understanding of quality. It is extremely exhausting to have to revise, complain and, in the worst case, even write off everything afterward. When selecting our furniture, for example, I took a photo of the items on display, printed it out and had the manufacturer sign it. In this way, I had hoped to get the same quality ensured. Despite my efforts, instead of receiving the seven closets and ten bedside tables in a light wood with a white *shabby-chic* effect, the finish on the furniture that was delivered looked completely different. Wood of the lowest quality was also used for production, which is noticeable in the smell, among other things. In addition, some cabinet doors do not open properly. There are no keys on some doors, and the door handles are missing on others. I wrote up a list of deficiencies —it has the same nature as the number PI: it is almost infinite. After several personal conversations and phone calls, but without any insight from the manufacturer, I have to accept that the promise of the *shabby-chic* furniture is not going to be honored and that we will have to settle for the *shabby* look. This cabinet scavenger has been driving me crazy for the past few weeks. I have wasted so much time with her, only to find myself back in the status quo with the substandard products in the end. It has been a thoroughly unsatisfying investment that has cost us not only a lot of money, but at least as much energy. Sami's expert advice to me: "Be flexible!"

My inward and unspoken counter-advice to him in this more than frustrating situation for me: "Then do your own shit!" All the same, I had better become master of my gruff inner voice and heed his advice. Because my bad mood in these moments changes very little in the circumstances, except that I deprive myself of my peace. Unfortunately, I am a perfectionist who cannot stand it if something does not go according to my expectations. And especially not when such a large amount of money is involved.

At least, the furniture maker of our beds is on the premises. As a carpenter, he is a real specialist when it comes to wood. The beds commissioned from him are manufactured directly on our construction site. The fact that the carpenter is on site has the advantage for us that we can always see what he is doing and how he is doing it. Nevertheless, what does not occur to us is to check the dimensions of the produced beds from the very beginning. The scope of his order includes a total of seven beds, in the standard lengths of conventional mattresses and in the widths that we explicitly gave him on a piece of paper. Perhaps we were a bit naïve in this respect, relying blindly on him. Yet, a carpenter should be trusted to know standard sizes and to reliably apply them to his projects. Now we find ourselves in the situation that we have three king-size and four single beds, which are visually beautiful, but are each 10 inches too short for our already purchased premium mattresses. The moment I put the mattress on the bed and realize there is a problem, and that the bed frames are too short, a part of me dies inside. I rant at God and the world, and for the first time I also get a little louder when speaking with one of our contractors. The consequence of this furniture mess is that the beds are worthless to us and have to be redone all over again. To make matters worse, we also have to find and pay a new manufacturer for this, since our trusted carpenter could not cope with this loss of face caused by incompetence and has since then neither appeared on the construction site nor been reachable. At least he could have kept his honor and left us a part of the already paid price. Often I no longer know whether to laugh or cry. Despite the constant search to discover a hidden camera on the property, revealing this all as a joke, I must admit to myself at some point that this is the bitter reality. Therefore, I decide to laugh, since I see no alternative but to fall back into sarcasm. Before that, though, I give free rein to my displeasure one last time. Sami's advice in this situation: "Be flexible!"

Incidentally, I am trying to take this advice to heart with regard to our fishpond in the garden. After tenacious research on the Internet as to what it should look like, we have found someone who is up to the task, to create it according to our ideas. He presents himself to me as a competent garden expert who knows exactly what to do to make all our garden dreams come true. As with the promising transaction with the furniture cobbler, I print out a picture from the Internet of the pond we want and have him sign it. In this way, I intend to ensure the quality and to prevent subsequent misunderstandings in advance. We agree on a price, which seems very high to me, but I still give him the order. Quality has its price.

A few hours later, he starts working diligently. First, he takes measurements of everything. Then he draws sketches of what is to be erected where and in what dimensions. But that is all for today.

A few days later, he shows up again. This time he's highly motivated. In view of his euphoria, I am about to high-five him and spur him on like a coach with a Go, go, go! After lunch, however, this euphoria already seems to have vanished because I do not get to see him the rest of the day.

Again, a few days later, he arrives at our site loaded with a lot of cement. This time he actually starts to build the foundation. After a few hours, he is gone again, just as quickly as during his short appearances before.

This goes on for three weeks and what I see so far looks more like the work of an unskilled child building a castle with cement instead of an aesthetically pleasing beautiful fishpond surrounded by rocks, decorated with flowers, plants and a small waterfall. But maybe that is just my perspective without any expertise or experience in this area. At least I am holding on to that hope right now.

When I observe him rigorously for an entire day and notice that he is spending more time loitering around the site and keeping the others from their work than pursuing his own project, I finally snap. I confront him with the question when exactly he finally intends to complete the project according to our demands. After all, we are running out of time. He is totally distraught and cannot understand my question at all. Shortly thereafter, he takes off.

Since he does not appear again in the following days and does not respond to my attempts to get in touch with him by phone, it becomes clear to me that we are dealing with a first-rate impostor and have been ripped off again. What he leaves us with is a fishpond of shame. The worst part is that the pond is not even watertight and is constantly leaking water. Unfortunately, the foundation of this concrete castle that looks like it was built by a child is useless. We therefore decide to tear the thing down as much as possible to remove all the bad energy of cheating and imposture from our facility. As if we did not have enough to do already, we build it ourselves on our own with the workers. We do our best within the limits of our capabilities. The result is only mediocre at best compared to the rest of our little paradise.

This is the common pattern throughout our building project. From the furniture, to our fishpond, to the construction of the water tank, to the building of the two-story wooden pavilion. The excuses are the same non-stop. The general understanding of quality is just not there. Again and again, I find myself in situations where I am unable to act and feel completely helpless. My scope of action is simply limited. Although I am now able to deal with setbacks better, I am slowly accumulating a lot of negative emotions that throw me off track at regular intervals. I long for a smooth process, but am constantly disappointed anew. These experiences are by no means teaching me any valuable lessons, rather they simply drive me to despair.

With regard to our fundamentally different cultural values in terms of communication, quality and reliability, Sami gives me some important advice: "In Bali always like that. You can learn a lot from it. This is not Europe, this is Bali. Again, be flexible. Sometimes we have no influence. You can only be responsible for yourself. What others think, feel and do is not your business! More important is how you react to it." He has been aware of my helplessness and the accompanying stress level for weeks. But I think he first tried to let me swim alone in the shark tank of the unreliable. Figuratively speaking, I drowned miserably. Of course, there is a lot of wisdom in his words. Even so, it is simply not possible for me to remain calm in this matter. I am simply too much of a perfectionist, too German for that. I have never longed for the quality feature *Made in Germany* as much as I do now.

2. Teamwork makes the dream work

*"I do not pay good wages because I have
a lot of money, I have a lot of money
because I pay good wages."*

[Robert Bosch]

The belief that we can turn our resort into a little heaven on earth is still alive, but we must not lose our sense of reality in the midst of all our dreams. Moreover, reality clearly tells us that money is slowly running out. All in all, everything has become much more expensive than expected. Not least because we failed in our planning to consider the constant cuts in quality and rip-offs.

In order to still be able to implement everything according to our ideas, I borrowed additional money from my parents after the last cent of my own savings was used up. Even though they were critical of my plans to go to Bali in the beginning, it now feels even nicer to have their unconditional support once again. The financial risk I am taking on our project so far is manageable, since I will have a secure source of income again beginning in January of next year due to my new job. The only risk is that Sami will not pay me back the money I have given him. Yet, I have no concerns about that. If I had such thoughts in the back of my mind, none of this would have made any sense to me, which is why they have never seriously surfaced so far, despite repeated warnings from those around me. I have great confidence in him —in every aspect.

In the meantime, Sami has also exhausted all his possibilities to raise funds from his family. Although we still have a real ace up our sleeve with the option of taking out a loan from the bank, we only want to do this in the case of acute financial need in order to continue to guarantee our financial independence and not expose ourselves to any pressure from the bank. Therefore, we have to tighten our belts in all areas at the moment.

Since Sami owns the facility, which makes him the supreme chief, and not only for that reason, his word is law at the end of the day. And he has decided that our business operations start on the day of the opening ceremony. There is no room for discussion to dispute with him on this decision. He does not even concede me a fair chance to bring this matter to a decision like real men with *Rochambeau*. For our business model of *Bali Chy Healing* this means that we have no time for financial rehabilitation and from this day on all fixed costs around the operation of the facility and especially for salaries of our employees have to be paid, which puts us under enormous pressure to succeed.

In any case, I would have preferred the opening to begin at a later date. But there is no turning back now. We have already sent out invitations to Sami's most loyal patients from all over the world, including the USA, Canada, Germany and Australia, offering them the chance to come to the opening ceremony and stay at our facility for free the following week.

This is also a way to express our gratitude for their trust and support over the years.

Apart from the completion of the retreat center, it is of utmost importance to have a solid team in place a few weeks before the start of the retreat. After all, before the opening of our retreat center, everyone must have been trained and instructed by me in order to know exactly what needs to be done and what role everyone on the team will play. Immediately after the opening, I will no longer be available on-site, which is why everything has to be arranged in advance.

Our team of therapists is already complete. This includes a yoga teacher, an energy healer, an acupuncturist, a natural healing specialist, and a local priest (the chief) who will be the tour guide for the trips and ceremonies included in the retreat package. They will all support Sami in his work as a healer and be on call for us.

We have already hired two cleaners, who will take turns cleaning the facility. In addition, it is certain that Sami's nephew will support us as a janitor and will help us with all necessary repairs. Based on an acquaintance's recommendation, we have also been able to recruit a gardener to join our team, who will also handle pool maintenance. We are currently in talks with a local chef, and I am confident that he is also eager to work with and for us.

On the subject of salary, we have agreed that we want to pay more than just the average wage for the respective occupational group and thus more than our competitors. Furthermore, we have decided that our employees will receive a bonus at the end of the year based on revenues. For me, the most important point is that our employees fully identify with our project and always demonstrate maximum motivation. And in addition to a warm and appreciative attitude towards each other, we believe that the best way to achieve this is through monetary incentives.

When it came to the most important personnel matter, the manager of our facility, Sami and I had heated discussions on more than one occasion. Due to our tight financial situation, we ultimately had no choice but to hire a local. A Western manager, with a monthly salary at least five times that of a local, would certainly offer us better quality in terms of reliability, public relations and sensitivity to the needs of our Western guests, but at the same time, with considerable fixed costs per month, would further increase our pressure to succeed. Although we already have Made, an absolutely lovely, committed, trustworthy, English-speaking local woman with experience in the tourism industry in mind for the position of manager, I would simply prefer to give this task to a Western person. I have great skepticism whether this is the right decision. After all, I will not be able to recognize neither issues nor opportunities from Germany, and will not be able to run the place myself. This makes me largely dependent on the work and flow of information from this employee. I have to be able to rely on her one hundred percent. Furthermore, this position requires a high degree of initiative as well as well-developed leadership qualities.

As time goes on, the pressure also increases surrounding whether we will be able to complete the facility at all by the opening ceremony. There are constant unexpected interruptions. For the past two weeks, work on the main building has been largely at a standstill, as most of the workers are away on a special Muslim holiday in their homeland on the neighboring island of Java. Our architect Pak Tude cannot really say precisely when they will return. And Sami is also getting a bit nervous about this now. After all, it is he who has put us under this time pressure in the first place with his wish to start the business with the opening ceremony in one and a half months. My advice to him with a mischievous expression on my face is, "Be flexible!"

3. Being lucky or being happy?

"Trying to be happy by accumulating possessions is like trying to satisfy hunger by taping sandwiches all over your body."

[George Carlin]

A short time later, our construction workers return from their homes in Java. One by one, they arrive back at our construction site. This is a great relief, after I already had the worst fears that they would not return —if at all —for a few weeks. If the construction progress continues at the same pace as before their departure, we will be finished at the very last minute, at best. The fundamental prerequisite for this is no more unexpected holidays or other setbacks. Considering the time we have left, I get scared and anxious when I think about all the tasks that still have to be done. In the next few weeks, the motto will therefore be: Driving at breakneck speed.

The roofing ceremony has already taken place some time ago. In the meantime, the main house with its walls, stairs and roof is more than just a structure and almost looks homey. The remaining work consists exclusively of finishing the interior. The floor is covered with light-colored tiles, all walls are painted white. The windows and doors are already installed. Thus, the first rooms can already be furnished and decorated.

The months of work on the construction site have bonded me firmly with our workers. Not only because I regularly supply them with cigarettes, but also because they know there is nothing I would not do to help, and I regularly get my hands dirty while working with them side by side. Sami has already told me several times that all the construction workers speak highly of me in my absence, and that for them this kind of relationship with the builder is an unprecedented experience. In fact, Westerners usually do not bother to lend a hand themselves, as labor in Indonesia is extremely cheap. The workers appreciate my honest work ethic.

I have a particularly close relationship with one of the construction workers. His name is André, and he is the only one who is not from Java or Bali. He is from Sumatra, the largest island in Indonesia. Perhaps that is why he seems like a bit of an outsider within the group. The people of the various islands are generally very different from each other. Not only in their appearance, but also in their character traits. André's introverted nature may also be decisive for his role within the group. At the age of twenty-seven, he has already been through quite a lot. I try to talk to him at every opportunity because, on the one hand, I feel sorry for him, but on the other hand, he has become a kind of friend in the meantime. André is one of the few workers who can speak English. He taught himself with English-language movies, music and an English book that he bought at some point. So far, this investment has apparently not paid off. I doubt that it was always his dream to slave away on a construction site for relatively little money, thus abusing his body. He is one of those who has been assigned to our construction site from the project's start to its finish. This is due to the fact that he has no training and does not specialize in anything, but is simply used as a human cement-mixing machine. Although it is hard to imagine that given the scope of the project, the building materials are not mixed by machine, the fact is that they are mixed manually with great effort using only a shovel. Since this task is required from the first to the last day, his work is also required for that timespan. I am happy about this, although I often feel sorry for him when I see how he slaves away there every day. Even though Pak Tude has already reminded me several times that cement mixing is his job and that I do not need to help him, I regularly feel obliged to join him in wielding the shovel or at least to supply him with cigarettes while he is working.

Perhaps our clandestine smoking in one of the outdoor bathrooms on the property further united us. I have great sympathy regarding his circumstances. André has tried so many different jobs in his life. As a street vendor of CDs, in a factory processing coconuts, as a driver, and so on and so forth. The fact that he is now content with working as a human cement mixer for the moment is solely due to the fact that he earns enough money in this profession. Settling for such a hard job does not necessarily show an abundance of alternatives, but reveals his lack of perspective. In my view, these are obvious reasons to be deeply unhappy.

André is working his butt off for us every day, and at the end of the day, he does not have much money to spare. He has to use his earnings to financially support his family in Sumatra, which includes his parents, his grandfather and his younger brother. They still live there as natives in a jungle far away from civilization. There, apart from growing their own rice, fruit and vegetables, they have no other source of income except André's. With a sad voice, André regularly lets me know that he misses his family very much. After all, he has not seen them for more than seven years. He cannot afford the long journey to Sumatra because a visit would also mean not being able to work and thus not generating any income. When I ask him how much money we are talking about for the flight, ferry and bus, he answers 3,000,000 rupees, which is the equivalent of about $190 dollars. Hearing that makes me want to cry because considering the sums I invest here in our project, this is only play money in my eyes.

I would love to make André happy and pay for his flight out of my own pocket. Unfortunately, my liquidity is currently coming to an end too. And paying him only a subsidy bears the risk that the money will be used for other purposes resulting in the temporary benefit of a few more packs of cigarettes. Moreover, it would also cause envy among the other workers, which, again, I do not want either. Most of them struggle at least as much as he does, and it is only due to their lack of English skills that their stories escape my attention. Furthermore, I want to interact with André not as a rich kid from the West, but rather as a real friend, characterized by empathy and compassion.

I try very hard to encourage him at every opportunity, hoping to motivate him to stay optimistic and to give him the strength and drive to get out of his predicament.

But when I look at the two of us, I have to conclude that, all in all, André is perhaps much happier than I am. He has accepted his circumstances and embraced them as part of himself. He is content with what he has and does not complain one bit about the hard work and pain he goes to bed with almost every night. If the sagging mattress on the board floor can even be called a bed. Not once has he complained that he has no real home and is regularly passed from one construction site to the next like a traveling whore. He has even accepted that. I see him laughing so often and every time he has a cigarette in the corner of his mouth, it makes it seem like he is content.

Comparing myself to him makes me think. Normally, we only feel worse when we compare ourselves with people who have more and who are better off in terms of health or social status. The envy that results from this constantly gives rise to new needs in us and, insofar as these are not satisfied, to new suffering as well as the feeling of lack. "So why do I feel bad even when I compare myself to someone who has virtually nothing and lives on the poverty line? Surely, I should be much happier than I am when I see what wealth and privileges I enjoy!"

For the umpteenth time in my life, I question whether it is actually things or external circumstances that make us happy, or whether that happiness can only come from ourselves.

These doubts about my previous search for happiness culminate one evening during my dinner with the workers. I consider it a sign of friendship and acceptance to be fed by them in the tin hut they build themselves on our site, which is why I gratefully accept the invitation.

All day long, for reasons of hygiene, I have had a bad feeling about whether the one and a half kilos of chicken meat would be better off in a refrigerated container than stewing on a plate in the blazing sun at nearly ninety degrees. I anticipate nothing good and envision myself spending the night on the toilet bowl of my hostel room with stomach cramps and a proper *Bali Belly*. At the time when the worker's day regularly ends, we let the shovels rest for the day and treat ourselves to the common meal as a reward for the sweaty work and the sensational progress of the last few days. There is no real kitchen available to the workers for the preparation of the meal. Instead, there is only a fireplace on which the pots and pans can be placed. Two of them have turned their attention to the meat, while another prepares the vegetables and takes care of the rice. First, the chicken is boiled for a long time before being pan-fried and then deep-fried. I did not expect them to have these cooking skills, as the roles in Indonesian families are clearly defined in terms of gender when it comes to preparing food.

We settle down in the workers' temporary home on the edge of our construction site and partake of our meal with our hands, as is customary in the country. According to the customs of the construction workers, we also have a good drink. The cheap rice liquor is on me, surprisingly they were able to take care of cooling it in advance. At first, I still try to resist this custom, but quickly I come to the realization that if I still want to be a part of this group, I must not lose face now as "Teetotal-Tom." And finally, I have to live up to my responsibility as a representative of the Wild West.

The food is excellent, and I have probably never eaten such deliciously prepared chicken before. As a thank you for the invitation, I have volunteered to cover the cost of the food. As I remember this, it occurs to me that I still owe André the money for the meat and all the vegetables. He was so kind and went to the local market in the capital Denpasar for us to get all the ingredients. When I ask him how much I owe him, he replies with his mouth full, "I get 80,000 rupees from you."

Given the equivalent of $5 dollars, I am surprised at how cheap that is. "Wow, that is cheap!" I express my amazement. After I gave voice to this assessment, the heads of all English-speaking attendees seem to lower a bit. André then informs me: "Cheap??? Yes, my friend, but only for you!"

Ouch, that one hit home.

The evening is really pleasant, and I enjoy the intimate atmosphere with our workers, but André's statement and the reaction of the group struck me hard. The question of the origin of happiness and satisfaction in life has not only occupied me since I became friends with André. I have been asking myself this question since my first stay in Bali when I was still a student. Although most of the people here live in poverty, most of them are seemingly happy and satisfied. Happier and more satisfied than we are in our Western society.

So, now I have been contemplating this for several days, recalling all the memories and everything I have learned from the past. I consider it appropriate to give the subject of happiness a separate chapter in my bible of knowledge. My philosophical vein pulsates at full speed and I record my thoughts as follows:

"Happiness is our true nature. Accordingly, we do not have to do or be anything special to reach the state of happiness. Essentially, we are always cheerful and happy. However, our subconscious mind has stored information over the years that tells us which events, circumstances or people allow us to reach this state. We are therefore programmed to know when we are happy and what conditions must be met for this to happen.

As part of a society driven by consumption and growth, we ourselves are to blame for why new expectations continually emerge and why we are never satisfied with what we have or who we are. This constant desire is like shackles that deny us true happiness. From an early age, we are taught to strive for more and more. It has become the centerpiece of our very existence. We therefore strive for all sorts of things, expecting them to bring us happiness. These may not only be concrete objects such as a nicer home, a new car, the latest technical equipment or simply more money. It can also be our desire to find an even better partner, to have more or better friends, or to experience feelings more intensely. As a result, we transmit a sense of deficiency through our constant desire, which we immediately experience on an emotional level. It is much wiser to focus on what we already have and see the good in it, in order to send out gratitude and live in abundance.

Happiness begins on the inside and manifests itself in the outer world. Our dependence on people or the material world limits us. Even if we find short-term satisfaction in things, nothing lasts forever. Things break and are no longer useful, and every person changes and eventually dies.

Contrary to our own beliefs, happiness meets us at every corner. It does not take any extraordinary incident to experience the sweet taste of happiness. It is in the little things that we find our happiness. And mostly they are the ones that money cannot buy. These include people we meet, time with children, kisses, laughter, or sweet memories."

In light of my findings, I almost feel sorry for how presumptuous I was to repeatedly give André cautionary advice regarding happiness. "What the hell have I gotten myself into? Compared to his life, I am a spoiled brat. While I grew up in a comfortable environment with all the daily necessities, his life is characterized by never knowing whether there will be anything on the dinner table in the evening or not. There is no social system available to him in case of emergency, no parents to provide for him, no savings. Instead, he lives a life in constant fear that something could happen to one of his family members, which would mean financial ruin in terms of medical expenses. So, how can I give that kind of advice to a person in such different circumstances, in such a different culture? Even if he does not know any other way, it is not my place to instruct him how to make the best of his situation. And certainly not how he can be happy. In fact, I should approach him and ask him to teach me his secrets for being happy.

I sink into a state of humility. The comparison of our different circumstances makes me realize how well I am doing. I can count myself lucky to have access to help from so many people, things and circumstances that I otherwise always took for granted and whose value I only now recognize after I compare my resources to those of a disadvantaged person.

Suddenly, so many things come to mind for which I can consider myself lucky. Starting with my family, who is always there for me. The love and care they show me. My friends who enrich my life incredibly and who always lend me a sympathetic ear. My financial and social security. I suddenly appreciate having insurance for liability, homeowner's insurance, occupational disability insurance, health insurance, unemployment insurance, long-term care insurance, and pension insurance. It would never be possible in the society I live in to fall so low as to even begin to understand what simple life in Indonesia feels like. I am grateful for the democracy and political stability I live in. For the peace and freedom. For being able to move around without restrictions and being mobile at all times. That I am free to travel the world and pursue my dreams on the other side of the globe. Until now, I have always taken all of this for granted. Suddenly, everything appears to me in an entirely different light.

The comparison downwards has opened my eyes. Many people would deeply envy my way of life. On the outside, I lack absolutely nothing. I now realize that compared to most people in this world, I live like a god. I am just infinitely grateful that I am allowed to lead such a privileged life, in which the conditions to be happy could not be better. For me, being happy means being who you are without wishing to be someone else. And to be content and grateful with what you have, and not to constantly strive for something else or anything more.

4. This is Bali

"God, grant me the serenity to accept the things I cannot change, the courage to change the things I can, and the wisdom to know the difference."

[Reinhold Niebuhr]

In view of our financial constraints, which have been looming for some time, we are now forced to take out a loan from the bank. Although we lose our financial independence, it is important to Sami and me, especially now at the end of the construction process, not to have to do without things to complete our little paradise.

In order to take out the loan, we expect two bank employees on our site at 2 p.m., who want to check our project and Sami's solvency. Sami does not inform me about the amount of the loan. For this reason, Sami has asked me to spare some time and support him at this appointment. After all, it looks much more serious when a Western businessman is involved in a project.

When the two bank employees arrive on time by local standards at 2:20 p.m., Sami calls me to join them downstairs in the garden. I am with Sami's nephew and we are in the middle of trimming branches of a tree which are sticking out over the second-floor parapet onto the balcony.

In swimming trunks, shirtless, tarred with sweat and sprinkled with tiny bits of sawdust on my torso, I introduce myself to the two suits. We take a seat in our garden pavilion and I explain to the group what our business will look like, how we are organized and what income we expect in the future. Both gentlemen look foreign in their loose-fitting suits. One man's pants are cut so wide he could easily pass for an *MC Hammer* lookalike: "U can't touch this, HAMMER TIME."

Even if they give their best, the two of them seem out of character in these costumes of respectability. In a typical Balinese way they are in a joking mood and with Sami, they have found someone who is in no way inferior to them and joins in directly. Therefore, the atmosphere is very relaxed right from the start, even if they continue trying to keep a serious face to ask the questions from the bank's point of view with as much insistence as possible. After half an hour, I am dismissed for now. They light a farewell cigarette before taking pictures of the facility for their documentation. I am quite satisfied with my performance, although I could have made a little more effort with regard to my visual appearance.

A few days later, we receive positive feedback from the bank. With the approval of the loan, the financial pressure is off to fund our project for the moment. It is reassuring to be able to fall back on financial reserves from now on.

Our retreat is nearing completion, just four days before the opening ceremony. A few last little things like the doors of the kitchen cabinets, the odd lamp or the fans in the dining area still need to be installed. Otherwise, we have really made it and defied all odds.

In the garden, we have planted beautiful flowers of various colors in addition to our medicinal herbs, fruits and spices. The kitchen is well-stocked with dinnerware, glasses and kitchen utensils. Fruit baskets with all kinds of exotic fruits give life to our huge dining table. Several colorful fish have found a home in our fishpond. The rooms light up with pictures and quotes on the walls. Branded pillows and bedspreads with the Bali Chy Healing logo decorate the already made beds. On top of that, the outdoor bathrooms are fully functional and equipped with all the necessary bathing supplies. We still have to do the basic cleaning in the next few days right before the opening.

I have been living in *Rumah Bapak Sami* for one week now. It is an overwhelming feeling. Especially in the morning hours when I have the place all to myself. There is total peace and a harmonious silence. Except for the murmur of the small stream and the chirping of the birds, there are no other sounds to be heard.

Since the site borders on a rice field on one side and is enclosed facing our neighbors on the other, I have pure privacy. This is indispensable for my nude morning routine, which includes a short walk through my paradise residence in my birthday suit, as well as nude yoga. I enjoy this freedom to the fullest and am proud to have brought nudism to Bali. Until the arrival of the first staff members around eight o'clock, textiles are strictly forbidden.

As much as I enjoy the morning hours, the hours after that annoy me. I no longer even have time for my afternoon nap, as I lack a place of retreat where I can hide from last-minute questions about the opening ceremony and final instructions regarding the facility. Sure, it makes me feel like the most important man in the resort, if not in the whole world. The fact remains, a man like me is nothing without his nap.

Unfortunately, the pool is not yet usable. We filled it up to the top with fresh water, then immediately jumped in and did a cannonball or two. A short time later, however, the fun is already over. There is still a real boss on the construction site, which we have to fight hard right now: Our power supply. Thanks to government regulation, we had enough electricity available during the months of construction to run the site. As of now, though, we unfortunately continue to have "only" access to this limited power supply for construction sites, which does not come close to meeting our needs for the additional electricity required for the day-to-day operation of the facility. As a result, neither the water pump in the pool nor the air conditioners in the rooms can be operated properly. Sami has been trying for several weeks to correct these shortcomings, so far unfortunately without success.

For a frugal person such as myself, this circumstance causes me few problems when living in the resort. Before moving in, I stayed at the small hostel *Arnawa Inn* and have not resided at the Hilton. I don't need any of the luxuries or frills. On the contrary, I have come to terms with the fact that I do not need air conditioning at all. Of course, it would be nice to have at least a cool retreat in my own room with these tropical temperatures. But to be able to stay within my own four walls, I gladly accept waking up drenched in sweat. On top of that, it also has the positive side effect that I no longer have to pay rent and can save on these expenses. The fact that not all lamps can be switched on without the fuse blowing only bothers me to a limited extent.

What gives me a big headache is the certainty that the first guests we invited for a free week in *Rumah Bapak Sami* will arrive in two days. This evening Eva, one of Sami's closest confidants from the USA, is already arriving. We are working hard to find alternative solutions. Despite our efforts, they are not available.

Sami is indisposed in the evening, which is why I meet Eva at the retreat. The pick-up service from the airport we've set up with our transportation partner has already worked flawlessly. I give Eva a warm welcome at the entrance to the facility. We already know each other very well, as she has already been to Bali twice during the year, just to see Sami. Her first words after entering the resort resound in a tone of voice that adds to her wide eyes of admiration: "Oh my gosh. This is amazing. Thomas, this is unbelievable. You guys are genius. I love this place. This is heaven on earth."

Like the emperor himself, I show her around with a puffed chest and show her everything we have created in the last few months. Her admiration never ceases.

As dusk slowly falls and the lights illuminate the premises with only half their usual power, Eva starts to feel a little uneasy. In the first days, I felt the same way, but with time, I got used to it. I can understand that Eva feels more and more uncomfortable with increasing darkness, because of the opening to the opposite rice field, as well as the generally rather remote location. I try to reassure her, after all I am still there and the neighbors on both sides are only a stone's throw away from us. Furthermore, I let her know with a wink that the Gods have been kind to us and that consequently nothing can happen. All the same, her reaction indicates that she does not appreciate my casual joking.

When she enters her room and the first moments resemble a visit to the sauna thanks to the accumulated heat, she storms back to me in the dining area in a rage with beads of sweat on her forehead and voices her resentment. The fact that at this moment a bat also scurries through the open entrance area is the final straw. Her nerves are on edge: "Thomas, I am really very sorry. But I can NOT stay here. I hope you understand that! Can you please call the driver? I will ask him to drive me to the hotel I used to stay the last times. Hopefully, they have a room available."

Somewhat shocked by the sudden change of heart, I comply with her request and order the driver back to take her to the hotel in Seminyak. When he arrives after a few minutes, she packs her bags right away and says goodbye, not quite as sympathetically as she had greeted me.

I watch the car drive away for some time. This is a real shock. A nipple pincher with one and a half turns. I am scared. Not of the darkness in which she abandons me, but that I have completely misjudged the situation. I firmly assumed that the dimmed lights, the unusable swimming pool, and the unusable air conditioners would only marginally affect our guests. After all, I myself have been staying there for a few days and undoubtedly considered it tolerable. Maybe I underestimated the fact that I had already gotten used to the heat during my previous nine months here on the island. In the rooms it is already very hot, and I do not know whether I could sleep without sweating in the months before here myself. In addition, it becomes clear to me what a deterrent the optical effect of the swimming pool has in the meantime due to the lack of the water pump. Instead of making the facility look like a wellness oasis, the green pool has the feel-good factor of a sewage plant. As I have found it like this every day, I have become blind to realize how expansive it actually appears. I get a stomachache when I consider that these circumstances could cause the same reaction in the other guests as they do in Eva.

I rack my brain as to how we can get out of this situation. The only way to save face and not entirely ruin our guests' vacation is to inform them of these shortcomings and let them decide for themselves whether they can cope with them and stay here or whether it would be better to move to another lodging.

I call Sami on my cell phone and tell him about Eva's sudden departure. Disappointed, I tell him that in my opinion, it is impossible to provide our guests with a nice vacation under these circumstances. I suggest that he contact the rest of the guests and tell them about the situation. He then replies to me: "You invited them, you have to cancel them. You are the manager, I am the healer. Self-confident and strong you need to be. Do not worry, my brother, they will understand."

I am uncertain if he really wants me to grow from this, or if he is just making it damn easy on himself. One thing is for sure, though: we are not getting out of this one. I feel so uncomfortable about this. First, we generously invite Sami's most loyal patients to stay at our facility for a whole week free of charge, only to ruefully limit our offer in this drastic way or withdraw it completely shortly beforehand. A flight from the USA, Canada, Germany or Australia is not cheap. And finding an alternative lodging in a hurry is not easy and can be costly. FUCK! I spend my night wide-awake and completely anxious.

Early the next morning, I muster all my courage and compose the following email in my nudist office at the dining room table, hoping not to meet with too much disappointment:

"Dear Bali Chy Healing family,
The last weeks at the construction site have been very intense and exhausting. Our goal was to have everything finished in time to welcome you to the opening ceremony and make Rumah Bapak Sami your new home for one week.
The good news is, we really finished everything.
The bad news is, our electricity that is supplied by the government, is not sufficient to run this big compound. That means that the air-conditioning is not working and the

swimming pool is unusable. Plus it might get a bit dark at night. Because of the weak power flow we can only use a limited number of lamps. If these circumstances are still acceptable for you, we would really look forward to welcoming you.

If you feel uncomfortable with this situation, please let me know. I will do my best assist you in any way possible to make the opening ceremony and your holidays in Bali a special time. In any case, please accept our apologies. Especially, for not informing you sooner.

Please share your feedback as soon as possible!

Warm regards

Thomas (and Sami)"

Understandably, this does not trigger a wave of enthusiasm among those affected. I am pleasantly surprised that the reactions are marked by profound understanding overall. Not a single person criticizes me. Ryan from Australia reacted most casually. From him, I receive only a very short, but all the more meaningful feedback, "This is Bali ;-)" which is accompanied with a smiley.

My relief in the face of their understanding responses is immeasurable. The fear of their reactions was unjustified, which is why it is a load off my mind. Nevertheless, it also feels awful not to be allowed to host single guest in the first inauguration week, when we had looked forward to and planned for a full house.

Lately, due to the multitude of tasks and the enormous time pressure, the work has given me less and less pleasure and has increasingly become a burden. After overcoming this now hopefully last obstacle, I therefore look forward to the opening ceremony. And soon it will be time to say goodbye to the Island of the Gods.

5. The gates open

"*We were born to make manifest the glory of God that is within us. It is not just in some of us, it is in everyone. And as we let our own light shine, we consciously give other people permission to do the same.*"

[*Nelson Mandela*]

The day of our opening ceremony has arrived. To my surprise, I have received support from my German home country. My good friend Simon spontaneously took two weeks of vacation. Thanks to him, I am no longer sleeping all alone in the villa. My nudist rules are still valid despite his presence, whether he likes it or not. My house, my rules.

In the morning, it is *Gotong Rojong* which means that all friends and acquaintances get together to join in the final preparations. A nice custom, which is why thanks to the manpower available to us through this, the work is completed quickly.

At noon, a local priest stops at our facility to hold a small ceremony. Everyone present is dressed in traditional robes. So are Simon and me. All the women are dressed as beautifully as I have ever seen them. With an eye for detail, they are perfectly styled from top to bottom. The blooming *frangipani* flower behind their ears completes the beauty of these lovely ladies.

Under the guidance of the priest, we pray together to the Gods and ask for assistance for the success of our business venture, as well as blessings for the facility.

Finally, in the evening, our gates open to the estimated ninety invited guests. About one third of them are of Western origin. They are former patients who either have traveled especially for the event or have their permanent residence on the Isle of the Gods. Among them are also the eight people we originally invited to *Rumah Bapak Sami* as our guests for the week after the opening ceremony. I am still tormented by my guilty conscience, which is why I apologize to them again as I welcome them to the facility with Sami by my side.

The rest of the guests are made up of friends, acquaintances and relatives, who of course cannot be left out of this spectacle.

Among the numerous guests, there are also some of our workers. Including my friend André. When I see him, I am deeply touched. I feel a profound attachment to him. I am grateful to my workers from the bottom of my heart because I know that beyond their wages, they have also put a lot of heart and soul into our project. You can undoubtedly feel that love throughout the facility.

It is not only meeting the workers that gets me extremely emotional. After all the stress, a lot of dead weight is now falling off me, and I am finally able to enjoy the moment of the opening and feel joy about the work that lies behind us.

For our guests, we have served up a great meal. A caterer prepared several large vessels and platters on our behalf with the best Indonesia has to offer culinary-wise. Fortunately, the caterer's price includes the serving and clearing service, so we can fully indulge in the festivities.

The entire evening is accompanied by music. Apart from the two bell ringers, who play traditional music to accompany the food, there is also a cover band playing afterward, which we have recruited from a bar in Kuta especially for this evening. The program is topped off by the performance of a traditional Balinese dance, presented by a group of ladies from our neighborhood. Finally, I give a short speech in which I once again refer to the development and construction of *Rumah Bapak Sami* and express our gratitude to all those involved.

The entire ceremony is only possible because our French neighbor from the house next door, with whom we have had an excellent relationship since the beginning of construction, has made his house's powerfully available to us for this evening. To our delight, he together with his wife and two sons accepted our invitation, so they also mingled with the other guests.

Throughout the evening there is a relaxed atmosphere, and you can see how happy everyone is and how happy people are for us. I am so exhausted that I stumble several times on some edges and stairs. It demands enormous strength from me each time to pick myself up again. I find it particularly difficult to stay awake at all.

To celebrate the evening, we treat ourselves to a bottle of gin that Simon has brought along from Germany as a housewarming gift and smuggled past me into the facility.

Quite secretly, somewhat apart from the last guests still present, we toast as if we were still under eighteen and doing something terribly forbidden. After all, we are in a healing center where we have to abide by the rules.

When at some point I have to go to the bathroom slightly drunk and sneak past Sami on my way there, he takes me aside briefly: "A great job you did, Thomas. I know how hard it was for you sometimes. I see it, I feel it. Really strong you already are. Are you happy?"

Exhausted, I let him know succinctly, "Yes, I am."

"And are you ready to go home?" he continues to ask me.

"Yes, I think so!"

A little later, the evening is over for me, too. With tired eyes and completely drained of energy, I lie down in bed. Without consciously noticing my inner joy about the successful opening ceremony, I fall into a deep sleep and don't wake up until noon the next day.

I have five days left until my departure, which I can use to take a real vacation with Simon to recover from the efforts of the last month, which was particularly exhausting. We decide to spend four days of it on the Gili Islands in the north of the neighboring island of Lombok, where there is no traffic and where one can only move around on bicycles or on foot. Far from all the scooter traffic, noise and any hustle and bustle, the islands offer us a real refuge to recharge our batteries. The islands are so small that they can be circumnavigated on foot in two hours each. Other than hanging out on the beach, snorkeling in the turquoise waters and eating, there is not much to do there. The total one-and-a-half-hour journey by scooter to the east of Bali and the two-hour crossing from there by speed boat are quite bearable and always worthwhile.

I spend the four days almost exclusively in the hammock on the beach. There I have all the peace and tranquility I need to review the ten months behind me in fast-forward. I realize that this is by no means enough time to really process all the encounters and impressions, all the experiences, downfalls and successes, all the lessons and my entire transformation. But one thing is for sure: I am not the same anymore. I have matured. I have built up a lot of self-confidence and I have gained strength. I feel settled and look to the future with optimism. I have gained a real understanding and grown considerably during my time here and have begun to appreciate life and myself better.

Early in the morning of my last full day, we return from the Gilis to Bali, completely relaxed. The return trip goes flawlessly, so we have ample time to have a quiet coffee as well as go surfing one last time. Sami asked me like a loving mother to come home for dinner at 6 p.m. He has invited several acquaintances and commissioned our chef to prepare a spectacular feast for my departure.

With all my intercultural competence from the last few months, I realize a few hours beforehand that I should not expect this farewell dinner to go as planned. Unfortunately, my thoughts are correct because even two hours after the agreed starting time for the preparation of the meal, the chef has still not appeared.

When I return from the beach shortly before 6 p.m., Sami not only asks me to forgive him for not having the farewell dinner at our resort and that we will have to go to an external restaurant, but also informs me that our cook does not want to work for us and will no longer be available in the future. My new "be-flexible" mentality renders this news as significant as a dropped bag of rice in China. Just Sami's intention to please me in this way makes me insanely happy. That is why my happiness is not affected at all, and we have a really nice last evening together in a nearby local *warung*. In a quite plain and simple atmosphere without any luxury, but with the best food on the island. Everything just to my taste.

When we are back home at the end of the evening, I sat down with Sami one last time on the stairs in the entrance area. Just as we used to do when we were still actively toiling on the construction site and sitting there to catch our breath. I can see his relief. After all, just like me, he has put in a considerable workload over the past ten months and has also borne the burden of being the role model and leader to his frequently lost son Thomas. "Look at this! Look what we created. This is a paradise. A special energy. So proud of you I am," he exclaims one last time, to arm me with a few final sentences for my return to Germany and my future path.

"You planted so many seeds for your future. On the right path you already are. Everything changes. You changed your way of thinking. Especially about yourself. Thoughts and feelings are not nothing, they create your reality. Every thought, every act and feeling in the present moment is a seed that forms your reality in the future. You are born as an image of the divine which means you are part of the divine. What you do, what you think, what you feel is all divine. But you are not aware yet. Everything is part of the divine. You are the creator of your life. Everything you are searching for is already within you. All you need to do is realize it. You have to be aware about it. Do not worry about it. Experiences that you have made are for your growth. For your spiritual consciousness. The vibrations you have send will show up in the material world at the right time."

We have a little small talk before I say goodbye with a deep look into Sami's eyes and a firm hug from him towards bedtime. One last time, I thank him. For guiding me, for his trust in me, for all the insights into the culture, and last but not least, for becoming a true friend to me in addition to being a teacher. I am melancholic and grateful at the same time because I know what a valuable change I was allowed to experience during my time in Bali.

After this last personal meeting for now, I am now finally ready to leave the Island of the Gods behind me. I feel strengthened and look forward to what lies ahead —in my home country, Germany.

PART 3

i.) A foreigner in my own country

1. Happy home

> *"They must often change, who would be
> constant in happiness or wisdom."*
>
> *[Confucius]*

A few short days before Christmas, I am on a plane back home. At regular intervals, I am musically attuned to my return with the Christmas song "Driving home for Christmas" by Chris Rea, which comes through the loudspeakers on the plane, and mentally prepared for the fact that Christmas is right around the corner. Somehow, it all seems so surreal to me right now —like a journey into the unknown. Even though I have spent most of my life in Germany.

A good friend picks me up by car from Frankfurt airport. Just in time for the Christmas holidays, the temperatures have dropped below freezing. Considering the ten months of continuous sunshine behind me, it feels like returning to Antarctica.

Apart from the inhumane weather conditions, I could not have imagined a more beautiful homecoming. My mother, in particular, is infinitely happy to be able to hold me in her arms again, unharmed. Her greeting is almost as emotional as if I had just returned home after years as a prisoner of war. It is only now that I really realize that my family and friends have really felt a huge gap, and that even the regular Skyping or the constant exchange of messages could only compensate for the physical distance between us to a limited extent. We are now catching up on all that at our own pace. I have a lot to tell. And on top of that, a lot of pictures that are just waiting to be shown.

My parents' concerns from the time before my departure have been forgotten in the meantime. What remains is the sheer pride in their son to have accomplished such a project — all alone at the other end of the world and completely on his own. Now, at the latest, it is clear to them that I am no longer their little son whom they have to worry about constantly, but that I have matured into a grown man who stands on his own two feet and purposefully pursues his own path.

In the first days, I immediately drop my social anchor by touring my entire network of family, friends and acquaintances. Everyone is happy to see me and eager to hear what I have to report about my time away. I am surrounded by people's warmth and feel confirmed that this is precisely the place where I belong.

In addition to enjoying social interactions, my return also has a culinary aspect to it. The Christmas season offers me just the perfect opportunity to fully indulge myself. That, too, means home to me. After eating almost exclusively rice plus X last year, morning, noon and night (and sometimes even at

284

night), I now enjoy the variety of German cuisine. Even the simplest dishes, such as a ham sandwich with pickled cucumber, evoke extraordinary feelings of happiness in me. Not to mention my favorite dishes from my mother's kitchen.

As strange as it sounds, somehow it also feels really great to feel cold again and not have to sweat all the time. Especially when I sleep, this is brought directly to my attention. My body and especially my skin thank me for finally experiencing a cooling down after being exposed to the sun for such a long time. There is something incredibly cozy about nesting on the couch in these freezing temperatures with a cup of hot tea, Christmas cookies and a thick blanket, and gathering your loved ones around you —that is the sweet taste of a real home.

Until I find my own place, I can temporarily move into my old childhood room in my parents' apartment. There are still *Tupac* and *Biggie* posters hanging on the walls there, reminiscent of my days as a wannabe gangster. One or the other dirty magazine should also still lie buried in gold digger manner within these four walls. My 130 square foot room is filled with all the furniture and odds and ends from my old household. So, the only room I have left is a small corridor between the door and the bed. To the right and left, everything else is stacked up tetris-like. There is not even a tiny spot to stretch out my yoga mat. But I do not want to complain, and I am incredibly grateful to my parents that they also offer me a spatial home for the transitional period.

2. Thoughts by the sea

*"The fruit of letting go is the birth of
something new."*

[Meister Eckhart]

After almost two weeks of settling in, the time has come and
my first day of work is approaching. While allowing myself a
little more spare time to reflect and process the experiences of
the past year a bit would have been nice, overall the joy simply
prevails that the transition back into professional life and thus
into Western society seems to be going so smoothly.

Since I'm returning to my old place of work in a new
position, the work environment is already largely familiar to
me. Even so, in controlling, a new department awaits me,
which presents me with new challenges in a variety of tasks
and topics. I already know all my new colleagues from my
time as an assistant in the Finance and Accounting
department. The relationship I have with them is a very
friendly one. We used to spend our lunch breaks together back
then.

For the first few days, I spent almost all of my time coming to
grips with the issues and absorbing the practical work
involved in controlling. With Excel, I am immediately at war.
Clearly, I cannot avoid this software in this field of work. No
question, I will try it anyway.

The settling-in phase is passing more quickly than I would like, which means that I am treated with kid gloves less and less, and I am gradually being given more responsibility. After just a few weeks, I find myself in a classic nine-to-five work routine: I get up, ride the subway for an hour to get to work, spend eight to nine hours at my desk in front of the computer working on calculations, and then spend another hour getting back home. To make matters worse, my daily commute does not take me to a spot of idyllic scenery, but leads me directly into the abyss of downtown Stuttgart, which from a traffic perspective is the *Mordor* of German cities.

The initial euphoria of returning home fades quite unnoticed with each subsequent working day. Everything that has been out of the ordinary for me and that I have longed for during my absence is slowly becoming a habit again. The ham sandwich has lost its magic. So have many other things. All needs have been satisfied for now. Unfortunately, the days have passed far too quickly, making that warm feeling very short-lived as well.

I am dealing with my situation in a very mature way because I have learned to accept what I am unable to change. I am aware that my reintegration — from the beach to the office, from heat to cold, from brightness to darkness, from professional flexibility to being tied down, from flip-flops and swimming trunks to loafers with pants and shirts — will not happen overnight. Yet, there is precisely this extremely constricting feeling of no longer being the master of my own life, but rather trapped in the structures of society that rob me of my freedom.

Because in practice, the transition turns out to be much tougher and harder than anticipated. Instead of continuing to do what fulfills me, to carry out my own ideas and to decide what I feel is right, I am now bound to the hierarchies of my employer. As such, all decisions must first pass through several levels before they are implemented —usually without the possibility of having a real say. In a figurative sense, it feels like being pushed off my very own stage, no longer pursuing my magic show with all my passion, but only dancing like a tramp for a few pennies in a backyard for a few men in suits. I feel myself diminished again, as my talents are only being used to a limited extent and I do not feel like I am passionate about my work. I know this precisely because working feels like working again, and I keep looking at the clock every day at ever decreasing intervals to see how much time is left until work is over. In Bali, mind you, I did not even wear a watch. But for the current situation, I bear the full responsibility myself. After all, no one forces me (except my need for money) to be here. And besides, it was clear to me from the start what kind of work environment I was getting myself into.

As time goes by, more and more obstacles come to light that are a challenge for me on my way to resocialization. While in Bali, I lived freely according to my own rhythm, here I am bound to fixed daily structures, and I am as flexible as if I were wearing a straitjacket. Here in Germany, I cannot simply take a walk on the beach in between to clear my head. Nor is it possible to start the working day with a sunrise surf or end it with a sunset surf. Instead, I am so inflexible that now I get annoyed if my daily schedule shifts back by a mere five minutes. Breakfast, lunch and dinner have their fixed times. Even on weekends. So, I do not eat when I am hungry, but rather when I find the time. Everything has to happen at a certain time. There is hardly any spare time for me. And in view of my living conditions, there is also no room. While in Bali, the world was open to me and I spent a lot of time at the sea with its endless expanse, my place of retreat here is limited to the bed in my crowded childhood bedroom.

Yes, even in terms of my mobility, I am currently experiencing drastic restrictions. In Bali, my scooter was a vehicle that gave me not only far-reaching mobility, but rather, like a Harley-Davidson, the feeling of boundless freedom. In this country, riding a scooter at these temperatures would be downright suicide. I do not own one anyway. Nor do I own a car. A purchase is currently out of the question, as I am as financially solid as a first-grader and therefore cannot afford it. Until further notice, I am dependent on public transportation, which always robs me of my freedom with its limited schedule and the other passengers.

Since I am currently staying with my parents, there are no rental costs for me at the moment. In this respect, I am able to put the majority of my salary aside. This is also urgently necessary because when I move into my own place, hopefully soon, I will have to take on larger investments, such as for a couch, a washing machine, a table, a wardrobe, chairs, a bed or a television. Furthermore, I still have to pay my parents back for the four-digit amount they lent me for our construction project in Bali. Although there is no rush for this, I still want to settle my debt with them as soon as possible.

Due to my financial limitations, I am consistently dominated by the feeling of deficiency, and I currently always have to think twice whether I can afford something or not. Therefore, it is not uncommon that I have to skip out on activities with my friends. Even if it is just going out to eat at an Italian restaurant. Every Euro is subject to my strict control, whether it is worth spending or not. It is an unusual and unprecedented situation for me to have no more money at my disposal. I have always been able to fall back on my savings and afford anything at any time. Money was simply always there and gave me a feeling of security and abundance. And now, for the first time in my life, that is no longer the case.

The only security I have right now is the certainty that I now have a fixed income again and that it is foreseeable that my debts will be paid back, and I will have rehabilitated myself financially. Regardless, it does not feel very good to live in this shortage. Yet, I do not regret anything and I stand fully behind the decision to have invested all my money in my dream in Bali.

The search for an apartment also turned out to be more difficult than expected. The housing market in the Stuttgart area is a disaster. Even for the most run-down holes, the proprietors still demand horrendous rents. Why? Because they can! There are simply too few apartments for too many prospective tenants. When I am among the last fifteen chosen at an apartment viewing, the blow hits me when the proprietor informs me that he has received over three-hundred and fifty inquiries for the apartment. Often the apartments are out of the question for me because of an underlying price-performance ratio. Provided that an apartment is a consideration for me, though, my offer usually fails because of the proprietor, who decides in favor of one of my competitors. I am faced with a real test of patience, in which even all my "be-flexible" attempts reach their limits.

In the meantime, there is not much left of the initially regular output of happiness hormones when I see my friends again. I am beginning to realize that I have changed a lot, while one or two others are still dragging their feet. These are precisely the friends who vehemently cannot understand that I am no longer willing to binge-drink my way through life on the weekends. I definitely do not want to miss that social time. And yet, it is no longer an integral part of my life (except for a few slip-ups).

It is also those same friends who ask relentlessly how much dough the entire Bali project earns me. As far as money is concerned, I keep a very low profile with my peers. I have signed a contract with Sami that guarantees me the repayment of my investments. Beyond that, we have never talked about the future possibilities of money flowing into my pocket. I cannot say why. Somehow, I just trust that he will reward me handsomely for my investments and efforts as soon as his financial situation permits. Perhaps I am now so indifferent about the return on investment because the project has become a real heartfelt affair for me. Something with which I can bring some good into the world.

If I were to put a monetary value on the change I experienced during my time in Bali, it would be worth much more to me personally than the time and money I have invested over the years. The knowledge I gained is priceless to me. Not to mention my deep spiritual experiences, which, by the way, I do not need to even begin to talk about with those very friends. They would not understand it anyway. For them, there is only the material world, which represents the absolute truth above everything. If I were to tell them about something like subtle energies or that we can decide what we want to become our reality by directing our focus on it, I would certainly be condemned and accused of belonging to a sect and would have to undergo the metaphorical burning at the stake.

In any case, it is becoming apparent that I will have to learn to let go of one or two friendships. That is probably one of the sacrifices one has to make when growth and change meet standstill. I find that hard to do. But with some of them, it just no longer feels like a real friendship. Instead, after every encounter, I feel like a complete idiot who believes in Santa Claus as well as magic fairies and the Easter Bunny. Although there are quite a few friends who completely understand me and support me in my inner journey, it feels like my social support is just breaking away a bit.

3. Happiness in the far distance?

"All difficulties and obstacles are steps
on which we ascend."

[Friedrich Nietzsche]

I am of course still following the business operations of our retreat in Bali with great interest, although only from a distance and without being able to directly influence them. I left my baby after the opening because I had no other choice. I was at the end of my financial resources and my money would not have lasted another month despite my only marginal expenses. Our plan was for me to hand over management matters to our manager Made as much as possible, but to continue to provide her with support. Particularly with regard to public relations and attracting new guests. In this way, we wanted to ensure that Sami could devote himself fully to his tasks as a healer.

However, working with Made as my right hand on site is proving more difficult than expected. Once again, plan and reality are light years apart. On the one hand, I underestimated my own workload as well as the difficulties of adaptation to which I am currently exposed and clearly imagined them to be easier. On the other hand, due to my work schedule at the office and the time difference of seven hours, it is a real problem to be available for communication during the week outside of *WhatsApp* messages. Nevertheless, I try to meet this double burden as best I can and am even willing to sacrifice parts of my weekend for it. At least until our on-site staff has learned to stand on their own two feet.

Our manager is really doing an excellent job. But unfortunately only up to a certain point. Whenever I tell her what needs to be done, she does it perfectly. But nothing more. Unfortunately, she lacks any initiative and always waits for instructions. And since I am not personally on site, it is becoming more and more common for me to be completely deprived of a great deal of information and to be largely unaware of what is going on there at all.

It was only sometime after the opening that we received the electricity supply from the government, which is necessary for the operation of the facility. As a result, the first bookings had to be cancelled. In the first weeks of the actual operation of the retreat, it became apparent that we could not even begin to guarantee the quality that we promise our guests. Something is always going wrong. Be it misunderstandings during a booking, an infestation of vermin, damage to the facility or unreliability in various services rendered. In my opinion, there is simply no one on site who actively takes the reins. That includes the lack of a true understanding of Western quality standards and the willingness to contribute and implement their own ideas.

On top of that, patients regularly stay in cheaper lodging and use Sami's individual services several times a week, thus creating their own low-cost retreat. I take responsibility for this gap in our system, as it was I who insisted on continuing to offer Sami's treatment at an affordable price to external guests also, thus accommodating the less well-off with an interest in his treatment. This was of such importance to me because in the past as a student, I would never have been able to afford the inclusive package including meals and lodging and thus would never have met Sami.

Despite the only moderate start of business in Bali and the only partly satisfactory conditions after my return to Germany, it is my inner yogi who quietly whispers to me that everything will be fine and that I should just stay positive. I believe that I have done this very successfully in the recent past. Not once have I lapsed into self-pity or complained about anything. This is true despite the fact that my overload, especially with regard to my part-time job in Bali, is becoming more and more pronounced.

It is the overall changes I've made that make me feel positive that I can lead a happy and content life in this country as well. I generally react in a relaxed way to my environment and remain completely cool even with negative people or situations. This is the phase of my life after Bali: more mature, calmer, more patient, more self-confident and with more confidence in life.

After three months of grueling searches and applications, I finally get the nod for a nice two-room apartment with a terrace and a garden. It was a bit rural and outside of Stuttgart, but close to my family. I can be in nature in all directions in less than five minutes. I am thrilled about this and fully convinced that this is the starting signal to finally arrive in Germany again.

Although I am largely at peace with myself, it is now high time to finally get back to myself. The eternal game of patience of the last weeks has by no means left no trace on me, and it will certainly take some time until I finally get used to the comfort zone of my old and new life.

4. If it does not work out plain and simple, it simply does not work

"We must be willing to let go of the life we have planned, so as to have the life that is waiting for us."

[Oscar Wilde]

Although I am still surfing on the wave of euphoria and approach my daily challenges with confidence and calmness, I am usually so physically exhausted after work that I lack any drive for even the smallest undertakings and end my days early due to a strong lack of energy and fatigue. My life takes place more or less only on weekends, although I increasingly use them to recharge my batteries. The weather certainly plays a significant role in this. The persistent freezing temperatures, the darkness and the dreariness have most likely caused a vitamin D deficiency as well as brought on a lethargic low.

I have not come in contact with a real ray of sunshine for weeks now. Like a computer nerd, I get virtually no daylight, as I leave the house during the week when it is still dark and do not return home until it is dusk. I hardly spend any time in the fresh air, but rather lock myself up in my dark apartment after work.

I am by no means satisfied with these circumstances. I know that I am responsible for my own life and that I can shape my life to match the life of my dreams. That is why I have integrated fixed rituals into my everyday life. This includes, above all, my morning yoga routine. Even before I go to work, I diligently do breathing exercises, sun salutations, and meditation in order to start the day energetically and positively. I also go to the gym once or twice a week and eat as healthy as possible. Despite that, as much as I try, somehow new obstacles keep coming up inside of me, causing strong negative emotions. Moreover, my lack of energy just does not want to turn into joie de vivre.

The fact that our Bali retreat triggers a permanent restlessness in me certainly also contributes to this. On the one hand, I wish with all my heart that the business would finally get the long-awaited boost, on the other hand, I feel powerless, since I cannot exert much influence from Germany.

For days now, I have been racking my brains as to why I have not received an answer from Made in Bali. Secretly, I have the hope that she is so busy that she can hardly find the time to answer. But this is more wishful thinking than a real assumption.

When I still do not get any feedback after a few more days, I snap a little because I consider proper communication to be elementary. After all, I am their boss and I have to be involved. Therefore, I turn to Sami to find out what is going on in our facility.

His answer also takes a whole day, which may well be due to his new smartphone, the use of which for him is equivalent to the complexity of rocket technology. In a brief message, he informs me about the current status: "Made, she quit. Not enough guests come. No work for her. Bored she was!" And not only that. As he further lets me know, her quitting is now also the trigger for why our generally very loyal janitor and all-around maintenance man is leaving the sinking ship and bringing our project down like a house of cards.

"And when was the gentleman planning to tell me this?" I ask myself. I was informed that Made was no longer completely satisfied. She had openly expressed that to me. Nonetheless, the fact that she now took this step and did not further comply with my request for patience simply knocks me over and takes me back to the good old days of endless disappointment.

"What am I going to do now? Without any onsite management at all? Fuck, I just should not have gone! Now I have put so much heart and soul into this. I just do not want this project to fail! Absolutely not. But what am I supposed to do from afar? Sami will find a way out."

My whole being shapes itself into a huge question mark. I have no idea how to go on from here. In light of this negative development, I do not even know how to respond to Sami's message now.

Instead of receiving guidance from him as usual and becoming optimistic, Sami increasingly turns into dead weight for me. Again and again I receive messages from him in the following days, asking for help. This puts me under even more pressure than I already was. Most of the time, these messages go around in circles and sound like this:

"I am sorry to tell you...I cannot run the retreat...have no idea about marketing and social media...I am so busy with all the treatments I give...I have to do all the garden work by myself...I have no time for bookings or e-mail contact with the guests...My friends also make pressure because I have to pay back the money I borrow from them...Please Thomas help me...Not enough guests come...So much money I have to spend per month...Please help me!"

Sami, who is usually so confident, always in control of his situation and always knows what to do, is now literally begging me to help him. I feel powerless because I feel responsible, but I have no possibility to change anything. Neither can I send him any money, since I have none myself, nor can I help him hire someone new. This would never work over the Internet, since there are usually communication problems anyway —not to mention the problem of training.

The thought that my dream is over, and the retreat is about to fail for good, is giving me the lowest of feelings. I am just too deep in it to abandon Sami now. After all, it was I who pushed him to turn this project into reality in the first place. Deep down, I would be happy if I could free myself from this responsibility. For some time now, it feels as if I am in over my head and continuously swimming against the tide. In these days of doubt, I keep reminding myself of a saying I came across on the Internet some time ago, which may also give me the answer to my current situation: "If it does not work out plain and simple, it simply does not work." Nevertheless, I continue to doggedly hold on to my dream. I have invested too much to simply give up now.

And so, the unavoidable happens: my body expresses to me, as it has in the past, that something is out of balance in my inner world. It is the total combination of all these circumstances. Actually, I should be grateful for this because I am aware that with the physical symptoms it is sending me a warning signal and demanding that I find a way to bring about change.

For a good week now, I have been suffering from insane neck pain that places tension in my entire shoulder, neck and throat area. Almost daily I get headaches caused by the pressure and pain on the surrounding nerves. I can only move my head to a limited extent, and it feels like I am wearing a permanent neck brace. It is pure torture when I have to sit at my desk all day at work. Even taking pain pills only provides limited relief. To make matters worse, my division manager seems to have no sympathy for my situation and has no qualms about putting me under time pressure with additional tasks and wearing me out. Sports and exercise are out of the question at the moment. Instead, I struggle through the workday, only to find myself completely burnt out on the couch in the evening, hoping to find relief laying down. As a rule, most of my evenings are spent in front of the television. Within my limited means, this is the most enjoyable way to just be entertained with meaningless crap and kill time before the day ends on its own as my eyes close shut. This offers no real quality of life for me.

My neck pain takes on such massive proportions in the meantime that I do not show up for work for several days. The usual routine takes its course. As required by the health care system, I first go to my family doctor with my complaints, who then gives me a sick note and refers me to an orthopedist. There I was x-rayed and then referred to a radiologist for an MRI to find out more. Two weeks and several hours at the doctor's office later, a more serious injury can be ruled out, but eventually it is not enough for a diagnosis and a real cause.

Another orthopedist is also unable to help me in this regard. I consider his advice to go swimming, if possible, to get over my neck problems a real impertinence in view of my immense pain. Briefly, I toy with the idea of destroying him with a Chuck Norris-style *roundhouse kick,* which would surely just be an expression of my general frustration. If I were not a peace-loving hippie with a permanent *Ooommm* in my ear, I definitely would have done that.

It is becoming apparent that I will have to run the same gauntlet as I did with my past medical conditions, with no cure in the end. Once again, my request for help feels like getting *pass A38* from *Asterix and Obelix,* who go through a nerve-wracking odyssey when completing this task due to the administrative apparatus, and it is always questionable whether this effort is worthwhile and whether this pass exists at all.

Since I am pretty confident that my physical ailments are due to stress and worries about our Bali retreat, among other things, I decide reluctantly to give up and tell Sami that I will no longer be available to him until further notice. It feels like I am admitting to myself that I have failed. But I just cannot do it anymore. I am at the end of my rope —physically as well as mentally. The degree of my overload is so great that I have no choice but to resign and take this step.

After weeks of suffering, I eventually get prescribed physiotherapy, which after all the examinations finally promises improvement. One of my buddies, who works as a physiotherapist, alternative practitioner and osteopath at the rehabilitation center of the Bundesliga soccer club VfB Stuttgart, spontaneously made a few more appointments possible for me. I feel like I am in good hands with him because he not only works with professionals, but is one himself.

Despite all his efforts, the hoped-for healing did not occur even after the second prescription and thus after the total of twelve treatment sessions. Even he cannot bring about much more than minimal relief. In the last session he confirms what I had already suspected: "I will tell you honestly, I cannot find anything physical there. I rather think that your problem is on a mental level. I mean the past few months have certainly been a big change for you. I think your body is now expressing this imbalance through your neck pain. After all, the neck also symbolizes flexibility and adaptation in life."

j.) I myself am my guru

1. Healing love

"The best and most beautiful things in
the world cannot be seen or even touched
—they must be felt with the heart."

[Helen Keller]

My life is just plodding along now. Unfortunately, I can only manage my neck problems to a limited extent. As difficult and depressing as the decision was to suspend my involvement in our Bali business for now, I now also feel freed from all the worries that had continuously haunted me while helplessly watching the events unfold from afar. Taking all the burden off my shoulders for the moment out of self-protection has certainly contributed to a healthy improvement. Now I hope to emerge enriched from this phase of my life as well.

For my buddy Matt's wedding in Cologne, I took an extra day off. Since his civil wedding will take place early on Friday morning, I have no choice but to arrive directly after work on Thursday. A few days beforehand, I used the online platform *BlaBlaCar* to organize a private ride from the Stuttgart train station to downtown Cologne. I cannot explain why, but the girl who will drive me from A to B for $21 dollars on this day seems to me to be extremely likeable and quite familiar just by exchanging messages and the process of making arrangements.

We have a plan to meet on Thursday after work at 4 p.m. Now it is already 5:30 p.m. and I am still waiting at the parking lot of Stuttgart's main train station to be picked up by a light blue Opel Corsa with Cologne license plates. At least my driver has informed me that she will be late because of a traffic jam. Despite her brief call, I find the ninety-minute delay to be a real impertinence and almost Indonesian in character for me. My experience in dealing with unpunctual people and my resulting acquired tolerance cannot help me in this situation. Because with each additional minute of sitting around, my level of annoyance increases. After all, I could have used the time more meaningfully than loafing around in the parking lot in the rain. The last thing that comes to mind is to work longer.

When the time comes and after one and three quarter hours of waiting, a light blue Opel Corsa with Cologne license plates finally pulls up, my mood has reached an all-time low. I would love to tell the driver in no uncertain terms what I think of this kind of reliability.

Despite it all, the moment her car stops in front of me and the door opens, all the anger is blown away. I am greeted by probably the friendliest person I've ever met. Because of the injustice of having to wait, I would still like to be angry with her, but I simply cannot. Because her radiant aura transforms my anger immediately. In addition to her enchanting positive aura, she is also damn pretty to look at. I look at her from the side as inconspicuously as possible (as inconspicuously as a man can look) and her beautiful full lips immediately catch my eye. Her blonde hair is braided back in a ponytail. We greet each other with the usual ride-sharing phrases.

"Are you Pia and are you taking me to Cologne?"

"Yeah, that is right," she answers.

"Then I will take you, provided you are Thomas. You can throw your stuff in the trunk."

I pack my suit and my small bag into the trunk, which is filled to the top. A shout-out for *Shotgun* is not necessary because the other two girls who will accompany us on this trip have already made themselves comfortable in the back seat, so I take my place on the passenger seat right next to Pia. I do not really feel like talking to the two supporting actresses behind us. Nevertheless, politeness dictates that I tell them my life story, including my origins, studies and profession, in rapid succession. I feign interest in their characters with my follow-up questions. The classic *BlaBlaCar* questions.

"Where are you from? What do you do for a living? What brings you to Cologne?" are quickly answered. Even if they are predominantly the same topics and patterns of conversation, they simply cannot be missed on a real *BlaBlaCar* ride.

With my driver Pia, on the other hand, I do not have to feign interest because it is genuine and also enormous. Pia is still studying and doing her master's degree in Healthcare Promotion near Stuttgart. She is headed to Cologne for a long weekend on a home visit. After the noises from the back seat with their annoying questions have died down, only she and I remain, and we talk about a lot of topics. My openness towards her is frightening. We get along so well, I do not even have to elaborate on my "I-live-my-dreams" stories from Bali, my food record of five *Nasi Goreng* in just one day, which I set there with Matt, or my sporting successes in handball. We tell each other the funniest stories and there is hearty laughter. When at some point I play the DJ and put on my groovy music, we both sing along to the songs with equal insecurity about lyrics and pitch. The girls in the back must think that we are an old-married couple and have known each other all our lives. For me, it feels more like going on vacation with my best buddy: Pack a case of beer and a few clothes, get in the car, put on some cool music and go. Only that we are going to Cologne and not to the South of France or Spain. And that we have only known each other for about three hours.

One thing is certain for me: I have to somehow make sure that this incredibly beautiful journey continues with her in more than just a figurative sense. Because we are slowly approaching our destination, and I am running out of time. The first small concerns arise. The thing on her right ring finger looks suspiciously like an engagement ring and makes me suspect her unavailability. In my head, I run through all the scenarios of how I might meet her again beyond the drive to Cologne. "Come on, think! Think ... think ... think ..."

Time is running out, as the other two passengers in the back seat have already been dropped off at their destinations. Now it is just the two of us in the car. When we arrive at the final stop agreed upon for me, I open the door, get out, and then lean back into the car with her: "I do not know how you felt, but I thought the ride with you was really cool. You already have my number, thanks to *BlaBlaCar*. If you ever feel like doing something with me in Stuttgart, just get in touch! You know…"

She smiles back at me, "Um, um, yeah sure."

For a short while, I play with the idea of kissing her. But then I decide not to want too much at once and to be satisfied with this step for now. We wave goodbye to each other. Then I stroll to the next kiosk to sweeten my twelve-minute wait for the train with a bottle of beer and reward myself for my courage. This is called positive conditioning through beer and is a thoroughly efficient spiritual exercise that I have taught myself.

The next day, Matt's wedding is in full swing. For his sake, I make an exception, abandon all reason and pop the corks. Really! There is dancing, fooling around and sipping one gin and tonic after the other. Late at night, I receive a message on *WhatsApp* that raises my mood to an entirely new level:

"Hi Tom, it is Pia. I hope you have a nice wedding party at your buddy's place. I was just playing volleyball and am about to go out for a drink with my girls. The ride yesterday was really fun. I did not actually understand it at first, but of course, I would like to meet you. Just in private and voluntarily. I look forward to hearing from you! Xoxo Pia."

She has taken the bait and I celebrate my catch, even if I have not yet landed it. I let her squirm until noon of the following day because due to my advanced drunkenness, I no longer consider myself in a position to write her a reasonably meaningful reply now. Let alone to write at all. At most, with one eye closed.

Our mutual familiarity continues when we exchange messages in the days that follow. And also when we talk on the phone. We both want to see each other again as soon as possible.

Already on the following weekend, we meet in a beer garden in Stuttgart. There, too, we have a lot to tell each other. She looks enchanting, and my already satisfied desire to see her again immediately turns into the desire to get closer to her. Since she has arrived by car, I have no ace up my sleeve to make her compliant with some alcohol. Yet, it is not necessary because I can feel her affection for me since the beginning of our meeting even without this remedy. At some point, conversations develop into kisses, as if on their own, which finally break the ice. Sitting in the beer garden turns into dancing in a nearby bar. As the evening continues, my driver to Cologne becomes my charming girlfriend, so to speak.

After almost ten years of loneliness without a steady partner, my search has finally come to an end. I cannot yet believe my luck. The long wait was worth it. And I have met her, just as I always hoped: In a completely natural way, without having to pretend, without having to woo her extensively and without having to create an uncomfortable and unpleasant situation, to approach her.

Because of Pia, I have defined a new category of woman, Category C, which has nothing to do with the dark categories A or B from the past: Category C is that of a real dream woman. Loud mouths and naysayers claim that I only succeeded in this insane catch because she was locked up in the smallest space with me, and thus she was denied all possibilities to escape.

Funny that I was already attracted to her the first time I wrote to her, which was still about organizing the trip to Cologne —without even knowing her or what she looked like. And in the weeks before that, I had somehow carried the feeling inside me uninterrupted, as if I had a girlfriend by my side. I could just feel that warmth. It was just there. I am convinced that the origin of all this is due to my time in Bali. What Sami meant by "You got HER already" is slowly becoming clear to me. It took time, but eventually he was right. I grew HER myself through the love I sent out. The seeds I have sown, they finally seem to be blossoming.

My life has thoroughly changed since that time and has been turned upside down by Pia in a positive sense. We spend every free minute together. Since we share the same interests, we have countless opportunities to do beautiful things together. The love and joy associated with this makes my neck pain present only in a very subliminal way. The pain eventually gets virtually no attention until it finally dissipates completely.

All the stress around Bali and my difficulties adjusting in Germany fade away and turn into a minor matter. Instead, I enjoy the preciousness of a partnership and relish the moments together and the feeling of finally having arrived, of being loved and of loving myself.

After only a few months of our relationship, Pia moves in with me. She found an internship in the Stuttgart region and has to go to her university at irregular intervals on the weekends.

At first when she moves in, it takes a lot of effort to get used to giving up my unrestricted freedom to a large extent. Finally, my toothbrush mug with the logo of my favorite soccer team had to make way for a container with a colorful flower pattern. Since then, the kitchen has been filled with baking utensils, something that had never existed there before. In view of all the make-up and beauty stuff, I no longer have any control over the bathroom anyway. Since she moved in, my *Spotify* account has been going crazy. The reason why my playlist of the week only consists of Cologne carnival songs and love songs can only be attributed to the fact that my account is secretly controlled by Pia.

The new rules regarding order and cleanliness in the entire apartment are also new to me and still take some getting used to. Much of what was previously decided by me as the sole ruler in my single dictatorship, must now be done under consultation. I did not know how to make concessions until then. Despite the long leash and tolerance within our relationship, I still feel massively restricted at times.

But now, as I get increasingly used to living together over time, this is not something that causes me problems any longer. Even in the small moments, it becomes clear to me how nice it is to have a partner. No more going for walks alone, or having to cook and eat alone are just a few of these things. Not to mention all the tenderness. I enjoy having in Pia not only an attractive partner, but rather a really good friend with whom I can both laugh and cry. It is what I have reproachfully held against several of my buddies for years: "Why cannot you be a horny chick? Then I would have the best buddy in the body of a beautiful woman. Always have fun, hang out together, talk shit and then in the evening be all over each other! But no ...." And that is precisely what happens in my everyday life now. Besides all the fun that has always been hidden behind this kind of reproach towards my buddies, I had secretly wished to find a partner and best friend in one person someday. All this has now become reality with Pia. I have arrived emotionally. Finally.

2. The end of the beginning or beginning of the end?

> *"The greatest glory in living lies not in never falling, but in rising every time we fall."*
>
> *[Nelson Mandela]*

I have been back in Germany for one and a half years now. The first six months was all about bearing it and enduring it until my difficulties in adjusting were a thing of the past. Then Pia came into my life and provided a positive upswing.

Although I am still in a very fulfilling relationship with her, I am not fully satisfied with my life right now. This is because I spend the majority of the day at work, where I encounter ever greater inner resistance. Although I have an outstanding group of colleagues in my department with whom I enjoy spending my time, my days are largely dominated by fussing with people outside our department and pursuing tasks that are neither fun nor in any way fulfilling.

If given the opportunity, I would love to make time stand still. Because it passes as if in fast motion. Months go by, and I have the feeling that I have not experienced anything special in the meantime. Day in, day out, I meet the same people. The topics are usually the same and go in circles —both professionally and privately. My tasks at work increasingly fail to challenge me because I have now developed a certain routine and they no longer demand anything of me. My everyday life is extremely monotonous. No, it is not just monotonous, it is boring as hell. The only change is the time I spend with Pia after work, which is very short due to my being away at work for at least ten hours a day during the week. Sometimes I am even happy about really shitty days. Simply for the reason that they offer a change of pace and variety to the boring routine — even if it is a negative one.

A big highlight of our still young relationship is our first vacation together, which I have longed for more than I have longed for anything in a long time. It does not take much persuasion to convince Pia to visit what I still consider the most beautiful place in the world for our first adventure outside Germany's borders: Bali.

On the day of our arrival, tired and exhausted, we reach the Island of the Gods, where Sami is already waiting for us at the exit of the airport. When I see him from a distance with his joyful smile on his face, I run towards him in slow motion like in a bad romantic comedy movie. We fall into each other's arms and I let out my emotions freely. We are both so moved by our reunion that tears come to our eyes. Real men show their feelings. Our shared experiences have simply welded us so closely together and turned us into brothers.

Our facility *Rumah Bapak Sami* is hardly recognizable. The small paradise in the making that I left behind still had a lot of concrete elements but it has now been completed to perfection. My pride in the life's work that we have created is immense.

The plants and flowers that I planted back then are now in full bloom and give the place a tropical touch. It is an indescribable feeling to see how the once knee-high papaya tree is now about twenty feet tall and bearing abundant fruit.

And just as the resort has evolved, the immediate surroundings have also embraced the thriving development of the Isle of the Gods and are now bursting at the seams. In the meantime, Canggu has become a real nest for hipsters. The new fancy cafés, restaurants and bars are definitely a gain for the region. The downside, though, is that without completely tattooed arms, a bun (or at least an undercut) and a customized motorcycle, you seem to be a nobody here. A surfboard is no longer the status symbol of the cool, but has become the unique selling proposition of owning a cell phone.

Rumah Bapak Sami offers us a wonderful home for three weeks. It feels good to be able to put our feet up in our second home, free of charge and free of all obligations. With my chest swelling with pride, I tell Pia all the stories related to the construction of the facility. She should know most of them by heart by now. Even so, to be on the safe side, I tell her again. Another reason is to hear them again myself and to refresh my memories. It gives me immense pleasure to be able to present my seemingly surreal story to her live.

Our retreat has meanwhile settled down to an acceptable, though not satisfactory, level. Sami and a friend of his run the place all by themselves. There is just rare PR through Facebook and Instagram because I do not see myself able to do more, but on the other hand, I would like to keep the community alive a little bit. The retreat package has been removed from our homepage in the meantime. Otherwise, Sami still offers his very popular individual treatments in the facility, through which he occasionally manages to inspire patients to book a stay. I am surprised that there is still a demand for the service, which is no longer actively offered. This shows me that the concept generally cannot be that bad and that there is a market for it.

If a retreat stay including lodging, food and treatment is booked, Sami and his companion take care of delivering the best possible quality to the best of their knowledge and belief. The only support they receive is from a cleaning lady. Otherwise, they do the gardening themselves, in addition to preparing and serving the food and Sami doing the actual treatment. Sami seems exhausted in view of the work he has to do apart from his vocation as a healer. I find it remarkable how bravely he accepts the situation and how positive he is despite it. I love having him near me again, being able to joke with him and also have deep conversations. It all still feels so intimate between us, despite all the difficulties we have faced with the operation of the facility.

During the vacation, we had the unprecedented opportunity to work with Cathy, a highly determined and competent hotel manager from Scotland, to give new impetus to the retreat. Sami was able to help her back on her path to wellness in several treatments, which is why she now wants to give something back to him as a thank-you. The fact that he waited a few extra weeks for me with this new start honors me and shows me that he still values my work very much. Now that I am on-site, I can finally play an active role again and live up to my responsibilities as manager. I am highly motivated, not least because I feel guilty for letting Sami down. Pia is very open-minded about the entire idea, as she herself is highly interested in such a project. Although she does not actively participate, she leaves me enough space to devote myself to the topics at hand.

In several meetings, we discuss which changes are necessary and what we have to do in the next weeks to finally get on track. Cathy has already put a lot of thought into this in advance, which impresses me at our first meeting. The tasks are clearly defined, and it takes some getting used to for me that I am not the one who distributes them, but rather that Cathy assigns them. But there is no room for my ego to be hurt. First and foremost, I want to make the most of this opportunity.

Together, we redesign the homepage and hire a new local manager, who, unlike the first time, does not report to me but to Cathy, our Scottish expert living in Bali. We also redesign the pricing system and offer different packages with the right incentives. The search engine optimization is done by our tough boss herself.

I realize that Cathy's professionalism is precisely what has been missing from our success so far. She has a lot of experience and knowledge in the tourism industry. I recognize the fact that I have neither each time she comes around the corner with another new idea and lets me know that this is standard in the tourism industry. As a potential investor, she is willing to become a permanent part of our team and lives locally in Bali, so this is a very promising venture for me, which is why I am again devoting a lot of time and energy to the project. I never stopped believing that the retreat would be a complete success. Not even when our former manager Made quit. Only one decisive factor has always been missing: a real constant, a Western manager, someone like Cathy. The omens could therefore not be better, and I have never been so convinced of the success of our plans as I am now.

That Pia has so much understanding for the fact that I spend my evenings dealing with the tasks Cathy has assigned me shows me that she is the right partner for me. She knows exactly how important the retreat is to me and what significance the project holds for me.

Despite all the work to be done, we do not miss out on our vacation. I have clearly communicated with my new boss that I will only be available up to a certain point and that I will do the rest of my tasks in Germany. It sounds crazy that I now have to be accountable to someone, since I have always been the sole ruler with Sami. Nevertheless, there has been a restructuring that I myself have helped to carry out. Even if I still have to get used to it.

So, we spend a few wonderful days, in which I take Pia to the most beautiful corners of the Island of the Gods and show her what it means to live a good life.

With an ambitious to-do list and the optimistic expectation to finally really get going with the retreat, our vacation is over after three weeks.

3. The dream is over

> *"Life is simple. Everything happens for*
> *you, not to you. Everything happens at*
> *exactly the right moment, neither too*
> *soon nor too late. You do not have to*
> *like it... it is just easier if you do."*
>
> *[Byron Katie]*

After our return to Germany, I invest every free minute to fulfill my tasks for Bali in a timely manner, despite the lack of spare time. Since this is the only ray of hope in my otherwise boring workday at the moment, I put all the more effort into it. Even when I reach the point where I feel that the double burden is having a negative effect on me. I pull this off for an entire two weeks and credit my workload and impressive productivity solely to my unrestrained will and my discipline. Since I am almost finished with my tasks and will discuss them with Cathy via Skype on the weekend, the goal is gradually in sight.

However, this is not meant to happen. A message via *WhatsApp* makes me stop abruptly. Cathy, in whom all my hopes have rested, announces to me in this quite impersonal way that she is taking on a new job as a manager in a five-star hotel without further ado. This leaves her no room to take care of our affairs any longer and thus she can no longer be part of the *Bali Chy Healing* family. She asks for my understanding and not to be angry with her. The generally very cool undertone in her message lets me guess that she did not really put her heart into it anyway. The fact that she will only be available to us very sporadically from now on to complete the changes we have started reinforces this feeling. With her departure, we must at the same time inform the newly hired local manager, even before her first day of work, that we are back to square one and that there is no spot for her in this scenario.

With just this one piece of news, all my hopes vanish into thin air. The new homepage has been revised, but will never be fully completed because the local programmer feels no further obligation to do so without Cathy's supervision. The newsletters are not sent out. Moreover, as for search engine optimization, I have no idea what Cathy has done.

Again, it was not meant to be. All efforts were in vain. Besides the immeasurable frustration, I am first and foremost upset about having wasted so much time on this pointlessly during my vacation.

The following days are again very depressing because since Cathy's exit, I continuously receive the same e-mails from Sami with the request to help him and the indication that all this overwhelms him. I would have gladly complied with his request, as I still feel obligated to him. But, due to the distance, my hands are once again tied. In addition, I lack the drive to engage myself further now, as I have finally lost faith in being able to save the retreat. This is precisely what I tell Sami:

"Dear Sami,

I have no idea how I could help you to change this situation. I feel so tired because we tried so much, but nothing works. I do not believe that we can be successful anymore. I am so sad.

I hope you do understand me. But life here in Germany is already very challenging for me. It is too much. It stresses me a lot. I am sorry to tell you, but I cannot do this anymore.

Yours Thomas"

For weeks, I don't get a response from him, and I have no idea how things are going in Bali now. The last information I received was that Sami has hired a realtor in the meantime, who is supposed to rent out the facility temporarily, until an alternative solution has been found. Because he too is no longer willing to continue the retreat under these circumstances.

Then after some time I finally receive feedback from Sami. His words are written in Indonesian. I am puzzled by this and understand them only vaguely. Regardless, I understand the core message: He has rented out our property *Rumah Bapak Sami* ... for twelve years. The ink is already dry, and the long-term lease of the property is thus a done deal. And not to just anyone, but to a Chinese businessman who has little to do with our vision of saving the world (or at least making it a little better).

In another email, Sami apologizes a lot and explains to me that he wanted to express his feelings with the right words and therefore used his mother tongue. Another apology email lands in my inbox and I notice how his guilty conscience towards me torments him:

"My lovely brother,
I have no other choice to run my retreat package.
I apologize about it.
I have to safe myself.
I do not like stress too much.
Really not easy to run the package without management.
Yours Sami"

I was aware that he had been having a difficult time since my departure. For me it was at least as difficult emotionally. But now hearing that he has already rented out Rumah Bapak Sami for TWELVE fucking years without having consulted me first or at least informing me, disappoints me very much. This is the last straw for me now — the dream is over. Twelve years is by no means only temporary, but almost a pact for eternity.

I have regularly entertained the prospect that I might someday have the courage to lead the retreat as the on-site manager. Yet, the fact is that some financial security is indispensable for me. Nevertheless, returning to Bali as the on-site manager was always an alternative in the back of my mind, in case I got sick again or was so unhappy with my life in Germany that I felt forced to take this step. And somehow I still had the subliminal hope that the retreat business would eventually lead to the chance to earn money for my livelihood.

But now I no longer have this option, and this robs me of some perspective in my life. I keep asking myself the same questions: "Is Sami really the right teacher for me? Is everything he taught me true? Why was he not able to master the situation? Why did he go behind my back and make this decision? I thought we were partners! Or rather, friends! Was he just using me?"

I seriously blame myself and think about what I could have done better and look for explanations to ultimately pinpoint the failure. My frustration that my Bali cosmos has now finally been stripped of its existence is endless. A wave of sadness overcomes me. As does the question that surfaces along with it, "What now?"

4. Spirituality in my head

*"Who wants to find themselves, cannot
ask others for the way."*

[Paul Watzlawick]

All of this is so confusing to me right now. I still feel even now that I did the right thing by bringing the retreat to fruition, and that I listened to the right signs. I am in despair, as I cannot find explanations no matter how much I think about it. Sami, after this bitch-move with renting out the retreat, does not come into question for the moment, either as a friend or as a teacher to ask for advice. My trust in him has been shattered by his behavior. So, I am left on my own with all these conundrums.

I am unsure what and whom to believe now. A lot of things I believed in and could hold on to, especially in difficult times, have died with the long-term lease of *Rumah Bapak Sami*. Especially, the conviction to follow the voice of one's heart and do what one believes in with total conviction has lapsed. All spiritual books speak about this. Even the Bible says that faith can move mountains. Although, for me, it feels like my mountain has not moved even an inch from its place.

The best-selling book *The Secret* says that you can have anything you imagine. That our thoughts are creative. All we have to do is put our focus on what we want. This is a dishonest fairy tale, in my opinion. There has never been any room in my thoughts even for the idea of failing. I was always firmly convinced that our retreat would be a huge success — for everyone involved and especially for our guests. I could see it in my imagination, I could feel it. Finally, my belief in it was enormous because I acted according to the ideas of those books. So, how does this understanding explain our failure?

The love and passion I put into the project, where did it go? Where is my karmic return? "Do good and good will come to you."

"Screw you, karma. My effort was always unconditional, as I did not earn a single cent from it until the end, and instead just invested a lot of money. That does not make any sense!"

I curse all spiritual influencers who, with their postings on various social media, not only make false promises to me, but spread all this influenza-style crap like a virus all over the world: "Follow your heart ... Same things attract same things ... The universe holds abundance for everyone ... You can be and achieve anything you want ... If you can imagine it, you can make it happen ..." Bullshit!

"And to you quantum physicists who think you have an answer to everything, let me tell you, you have failed. Resonance (that we attract what we emit as vibration) is, in my eyes, nothing more than an empty word." This is all nothing more than pure theory to me. It does not have much to do with reality. At least not with mine.

Regarding my bitterness, I have come to the conclusion that while the entire spiritual theory may certainly be true, it is not equally valid for everyone. The authors of these works have laid down truths from their point of view, through which one gets at best inspirations. They serve as a guide. The fact is, they never represent a final truth. And certainly not for one's own general validity.

In my spiritual path, I am no longer willing to trust the promises of others, but only to trust what arises from my inner self. For me this is about finding my very own truth. And I find this only in life itself and in the experiences I have—and not in the teachings about it. I myself am my guru. Yes, I am convinced of that. Only I myself can know what is best for me. It is only I whom I can truly trust. My soul will find its expression. Through my inner voice, it will show me the right way and give me impulses to make the right decisions. It will send me feelings about what is the right thing to do.

With these convictions, I now surrender to my situation. I need the certainty from deep within me to decide what to do with my future.

I wait and wait until the appropriate signs appear to me to provide explanations and especially to bring about a change in my life. Secretly, I hope that some condition of life might occur that will bring about a positive change. For example, a third-degree uncle, whom I have never heard of until now, could start things off by leaving me an inheritance of several million. Instead, nothing but stagnation. My patience is at its end, and I am terrified of not finding my way and continuing to waste my lifetime with this lifestyle. This waiting is exhausting until my inner voice finally speaks up —which eventually is just spiritual theory again, even if it comes from myself.

k.) The success of failure

1. Wasting my lifetime

> *"You often feel tired, not because you've done too much, but because you've done too little of what sparks a light in you."*
>
> *[Alexander Den Heijer]*

There is not much left of the former dreamer who travels to the other side of the world, puts himself in the hands of an extraordinary healer and with all his courage and vision, puts all his money on one card to find happiness. Rather, I now feel like a sad clown whose circumstances have caused the corners of his mouth to droop into a frown as well as a huge tear on his cheek. The Peter Pan in me is dead. Instead, I have mutated into a real adult. Sometimes I am a bit narrow-minded and bitter. Often I even seem like a smart-ass. And as everyone knows, no one can stand those. All I need now is a condominium with a balcony, so that I can live in monotony for the rest of my life. That is the perfect nightmare. And I am about to live it.

The longer my depressing life drags on like this, the more hopeless the situation seems to me that I no longer have any real dreams. For the first time in my life, I had a real master plan of what I wanted to do with my life and promptly experienced a bitter disappointment that has now left its scar on my soul. Right now, all I have to do is endure the present. But that is even worse: I have no idea what my future should look like. Without real dreams and goals, my life is not worth living. I have reached a new low point.

Inside me, there are the same phrases over and over again, which seem to reinforce my situation with every utterance and increasingly test my patience: "What do I earn my money for? What for? I have no goals! And certainly no profession in which I am even remotely happy. I am professionally trapped in this line of work. Or what else could I realistically earn my money with? It is hopeless! This cannot be all that life has in store for me! Not after this positive transformation. Not after all the hurdles I've overcome."

When I consider that I have thirty-five more years of work ahead of me in an office, I break out in a sweat that smells directly of doom. The signs that spring from my inner self make themselves known and provide me with unmistakable signals as to what they think of the continuation of my current lifestyle:

My head says, "Baaaaaa!!!!"
My stomach says: "Arrggggghhhh!!!!"

And my heart: "Aaawwwww!!!!"

But particularly I see that in the medium term it will make me sick again to do something that does not evoke any joy in me and does not correspond in any way to a destiny. The thought of having to spend my life in this monotony, without being able to express myself even rudimentarily, deprives me of my sanity.

I have no choice but to continue to be content with what life has to offer me at the moment. Certainly, a positive mood would allow me to name a lot of things. In connection with my continuing lack of perspective, however, I am currently blind to these things.

My monotonous office job is eating me up inside. Again and again, even the smallest things cause my barrel of negative emotions to overflow. I am highly sensitive and explosive in my reactions. I never avoid conflict, but am usually the one who instigates it in the first place. Since I have virtually no appointments at work (which I consistently perceive as an expression of my insignificance in the company), I spend my workdays almost exclusively in front of my computer.

During the summer days, when I have virtually nothing to do, my situation becomes even more acute and reaches its negative peak. I find myself in the constant tension of looking busy, while in reality I try to kill time as best I can. I have already offered my help to my colleagues, but they are not taking me up on it because of their own summer slowdown. I do the most stupid things (such as filing) as occupational therapy, just to get the time until closing time over with as quickly as possible. I also take a coffee break between every task. And every time I check my watch, only a few minutes have passed, even though it seems like an eternity. It is not that I am avoiding work —there just is none at the moment. It completely kills me. And with every day that passes, I question my life more fundamentally.

I am constantly waiting for my inner voice to get louder and tell me what to do next in my life. Hoping to see a light on the horizon of boredom again. But this voice refuses to appear to me. Instead, I spend most of my days in front of a computer, pressing the buttons on my mouse to make my co-worker think I am busy with the clicking sound. In reality, though, I sit in front of the computer doing nothing, staring at the screen and hoping that time will pass. I await the end of my working day, in order to serve my lifetime again the next day. It is not so much the situation itself that makes me experience this suffering, but rather my negative assessment of it.

Lost in thought and staring at the screen, I imagine what it will be like when I look back on my life in old age and, with the Grim Reaper breathing down my neck, imagine how I have trampled on the precious years of my life and wasted them senselessly. "Is this really the life I want to look back on? Would I be able to look back and say I had a good life?"

"Time is so precious, do I seriously want to waste it just sitting in front of the computer? So that time passes and I get another month's worth of money transferred into my account that I do not know what to do with anyway?

NO!

NO!

NOOOOO!

I want to live! I want to feel alive! I want to develop my full potential! I want to make a difference in my life with my work and my impact! I want to be an inspiration and help others! I need dreams and visions again! Just for the reason that I will know what I spend my time on and earn my money for. I need a direction to move in. I want to look back in my old age on a life I am proud of —knowing I have always lived at the limit, always seized every opportunity, and always made the most of everything."

With this in mind, it is impossible for me to continue to be content with my role as a victim and my passive existence. I will no longer surrender to my fate and actively work to change it. Therefore, I allow myself to seek external help, even if it contradicts my conviction that only my inner guidance can give me the right answer. Experiencing a different perspective than Sami's will certainly do me good. He is so far the only one I have confided in regarding my spiritual quest. I am curious where my first steps without him will lead me.

2. Tutoring

"Begin," says the Master,
"then you will learn."
"I don't know enough yet,"
replies the student.
"Then wait," says the master.
"How long?" asks the student.
"Until you begin," says the master.
[Zen Story]

Of course, I cannot entrust myself to a conventional therapist in my search for support. He has to take a holistic approach in order to breathe new courage into me and help me on my way out of my victim role.

My research on the Internet leads me to the weirdest coaches, therapists and healers. I quickly discover that it is not an easy task to decide on the most suitable support in this vast abundance. In the process, I come across various people, from whom I immediately sort out those who seem a tad too esoteric even for my taste. No one can really win me over right away. A certain skepticism is permanently present. This may also be due to the fact that I secretly compare each of them with Sami and am not sure whether they can hold a candle to him in terms of his abilities.

In the end, I decided on a systemic consultant and awareness coach in Stuttgart. I follow the advice of a buddy who recently met with her and about whom he literally raved. That is enough for me to accept it as a real sign.

Less than two weeks later, I have an appointment with her. After a short introduction on her part, she asks me to describe my request. I tell her about my experiences in Bali, which basically start with building *Rumah Bapak Sami* and end with the lack of dreams and perspectives in the present. She charts my status quo in relation to my family and what I have experienced and subsequently lets me know how I relate systemically to my fellow human beings and also to Sami. This allows valuable conclusions to be drawn. Her questions strike an amazing resonance in me: "You said that you put all your heart and soul and 110 percent of your passion into it and it still did not work. How much more effort on your part do you think it would have taken to make it a success? Do you not think that this could also be due to the constellation? With Sami as your boss, who as a healer dictates decisions to you even in management matters? With the very concept of the retreat, these facilities and in the stage of life in which you have only just matured? And all this in a short time and in a foreign culture? Do you not think that your failure as you call it could be due to his systemic environment?"

She recommends that I reflect and question all this again in peace, without continuing to blame myself for the failure. Because I simply could not have brought more to the table in terms of commitment, courage, passion and knowledge at that time. And with that, I completely agree with her.

She points out to me that it is very important to process what I have experienced and not to simply sweep the emotions associated with it under the table. To this end, she advises me to recall all my experiences —especially the painful ones —as vividly as possible and then to make peace with them. And last but not least, to develop love for what lies behind me and can no longer be undone. It is time to conclude what I have experienced in a harmonious way and to let it go. Only then it would be possible for me to create space for something new and to open myself to all the happiness that is waiting for me.

Somehow, this is exactly what I want to hear. Somehow what she is telling me feels right.

The first step of my mental cleanup begins with reaching out to Sami to bury my unspoken hatchet with him. Because I am still pissed off at him and full of reproaches after the treason with the long-term rental of *Rumah Bapak Sami*.

3. Beginning of a new journey

> *"I have not failed. I have just found*
> *10,000 ways that will not work."*
>
> *[Thomas A. Edison]*

I see that Sami is online on *WhatsApp* right now, so I take the opportunity to write him without further ado:

"Hi Sami, to be honest, I am still very disappointed that you rented out Rumah Bapak Sami for 12 years. For the first time in my life, I knew what I really want to do. I listened to my heart. And I followed my heart. However, in the end we failed! Since this happened I feel lost. I do not know what I should believe. Everything that you taught me makes no sense. I do not understand why I am again here in Germany wasting my time in front of a computer. I feel that I am getting sick! Again!"

Message sent. Without a big hello and goodbye and asking how-do-you-do. I let my emotions speak and tell him how I really feel.

The first tick appears in my message — so it has been sent.

The second tick appears — consequently, he has received the message.

The two check marks turn blue — so he has now read my message as well.

Now it is up to him. I am extremely curious about how he will respond. I feel like I am back in the old teenage days, when waiting for a reply from a loved one after writing a declaration of love caused a similar tension in me. Only now without love, but with a liberating and also indirectly reproachful message from me. And promptly I see in the display: "Sami Healer writes ..."

Minutes pass and in the time that has already elapsed, one could easily have written the first part of *Harry Potter*. More minutes pass.

Still, "Sami Healer is writing ..." Then a message pops up and I finally receive my eagerly awaited reply. Sadly, unlike what I had hoped, he neither really takes a stand nor tries to explain the mystery of "life" to me. Two simple words are all he has to offer me. "Why failed?"

Before I let the content of his message sink in, I wonder what he has been up to all this time and whether it can seriously be true that a talented and educated person like him takes so long to write two simple words.

Next, as I become aware of the concentrated wisdom of his words, I briefly doubt his common sense. I think to myself, "Boy, are you perhaps a little slow on the uptake? Why failed? So where I come from, even with all the positivity in the world, there is no denying our failure. This is like when your soccer team got beaten by 5-0 and afterwards nobody wants to admit the defeat." I mentally elaborate on my answer. The tone of my inner voice can hardly be topped in its flippancy: "What failure am I talking about? Well, that we have invested not only love, sweat and time, but also a lot of money in something for ten months and at the end of the day, nothing has worked. That dreams have been shattered and simply everything I believed in no longer makes sense now — this FAILURE!"

But I pause and answer almost eloquently compared to his message, "Renting out *Rumah Bapak Sami* for 12 years."

"Again, why failed?" he replies to me in probably a new best time of under five minutes of writing. But then the messages hit home as if he had written them before in preparation for this conversation:

"Happiness is a process!"

"Are you proud of what you created?"

"What you learn from your experience in Bali?"

I quickly run through the questions:

"Happiness is a process!" — "OK, I see."

"Are you proud of what you created?" — "Yes!"

"What you learn from all your experiences in Bali?"

"Good question ... excellent question! A lot, definitely."

Then another message pops up, abruptly ending our conversation for today:

"Good night, brother!"

I put my phone aside and remind myself of the positive change I have experienced over the years and how I have emerged stronger as a person. Openly confronting what I have learned from this experience makes me see it all again from a much broader perspective.

"I have experienced so much pain over the past few years. Physically and mentally as well as emotionally. I know what it means to be sick, powerless, lonely, unhappy and not particularly confident. However, I found a way to change that —to change me. In Bali. With this very project. I learned so much about yoga, meditation, philosophy, Ayurveda, spirituality, emotions, our mind, the polarities of life, the five elements, yin and yang, subtle energy and all the healing techniques in my quest for love, health and happiness. And last but not least, I understood that if I want to change my world, I have to start with myself and change myself." Even so, the conclusion of what I have learned from the failure of our business is missing. And thus, it's the same old, same old. Because all the other insights are nothing new to me. I have just never been so aware of them before.

I answer Sami, even though he is probably already immersed in his dreams due to the time difference:

"I learned how to love myself. I learned so much about body, mind and spirit, about healing and how to be happy. But I still do not understand why in the end the project failed, why *Rumah Bapak Sami* failed. I really did my best."

I get up and go to the kitchen to make myself something to eat. When I come back, three new *WhatsApp* messages are flashing.

All of them are from Sami. So it seems he is still up to his old mischief after all:

"Failure is part of the process how to be HAPPY. Because from every failure you learn. How to be strong. How to trust and love yourself."

"From every failure you learn how to be successful. That is part of life. From everything you learn. Failure is not the opposite of success. It is part of the success."

"Even it might feel bad. You have to be aware about the lessons it teaches you."

"And what do you think I might learn from my failure with *Rumah Bapak Sami*? None of this makes any sense to me!" I continue to show my confusion, not yet fully understanding the context.

"This is something you have to ask yourself!"

So I confront myself again with what I asked Sami: "What did this experience want to teach me?" Actually, I no longer need to ask myself this question. Because inside me there is already the feeling that all of this has happened to me to prepare me for my destiny. Therefore, I intuitively rephrase the question: "Do I have the gift to support people on their way to personal happiness? Is this what I am searching for?" It has never occurred to me to embark on such a path, as I was usually the one who had to rely on others for support with my problems.

It feels like opening the cage I have locked myself into by stubbornly clinging to the success of our retreat center. I am experiencing a release after all the suffering and disappointments that have haunted me in the past. The feelings of happiness that flow through me are an expression of the knowledge that I have finally found what I was searching for. No resistance, no doubts. Not even my mind has anything to oppose this conviction now.

4. All's well that ends well

"Choose a job you love and you'll never have to work a day in your life."

[Confucius]

What Sami had told me several years earlier in my search for love, health and a happy life, has all come true in retrospect: "Start from economy. With what you studied. Still very young you are. You need some experience. You will find it. Happiness is a process. One day you will know what I did for you. One day you know what I want you to do. You need to listen to yourself. I know who you are. And what you need to do. You are not doing something special for yourself. You need to know yourself. Go your own way. Make your experiences. Then you will find what you need to do."

As much as I thought about it at the time, his words always remained a mystery to me. He always had a deeper understanding of things, which I was not aware of at all.

All my experiences now appear in a different light. Everything I experienced has its justification and is part of the puzzle, which I am now able to recognize as a beautiful picture. Everything makes sense at once. Simply everything. In the process, I regain my faith in what I have learned over the last few years. Moreover, suddenly I discover what enormous value this failure has for me: "Assuming our retreat center had started successfully, where exactly would I have found my place in it? Even if I had earned money at some point in my role as a manager, what specific tasks would I have taken on? The work that would have awaited me there, in addition to marketing and bookings and correspondence, would not have filled my day and would not have provided me with fulfillment in the long run. It would have been inconceivable for me to live in Bali all year round. I feel too foreign there and simply too comfortable in Germany. Even if I had commuted back and forth between the two countries, what would I have done professionally during the periods in Germany? Without a real job, I would not have been happy here either. My free time would have become my everyday life and would have lost its value at some point due to boredom. And above all, I would have always diminished myself behind the uniqueness and exceptionality of Sami, without letting my own light shine."

All the experiences and feelings I went through were not in vain. Although they threw me into a crisis at the time, I do not regret them or want to forget them. They have shaped me. They have made me strong and allowed me to mature as a person. Life has cut me like a diamond. The only way to stop believing and to gain knowledge and understanding is through experience. No one can take this knowledge away from me anymore. The empathy that I can show to others as a result is my greatest asset and will enable me to help many people on their way.

I proudly write to Sami to share this revelation with him:

"Hi brother, I finally got the answer. I found my calling. I am some kind of healer, too. Finally, I know what I want to do with my life. I now understand why this all happened. It all makes sense to me. I finally got it! Thank you so much for everything you did for me.

In Love, Thomas"

His answer amazes me like so many things that have happened to me in the last almost eight years with him:

"Finally brother. I know already since the first time you meet me. Be patient. Everything in process already. Always remember: Don't worry, be HAPPY."

As the Buddha so beautifully says, "We are never at the destination. The journey is the destination." Having virtually stopped moving forward since returning to Germany two years ago and doggedly sticking to our retreat project without moving an inch forward, I now have renewed vigor. It does not matter how rocky this path may be, I will follow it consistently. Instead of waiting for a change to happen in my life, I will take an active role and lay the foundation for my new dream: to accompany people in letting go of their own negative patterns, to accept themselves in love, to unleash their full potential and to let their hidden light shine. I want to touch hearts with what I do.

"The journey is the destination." Definitely! However, the journey only begins with walking. So I grab pen and paper and start making initial sketches that will be the basis for this very book. Who knows where this new project will take me. Whether my autobiographical novel will eventually climb to the top of all the bestseller lists or just find its way into the drawers of a few. One thing is already certain for me: as long as I create something with love, passion and joy, there can be no failure. Failure only occurs when I no longer do what I want to do, but what I HAVE to do.

Acknowledgement

"There is no excess in the world so commendable as excessive gratitude."

[Jean de La Bruyère]

I would like to express my sincere thanks to all those who have contributed directly or indirectly to the creation of this book and who have supported me.

My thanks therefore go to:

... my family and my friends. I love you!

... Sami, for whom it was really not always easy with me. Thank you for your patience, for your teachings and for your guidance.

... my wife Pia. Your positive feedback on the book was my motivation. But as the best wife in the universe, what else could you have said? I want to thank you and our two daughters for being who you are. Through you, I can experience anew every day the meaning of love and happiness.

... to all readers, who I was allowed to take with me on my very personal journey. If you liked the book, please leave me a review on Amazon. I am very happy about sharing my story and appreciate your review which will help me to make the book more visible!

Glossary

Alcopops
Sweet alcoholic mixed drinks that were very popular until shortly after the turn of the millennium.

Bali Belly
Diarrhea in Bali.

Biggie
Short for *Biggie Smalls* or *The Notorious B.I.G.*, one of the best-known US rap stars of the 90s. Unfortunately, he was shot in 1997.

Bintang
Beer brand from Indonesia.

BlaBlaCar
Online carpooling service.

Bud Spencer fist punch
In reference to the Bud Spencer and Terence Hill movies, in which many beatings were handed out.

Chakra
Subtle energy centers between the subtle body and the human physical body.

Chuck Norris roundhouse kick
What is the last thing that goes through the mind of Chuck Norris' victims? His foot!

Clark Kent	Journalist and Superman's alter ego from the movie of the same name.
Endless-Summer	Based on *The Endless Summer*, a 1966 surfing movie in which the cast follows summer around the world —always in search of the perfect wave.
Feng-Shui	Chinese theory of harmonious living and home design.
Gandalf the White	Wizard from the novel and film series *The Lord of the Rings* as well as *The Hobbit*.
Hip dysplasia	Abnormality or disorder of ossification of the hip joint.
Hulk	Main character from the eponymous Marvel comic book and movie. Every time he gets angry, the character transforms into the huge, green raging monster Hulk.
Iliopsoas	"Muscle of the soul." Essential muscle for bending the hips.
Line-up	Ideal spot in the water where surfers wait to catch a wave.

Lumbung	Traditional Balinese hut that looks like an open pavilion.
MC Hammer	US rapper who had his biggest hit in the 90s with the track "U can't touch this." Legendary for his wide cut pants.
Mr. Myiagi	Karate Master from the *Karate Kid* movies.
Mordor	The realm and base of evil in the movie *The Lord of the Rings*.
MTV Cribs	MTV reality TV show where wealthy celebrities give a tour of their ostentatious homes.
Nasi Goreng	Most famous rice dish from Indonesia.
Obi Wan Kenobi	One of the most famous and powerful Jedi masters from the *Star Wars* film series.
Ooommm	Phonetic spelling for the sacred syllable OM or AUM. It stands for the essence of all being as well as the harmony between body, mind and soul.

Prana	Hindu term for life energy or life force.
Shotgun	Word used to claim the passenger seat for oneself.
TripAdvisor	Tourism platform where personal reviews are shared.
Tupac	One of the most famous US rappers from the 90s. Unfortunately, he was shot and killed in 1996.
Warung	Indonesian term for a food street vendor stall.
Yoda	Small, green Jedi grand master from the *Star Wars* film series.
Zen	Japanese movement derived from Buddhism. Attempt to experience the unity of all being through meditation.

About the author

Thomas Krause was born in Stuttgart (Germany) in 1985. After his studies of economics, he had to come to the bitter realization that it is not his nature to spend his working day in front of a computer and crunching numbers. Neither as a controller, nor as an assistant, nor in any other employment in the financial sector. Because within him is the urge for freedom and autonomy, as well as the desire to be of help to other people with his work.

Today he lives in Cologne, and as a coach, supports people in overcoming their challenges and finding their personal balance. In his philosophy of "East-meets-West," he brings together Far Eastern wisdom teachings with modern approaches from the West and makes them applicable to everyday life.

Newsletter

Do you want to stay up to date?

Just use the QR code or send me an email with the subject "Newsletter Bali Chy Healing" to Balichyhealing@gmx.de.

@Balichyhealing_Dtld

@Balichyhealing

#Balichyhealing_book

www.Balichyhealing.com

PERSONAL VIDEO
FOR YOU

Use the QR Code to watch the short video with impressions
from Bali, an introduction of the author and exciting insights
about what happened after the end of the book's story.

Printed in Great Britain
by Amazon

27043642R10207